EUL VERLAG

EINZELSCHRIFTEN

Fabian Diering
**Kritische Analyse der deutschen Hinzurechnungs-
besteuerung**
Lohmar – Köln 2015 ◆ 132 S. ◆ € 43,- (D) ◆ ISBN 978-3-8441-0423-3

Michael Möcker
**Ambiguitätsaversion und Zeitinkonsistenz in Prinzipal-
Agent-Beziehungen**
Lohmar – Köln 2015 ◆ 260 S. ◆ € 57,- (D) ◆ ISBN 978-3-8441-0425-7

Gerrit Böhm
**Entwicklung geschäftsmodellspezifischer Bilanzrating-
modelle** – Leistungssteigerung durch Bilanzhomogenisierung
Lohmar – Köln 2015 ◆ 284 S. ◆ € 58,- (D) ◆ ISBN 978-3-8441-0428-8

Jantje Halberstadt, Christian Jakob, Michael Schuricht (Hrsg.)
Jenseits des Elfenbeinturms – Universitäre Forschung und
praktische Relevanz
Lohmar – Köln 2016 ◆ 360 S. ◆ € 64,- (D) ◆ ISBN 978-3-8441-0442-4

Michael Meyer
**Einfluss und Wirkung von Nachfragemacht auf Preisent-
scheidungen** – Eine experimentelle Untersuchung der Ausübung
von Einkaufsmacht
Lohmar – Köln 2016 ◆ 244 S. ◆ € 56,- (D) ◆ ISBN 978-3-8441-0444-8

Judith Ponnewitz und Tobias Kienzler
Marktfähigkeit von Mikroapartments – Ein Leitfaden für eine
Projektentwicklung
Lohmar – Köln 2016 ◆ 248 S. ◆ € 56,- (D) ◆ ISBN 978-3-8441-0451-6

Luisa Henrike Schäfer
**Employees as Key Success Factors for Sustainability
Strategies?** – An Empirical Study on the Influence of Human
Resource Development
Lohmar – Köln 2016 ◆ 140 S. ◆ € 43,- (D) ◆ ISBN 978-3-8441-0452-3

JOSEF EUL VERLAG

Luisa Henrike Schäfer

Employees as Key Success Factors for Sustainability Strategies?

An Empirical Study on the Influence of Human Resource Development

With a Preface by Kathrin Bischoff, M. Sc. BA,
University of Wuppertal

Bibliografische Information der Deutschen Nationalbibliothek

Die Deutsche Nationalbibliothek verzeichnet diese Publikation in der Deutschen Nationalbibliografie; detaillierte bibliografische Daten sind im Internet über <http://dnb.d-nb.de> abrufbar.

ISBN 978-3-8441-0452-3
1. Auflage März 2016

© JOSEF EUL VERLAG GmbH, Lohmar – Köln, 2016
Alle Rechte vorbehalten

JOSEF EUL VERLAG GmbH
Brandsberg 6
53797 Lohmar
Tel.: 0 22 05 / 90 10 6-6
Fax: 0 22 05 / 90 10 6-88
E-Mail: info@eul-verlag.de
http://www.eul-verlag.de

Bei der Herstellung unserer Bücher möchten wir die Umwelt schonen. Dieses Buch ist daher auf säurefreiem, 100% chlorfrei gebleichtem, alterungsbeständigem Papier nach DIN 6738 gedruckt.

Preface

As a result of the severity of global challenges and the augmented societal request, the business sector is increasingly moving towards implementing responsible and sustainable business strategies. Sustainable business development implies that companies meet in their business activities the needs of the present stakeholders without compromising the ability of future generations to meet their own needs. Thus, companies are prompted to integrate social and ecological issues voluntarily into their business activities and interactions with their stakeholders. While there is widespread consent that integrating sustainability into their business strategies is important, organizations frequently struggle with *how* to establish concrete sustainability strategies as win-win situation for themselves and society on the whole.

In this context, the role of human resources in order to successfully implement a sustainability strategy in a company has to be emphasized. A sustainability strategy can solely be deeply anchored, if the employees are aware of it and share its underlying values and beliefs. Moreover, employees have to be motivated and committed to embedding sustainability in their working environment and corporate context. Whereas prior research has revealed the importance of employee identification with employers and the positive impact of corporate social engagement on employee satisfaction, thus far little research has been conducted on the role that employees themselves can play as key success factors to sustainability strategies.

The study of Luisa Schäfer addresses this research gap by empirically examining the influence of human resource development on the success of sustainability strategies. The author thereby employs a highly structured and analytical analysis approach and investigates the topic in an advanced level of depth. The literature review is based on a systematic literature search and the employed empirical research methodology is sound, rigorous and suitable. The argumentation is comprehensive and logical with an own contribution being highly visible. All findings are ultimately presented and discussed in an in-depth manner and profound implications for theory and practice are drawn.

This work makes an excellent contribution to research on the overlap of sustainability and human resource development and is of outstanding value to researchers and practitioners who are interested in gaining further insights on how human resource development professionals can contribute to successfully implementing corporate sustainability strategies.

Cologne, February 2016   Kathrin Bischoff, M.Sc.BA

Foreword

The concept of sustainability has quickly evolved into a norm for corporate strategies, and it appears that the technical term has become an ambiguous metaphor for current problem descriptions. Exploring human resource development initiatives for corporate sustainability is still a novel path, all the more if sustainability is understood as a holistic concept. The thesis at hand is characterized by the question of why sustainable development is not imprinted in every employee's mind and how this can be achieved. During the six months of my research, I learned that sustainability is an issue of moral orientation and that employees should be free to determine intentions; they lie within their control. Immanuel Kant (1788) developed the notion of morality based on his 'categorical imperative'. Indeed, the hidden agenda of sustainability follows Kant, as the idea of instilling a corporate sustainability culture and mindset is confronted with the complexity of assessing and steering individual attitudes. Hence, I consider encouraging employees to use their own understanding in improving their responsible behavior as essential plea.

I want to express my highest gratitude to my supervisor, Anne Kathrin Bischoff, for her inspiring advice and excessive time spent on guiding me through the writing process of my thesis. Furthermore, I want to thank my first examiner, Prof. Dr. Christine Volkmann, holder of the Chair of Entrepreneurship and Economic Development & UNESCO-Chair for Entrepreneurship and Intercultural Management at the University of Wuppertal, and my second examiner, Dr. Marc Grünhagen, for their special effort. Finally, I am grateful to the employees of the Josef Eul Verlag for their continuous help during the publication of my thesis. As every piece of writing, this one was supported and influenced by the encouragement and discussions with a number of people especially in my private environment, to whom I wish to express my sincere appreciation.

My thesis shall be considered with a prior reflection of Kantian thought, which enlightens that sustainable, responsible individual behavior is particularly a demand of ethics and of reason of a human society interested in its long-term preservation including also economic welfare.

Cologne, February 2016   Luisa Henrike Schäfer

"Act only according to that maxim whereby you can at the same time will that it should become a universal law without contradiction."

Immanuel Kant, 1788

Table of Contents

List of Figures

List of Tables

List of Abbreviations

CA   Competitive Advantage

CR   Corporate Responsibility

CS   Corporate Sustainability

CSR   Corporate Social Responsibility

CSV   Creating Shared Value

GRI   Global Reporting Initiative

HR   Human Resources

HRD   Human Resource Development

KSF   Key Success Factor

MNC   Multinational Corporation

NRW   North Rhine-Westphalia

OD   Organizational Development

ROI   Return on Investment

SME   Small and Medium Enterprises

T&D   Training and Development

TBL   Triple Bottom Line

1 Introduction

1.1 Relevance of the Topic

In the course of globalization and powerful systemic, technological and capital market changes, competition and pressure for companies have increased tremendously. Alongside the macro-economic context, environmental issues and societal changes as well as their respective demands on companies and impacts of entrepreneurial activity have to be kept in mind (Wall & Leitner, 2012). From a classical management perspective, sustainable business strategy ensures the long-term survival of a company (Porter, 1987). Nowadays, companies have recognized the superior need for a comprehensive corporate sustainability strategy. Adequate strategies integrate economic, social, and environmental dimensions for successful corporate performance not only due to external influences but also with respect to changing individual and organizational factors (Pfeffer, 2010). Fully integrating sustainability into a corporate strategy has progressively become the ubiquitous norm for businesses. This is also evident when considering the amount of published sustainability reports within Germany: In 2013, a total of 173 reports based solely on the Global Reporting Initiative (GRI, 2015) were published. Moreover, a clear majority of companies in the DAX segment and a remarkable amount of MDAX and SDAX companies disclosed sustainability activities (see Figure 1).

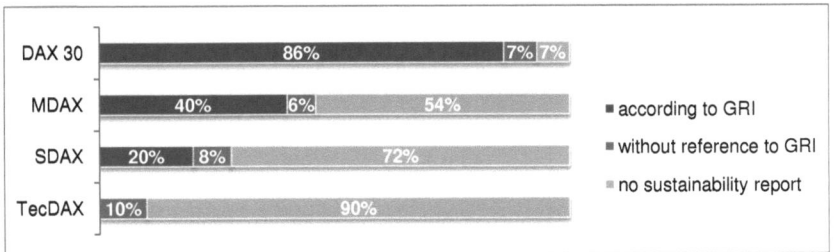

Figure 1: Publication of Sustainability Reports in DAX Segment
Source: Adapted from Ernst & Young, 2014, p. 8.

In a recent poll of 300 sustainability specialists and participants of the German Sustainability Award, these experts were asked, if companies are on the right track to achieve sustainability goals (A.T. Kearney, 2015). Strikingly, experts are apparently optimistic regarding sustainability of resources, employees and profitability (see Figure 2). However, other spheres are met insufficiently: 51% of experts are skeptical about the achievement of climate goals, 58% concerning nature and 52% concerning society. Companies may have solutions and tools but do not use them effectively to meet the sustainability challenges. A study by the Society of Human Resource Management (SHRM, 2011, pp. 24) reflects that only 6% of HR departments are involved in the creation and 25% in the implementation of sustainability strategies (n_1 = 395; n_2 = 390). Certainly, as Scully-Russ (2012) argues, "... Human resource development (HRD) and sustainability lie in a mutually co-constructive relationship" (p. 399). While the need for and benefits of sustainability strategies are universally acknowledged, the relationship with human resource development (HRD) still has substantial gaps.

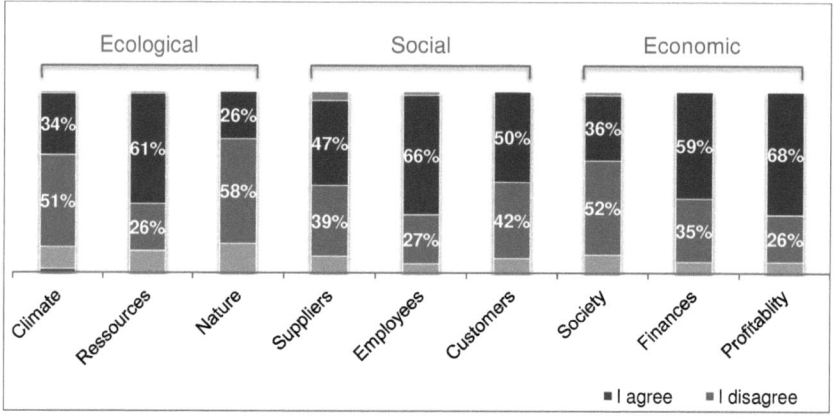

Figure 2: German Corporations on the Pathway to achieve Sustainability Goals
Source: Translated from A.T. Kearney, 2015, p. 6.

However, without employee support, actions concerning sustainability strategies risk being perceived as insignificant public relations practices. Garavan, Heraty, Rock and Dalton (2010) put it this way: Despite the existing research on corporate social responsibility (CSR) and corporate sustainability (CS) "... there is significantly less on the influence of employees on the adoption of CSR and CS initiatives. Given the centrality of employees as stakeholders in CSR/ CS adoption, it is important to understand how barriers at individual, organizational and institutional levels of analysis influence the adoption of CSR/CS initiatives" (p. 587). Due to the economic, environmental and cultural changes, firms encounter new challenges which they need to adapt to and "... HRD has a central role to play in promoting and supporting the development of a learning environment to create and nurture knowledge" (Valentin, 2006, p. 18). Quality training and learning opportunities positively influence employee engagement which is required for the success of sustainability endeavors (SHRM, 2011). Thus, for any holistic sustainability strategy to be effective, the company's employees need to be aligned and engaged behind it. Altogether, the apparent lack of attention given to the relevance of HRD in the context of sustainability strategies is in sharp contrast with the importance of it.

1.2 Research Questions and Objectives

This thesis examines to what extent HRD is a constitutive element of employee performance with regard to sustainability strategies. Taken from the introduced current research gap, the need to understand interdependencies is seen: Employees have to be committed and involved for sustainability endeavors to be successful. As stated before, a positive relationship between a firm's employee training and its performance in sustainable development is most likely. Assuming that HRD has strong positive impact on employee engagement for sustainability, it is postulated that HRD departments need to ensure that all members of the company hold the appropriate mindset for such behavior.

Considering the increasingly complex, globalized world, Lee (2007) argues "As we conceive of, or operate within, that which we call 'HRD' we are not working in isolation" (p. 97). It was described above how the request for CS embeds HRD in the context of global change. Thus, rather than limiting it to mere training and development, HRD should also take economics, politics, philosophy and corporate strategy into account, and "… become a partner in the struggles of the world to promote core aspirations of fostering a sustainable environment in which the needs of people are balanced" (ibid., p. 108). Accordingly, this study claims for an involvement of HRD and an understanding of sustainability as a comprehensive mindset of employees, which regards macro and micro-economic requirements holistically. Primary attention is given to the HRD processes and methods companies are implementing for sustainable practices. Hence, this study will contribute to the emerging literature linking HRD and sustainability. As sustainability has rarely been connected with HRD research, this research is considered exploratory and the central objective is not testing theory. The aim is rather to improve the understanding of HRD's influence on cross-company sustainability initiatives' success and to highlight its relevance. Therefore, the types and effects of personnel training and development (T&D) on sustainability strategies' success are examined and the following questions are addressed:

> ➢ *Question 1: Which forms of HRD are used to support sustainability strategies?*

> ➢ *Question 2: How effective are HRD interventions and which factors have an influence on transfer into practice?*

> ➢ *Question 3: Are results of training measured and if so, how? Is internal or market-related performance enhanced after an HRD intervention for sustainability?*

Due to the lack of empirical evidence currently available about the topic, the objective is to gain practical insights through qualitative expert interviews with HRD professionals of large

German companies. The final goals of this research are first, to present if and how HRD activities are helping to implement sustainable practices, and secondly to offer HRD managers knowledge to enhance their ability to play a more prominent role in implementing sustainability practices. More precisely, such research may yield practical advice on how to progress toward training for sustainability, based on analysis of organizations clearly committed to sustainability that might have started engaging HRD implementation efforts already. Moreover, this study can lead to further research on the steps necessary to train HRD managers to become champions in making sustainability part of their organization's culture.

1.3   Structure

Subsequent to the introduction this thesis is divided into six further parts. To give answers to the questions set out above, the subject has to be put into perspective of the basic theories and concepts of sustainability on the one hand and of HRD and its role on the other hand. *Chapter 2* comprises the initial theoretical foundation of this thesis, portraying a structured review of the current state of theoretical and practical research. Then, *Chapter 3* explains the appropriate methodology including the research paradigm and design, data collection and finally data analysis. *Chapter 4* presents the findings of the empirical research which was conducted in order to bridge the concepts of HRD and sustainability strategies. The inductive categories established from empirical facts and statements are a central interest of this work. Following this, *Chapter 5* provides important guidance for academia and practice to increase their contribution to sustainability. *Chapter 6* highlights theoretical and practical contributions of this study and their implications. It will also discuss limitations of the realized empirical study. The chapter concludes with suggestions for future research. Finally, *Chapter 7* summarizes key insights and statements of this thesis and gives assumptions about the future evolution of HRD in the context of sustainability strategies.

2 Human Resources Development towards Sustainability Aims

This chapter comprises the theoretical foundation of this thesis, portraying the findings of a literature review. The second and third sections discuss relevant concepts and theories to form an understanding of the novel interface of HRD activities to implement sustainability.

2.1 Structured Review Methodology

Initially, this chapter outlines the research methodology which was applied in order to gain theoretical insights into the problem posed. The realized review process is analog to proposed review methodologies in that it covers the necessary stages suggested by Cooper (1998), Fink (2005) and others. The first step of formulating the research problem was undertaken in the previous chapter. As the process flow in figure 3 indicates, the procedure continues with an identification and selection of literature and concludes with an evaluation and synopsis of the findings. Cooper differentiates between two types of scientific literature review: theoretical review and research synthesis. *Theoretical reviews* expound theories to explain a certain phenomenon. *Research synthesis* focuses on empirical studies and aims at presenting "... the state of knowledge concerning the relation(s) of interest and to highlight important issues that research has left unresolved" (Cooper, 1998, p. 3).

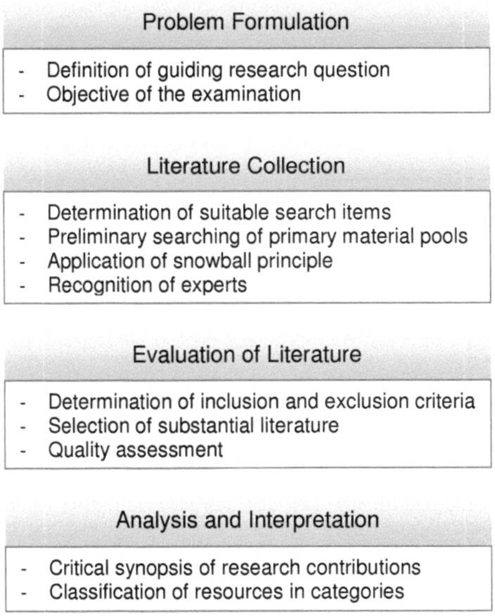

Problem Formulation

- Definition of guiding research question
- Objective of the examination

Literature Collection

- Determination of suitable search items
- Preliminary searching of primary material pools
- Application of snowball principle
- Recognition of experts

Evaluation of Literature

- Determination of inclusion and exclusion criteria
- Selection of substantial literature
- Quality assessment

Analysis and Interpretation

- Critical synopsis of research contributions
- Classification of resources in categories

Figure 3: Literature Review Process
Source: Own representation based on Cooper, 1998, pp. 5.

Another frequently used term to describe the latter process is *systematic review*. At a meta level, this process is viewed "… as a self-contained research project in itself that explores a clearly specified question" (Denyer & Tranfield, 2009, p. 671). Otherwise put, the aim is to locate and choose existing primary material according to predefined relevance and quality criteria, whereupon a concise evidence-based conclusion is drawn (ibid.). In contrast to this approach which should provide a systematic analysis of empirical data and in contrast to a solid, exhaustive presentation of theoretical literature, the subsequent deliberations emphasize distinctive aspects only. The applied *comprehensive literature review* regards both theoretical backgrounds and current research outcomes and attempts to build bridges between the topic areas. Overall, critical knowledge is extracted in view of its relevance for the empirical study following in later chapters. As this review shall merely introduce the new primary study, it will be restricted to those theoretical works and empirical studies pertinent to the specific interface of HRD approaches for sustainability.

2.1.1 Literature Search and Selection

To gather relevant secondary literature, both databases and library catalogues where sifted through. On the one hand, the research area of economics was investigated primarily by using Business Source Elite (EBSCO), Web of Science, EconBiz, ScienceDirect and Abi Inform/Proquest. On the other hand, the psychological research field was explored by focusing on the databases PsycARTICLES, PSYNDEX and PsycINFO. Lastly, the university's library catalog DigiBib/ BetaCatalog of BUW and Google Scholar were consulted. By using the search engine scholar.google the vast number of readily accessible documents on the internet was filtered solely by considering reliable scientific articles and not sources like blogs, tweets or forums.

Identification of Articles

The synonym keywords partly named in table 1 were combined with Boolean operators[1] in a successive manner. The combination [sustainab* AND "human resource development"] was found to effect notable literature. Hence, table 2 below shows this combination's results. Conversely, the German equivalent [nachhaltig* AND Personalentwicklung] did not yield results. The overall hits revealed in the title category were 37,944 for the term "sustainab*" and 1,236 for the term "human resource development". Indeed, as displayed in table 2, only 39 articles about the guiding research question which combines the two topics were identified.

---

[1] Boolean syntax operators "allow the searcher to use set theory to help define the items that will be retrieved by a search" (Cooper, 1998, p. 50).

Sustainability	HRD	Employees
- CSR - Responsibility - Nachhaltigkeit	- Teaching & Training - Education - HRM - Personalentwicklung - Mitarbeitertraining - Fort- & Weiterbildung	- Personnel - Staff - Human capital - Mitarbeiter

Table 1: Overview of Keywords used in Literature Identification
Source: Own representation.

Selection of relevant Articles

As mentioned above, 39 articles about the guiding research question were identified (see Table 2). For an efficient evaluation of the data found, both *inclusion* and *exclusion criteria* to the literature in the further review process are needed (Cooper, 1998, p. 78). Primarily, results were inspected on their content-related relevance by screening title, abstract and all text on decisive factors concerning the directive research question. Only scholarly peer reviewed journals in English and German were considered whereas all publication types and publication dates were included. By application of the snowball principle, recognized literature's references were scanned for further pertinent literature. Finally, to assess the validity of a certain paper, the number of its Google scholar citations and ideally the scientific quality of the publishing journal which is "... defined as the degree to which the journal in question advances business research as an academic discipline" (VHB[2], 2015) were taken into account. Upon completion of this thesis, over 100 papers about relevant subjects identified through literature research and snowball principle were read. Of these papers, about 25 deal explicitly with sustainability and about 80 with HRD-related issues or the joint subject area of HRD approaches towards sustainability aims. The third step of analysis and the synthesis of findings as final step within the review process are expounded in the next chapters.

2.1.2 Overview of Secondary Research Findings

This section briefly outlines crucial topics surrounding the complex of themes. Since the research on sustainability and HRD stems from various academic fields, the perspectives are quite diverse. By far the most extensive literature on sustainability and HRD or their interface arises out of the US and the UK. The predominance of US or UK-based topical research is reflected in the amount of papers published in journals.

---

[2] VHB is the German Academic Association for Business Research (Verband der Hochschullehrer für Betriebswirtschaft e.V., Göttingen).

	Database	Keywords	All text	Abstract	Title
economics	EBSCO	sustainab*	75,336	29,216	11,916
		"human resource development"	6,092	1,620	489
		sustainab* AND "human resource development"	954	124	<u>33</u>
	ScienceDirect[1]	sustainab*	279,323	38,111	13,083
		"human resource development"	8,777	193	62
		sustainab* AND "human resource development"	1,875	21	<u>1</u>
	Abi Inform/ Proquest	sustainab*	36,272	25,056	10,216
		"human resource development"	1,769	812	356
		sustainab* AND "human resource development"	34	21	<u>0</u>
psychology	Psyc ARTICLES	sustainab*	1,510	133	30
		"human resource development"	331	7	2
		sustainab* AND "human resource development"	21	0	<u>0</u>
	Psyndex[1]	sustainab*	491	194	192
		"human resource development"	46	17	13
		sustainab* AND "human resource development"	0	0	<u>0</u>
	PsycINFO	sustainab*	8,847	7,556	2,024
		"human resource development"	2,129	1,018	290
		sustainab* AND "human resource development"	47	27	<u>5</u>
overall	DigiBib/ BUW BetaCatalog[2]	sustainab*	1,293	-	483
		"human resource development"	32	-	24
		sustainab* AND "human resource development"	0	-	<u>0</u>

Note: [1] Explicit limitation on peer reviewed articles not possible. [2] Abstract search option not available.
Table 2: Literature Search Results per Database
Source: Own representation, retrieved on 07 May 2015.

The review of these sources revealed that extant literature discusses definitions of sustainability, CSR and related concepts (Aguinis, 2011; Carroll, 1999; Elkington, 1997). Searching for ["human resource development"] generated less literature, to be exact 3,667 results within the title (see Table 2). The derived classification shown in table 3 includes both the research areas of sustainability, HRD and their incorporated emergent stream. It shows that the concept of sustainable development is usually three-dimensional and consists of ecological, economic and social goals (Elkington, 1997). Concerning HRD the three domains of (1) training and development, (2) organization development, and (3) career development are frequently named (Swanson & Holton, 2001). The focus of the research question at hand can be subsumed at a macro level, which concerns HRD instruments' support during the implementation of sustainability strategies. On the one hand, this summarizing taxonomy facilitates classing the research objective of the study and on the other hand it serves as structural preview for the defining terms and concepts following in the next chapter.

Sustainable Development	Human Resource Development
- Balance of ecological, economic and social aims	- Training and development - Organization development - Career development

Integration of Sustainability and HRD
I. Micro level: HRD as an element of the sustainable HR strategy **II.** Macro level: HRD instruments' support during implementation of sustainability strategy

Table 3: Taxonomy of Themes Addressed in Literature
Source: Own representation.

2.2 Foundation Concepts

The question of definition of sustainability is a crucial, yet complicated one. As it is relevant that the concept is understood when linking it with HRD, the role of this chapter is to give some clarity about sustainable development.

2.2.1 Evolution of Sustainable Development and Corporate Responsibility

It is significant that the terminus 'sustainability' is widely used as the research demonstrated above underlines: The application of [sustainab*] generated 37,944 results within the title and 403,072 results when searched through the entire text. Historically, the source of *sustainability* lies within forestry and was first mentioned by Hannß Carl von Carlowitz in his book 'Sylvicultura oeconomica' in the context of uncontrolled deforestation for silver mining (1713, pp. 105). In his work, the author describes economic planning that attempts to foster economic growth while preserving the quality of the environment. Today's dissemination of the term goes back to 1987 when a team led by Gro Harlem Brundtland discussed the issue of sustainability publicly in the so called Brundtland report of the World Commission on Environment and Development (WCED). The purpose of the report was to develop an agenda for global change and a common future for mankind. In this report 'Our common future' of the

WCED *sustainable development* was defined as "... development that meets the needs of the present without compromising the ability of future generations to meet their own needs" (WCED, 1987, p. 41). In 1992, the Rio declaration on Environment and Development concretized the term sustainable development into a three-dimensional concept which included a balance of ecological, economic and social aims (United Nations Conference on Environment and Development, 1992). This three-dimensional concept is better known as the *Triple-Bottom-Line* (TBL) from Elkington (1997). In a newer comprehensive review, Bansal (2005) translates the TBL into the notions of environmental integrity, social equity, and economic prosperity.

The framework of *corporate responsibility* (CR) goes back even further. In 1953 Bowen defined it as "... an obligation to pursue those policies, to make those decisions, or to follow those lines of action that are desirable in terms of the objectives and values for our society" (p. 6). Historically, a myriad of terms has been used to refer to corporate responsibility, some of these include: CSR, CS, corporate ethics or corporate citizenship (Aguinis, 2011). Thus, CSR is a term related to sustainability and in some cases even used as a synonym (Steurer, Langer, Konrad & Martinuzzi, 2005; Van Marrewijk, 2003).

In an attempt to determine sustainability or sustainable development for the corporate level, Dyllick and Hockerts (2002) define *corporate sustainability* (CS) as "... meeting the needs of a firm's direct and indirect stakeholders [...] without compromising its ability to meet the needs of future stakeholders as well" (p. 131). Steurer et al. (2005) separate the concepts of CSR and CS by the fact that CSR is stakeholder-focused and lacks the long- term perspective inherent in CS. The social dimension of the CS concept is often used synonymously with the terms CSR or ethics (Jones-Christensen, Peirce, Hartman, Hoffman, Carrier, 2007). Concerning corporate responsibility, Aguinis (2011) finds the term *organizational responsibility* more encompassing as it includes any type of organization. Thereafter, the author defines organizational responsibility as context-specific actions and policies that consider all pillars of the TBL and stakeholders' expectations at the same time (ibid.). The concept of corporate responsibility will not be disregarded within the empirical research. It will be taken into subordinate account based on definitions which incorporate ethical consciousness in treating the firms' stakeholders in a responsible manner (Carrol, 1991; Hopkins, 2003). Likewise, a more recent definition of CSR by the European Commission applies for the purpose of this study: "... the responsibility of enterprises for their impacts on society" (European Commission, 2011, p. 6).

2.2.2 Elements of Corporate Sustainability Strategy

In today's global market environment, competitive strategy has become a crucial mechanism to differentiate and achieve long-lasting *competitive advantage* (CA). Johnson, Whittington and Scholes (2010) debate that many industries are marked by *hyper competition* making it hardly possible to achieve CA. Weston, Mitchell and Mulherin (2004) put it as follows: "Strategies seek to provide a framework for continuity and adjustments in evolving environments and competitive conditions. The goal of strategy is to guide a firm to acquire capabilities and other resources to achieve a sustainable, competitive advantage" (p. 102). Due to the fact that the concept of sustainability includes broad and various fields of activities, Baumgartner and Ebner (2010) argue that "Although many companies investigate sustainability management and publish sustainability reports, their main focus in this endeavour remains unclear" (p. 1).

The question to be answered is why sustainability is considered a strategic issue. Besides diverse benefits of pursuing sustainability like saving energy, differentiation or attracting the best employees, Hitchcock and Willard (2009) name environmental issues or health concerns as reasons. In an intertwined circular reasoning, both the causes for and benefits of sustainability strategies involve optimizing economical, environmental and social elements. As Lee and Ball (2003) point out, there is little evidence to suggest that corporations will become more sustainable voluntarily, but rather that "… corporate contributions to sustainability must stem from self-interest and survival instincts" (p. 89). Jaffee (2001) underlines a defining feature which is that "The organization does not emerge accidentally or informally but is constructed a priori to achieve an objective" (p. 6). According to Porter (1987), diversified companies have a *corporate strategy* which "… makes the corporate whole add up to more than the sum of its business unit parts" (p. 43) to create *competitive advantage* (CA). "Yet corporate strategy should not be a once-and-for-all choice but a vision that can evolve" (ibid., p. 57) meaning that a company should determine a long-term vision and proceed toward it. Contrary to the classical point of view, from a recent point of view ecological and social actions do not necessarily interfere with the aim of economic success (Fowler & Hope, 2007; Porter & Kramer, 2011). The connection between CA and social issues is explained by Porter and Kramer (2011) as the principle of *creating shared value* (CSV). The idea is to create economic value and concurrently value for society. However, this concept should not be confused with sustainability or social responsibility. It is regarded as a way to achieve economic success by recognizing "… societal needs, benefits and harms that are or could be embodied in the firm's products" (ibid., p. 68). Therefore, *value* is defined relative to costs, because societal problems can interfere with internal costs in the company's value chain (ibid., p. 68). As sustainability is seen as system-scale term it is debatable whether the impact of organizations on a system as whole can be assessed (Zadek, 2001). It is therefore more suitable to use the term 'sustainability-promoting corporation' as defined by Diesendorf (2000): "... a corporation which is successfully integrating sustainable development into its strategy" (p. 6). Although the aim of this research is not to label individual organizations as sustainable or unsustainable, Diesendorf's definition is applied to identify companies that integrate sustainability with strategy.

Within the meaning of corporate sustainability (CS) three principles are generally accepted (Gminder, Bieker, Dyllick & Hockerts, 2002, p. 96): Capital maintenance, permanence and three-dimensional creation of value. *Capital maintenance* indicates that a corporation should subsist by only using its income and not its capital. This principle is well-known in its economic sense but should be applied to all three dimensions of sustainability. The second principal of *permanence* claims a business development to be retained in the long run. Lastly, the three-dimensional *creation of value* requires a maintenance and equal creation of value in social, ecological and economic terms. As Dyllick and Hockerts (2002) declare a single focus on economic sustainability only functions in the short run; in the long run a satisfaction of all three dimensions should be achieved. In economic terms sustainability means that companies guarantee "... at any time cash flow sufficient to ensure liquidity while producing a persistent above average return to their shareholders" (Dyllick and Hockerts, 2002, p. 133). The objective of ecological sustainability is attained if the following three criteria are fulfilled: (1) renewable natural resources are only consumed as far as they can be reproduced; (2) non-renewable resources are only consumed as far as they can be substituted by other resources; and (3) the amount of emission caused by a company does not exceed the amount of emission which can be assimilated and absorbed by the natural system. In social terms a company can increase the human capital of a society and further its societal capital (ibid.).

The intersection between society and corporate performance is depicted in figure 4. If a company pursues a CS strategy, the purpose is to create shared value not only profit. Baumgartner and Ebner (2010) specify that "External influences also affect the corporate orientation on sustainability. Moreover, CS also has positive effects on society in the long term" (p. 77). That is, diverse macro-economic factors have to be regarded in order to fulfill the balance of economic, ecological and social sustainability. In the long run a company can build a CA, for instance through cost reductions or a better employer image (Ramus & Killmer, 2007).

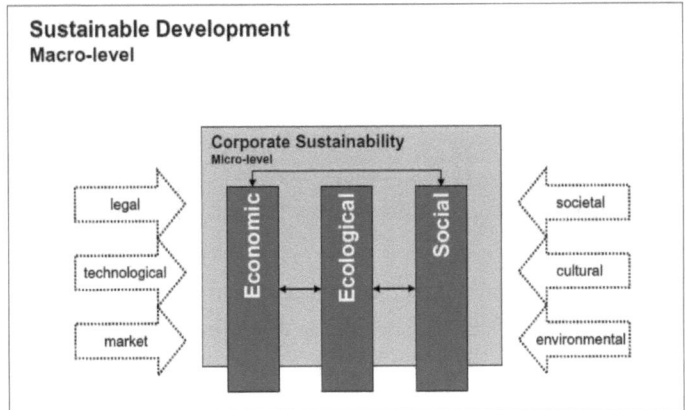

Figure 4: Corporate Sustainability and its Interdependencies
Source: Ebner & Baumgartner, 2006, p. 13.

Regarding the comprehension of sustainability strategy for the envisaged expert interviews, a focus is put on the TBL, i.e. the balance of ecological, economic and social aims. Furthermore, a broad consideration of sustainability in all managerial decisions is aimed for. In the sense of the afore mentioned shared value concept, the idea is that employees' behavior is influenced by a mindset of sustainability at all times. According to Goodpaster (2007), mindsets are a set of "... beliefs and attitudes which govern someone's behavior and outlook" (p. 37). The idea of a *global mindset* implies that human and organizational mental models are adapted to the thought of sustainability.

2.2.3 Human Resources and their Development

Although McGuire and Cseh (2006) argue that a disciplinary base is essential to develop research and practice in HRD, they also assess that no definite perspective exists. This absence of a clear understanding and consensus on the constituent components of HRD results in a diversity of conceptual frameworks. In her article on the refusal to define HRD, Lee (2001) challenges definitions as a thing of being rather than "... what we would like HRD to *become*, in the knowledge that it will never *be*, but that we might influence its *becoming*" (p. 338). According to Kuchinke (2001), HRD should not be seen as an isolated discipline in the academic sense: "... HRD does not count as a discipline but rather as a field with multiple disciplines as its roots or foundations" (p. 292). HRD is an interdisciplinary research field which can be subsumed under social sciences and involves economics, psychology, sociology, anthropology and political science in equal shares (Kuchinke, 2001). Swanson (2001) calls for conclusive theory building in HRD to ensure further maturing of the discipline. Thereafter,

Swanson (2001) states that HRD relies on psychological, economic and systems theory. Regarding the application of resources the author concretizes that psychological theory captures the development of human resources, the economic perspective obviously deals with their efficient, effective utilization and systems theory treats the dynamic interactions of micro and macro-variables (ibid.). In an attempt to provide a solid philosophical foundation, Kuchinke (2010) argues for the inclusion of *human development* ideas. The author stresses the need of HRD to formulate goals and responsibilities as a unique set of values in order to satisfy changing requirements in the era of global mobility. The core idea presented is that – under the premise of HRD being classified into the wider human development concept – human flourishing should be the leading value of HRD (ibid.). The term resource generally refers to "… something that the organization can draw upon to accomplish its aims" (Helfat et al., 2007, p. 4). Thus, all human characteristics that can achieve an economic profit are recognized as *human resources* (HR). Barney (2002) defines human capital as "… the training, experience, judgment, intelligence, relationships, and insight of individual managers and workers in a firm" (p. 156). However, it has to be noted that human resources are active subjects with individual needs and wants (Brewster & Larsen, 2000). Human characteristics involve both formal professional and less formal skills like experience or motivation (Tomé, 2011). Consequently, HRD is the activity by which HR are fostered. Likewise to its disciplinary foundation, there is no clear discretion on the facets of HRD (McGuire & Cseh, 2006). By unifying the idea of guiding norms and the previous consideration of theory being particularly important for the advancement of HRD, Swanson puts forward a theory of ethical intent (Swanson, 2001). It must also be highlighted, that definitions of HRD are influenced by the cultural context in which they emerge and are not self-evidently appropriate internationally (McLean & McLean, 2001). In spite of that, McLean and McLean claim their definition to be holistic, so that it serves the purpose of this study:

> *Human resource development is any process or activity that, either initially or over the long term, has the potential to develop adults' work-based knowledge, expertise, productivity and satisfaction, whether for personal or group/ team gain, or for the benefit of an organization, community, nation or, ultimately, the whole of humanity. (McLean & McLean, 2001, p. 322)*

As recognizable in figure 5, HRD is a process within the larger environmental and organizational system which HRD is supposed to harmonize and shape (Swanson, 2001). Lee (2010) examines HRD in relation to challenges it faces, among them changes of technology, demographics and the working situation.

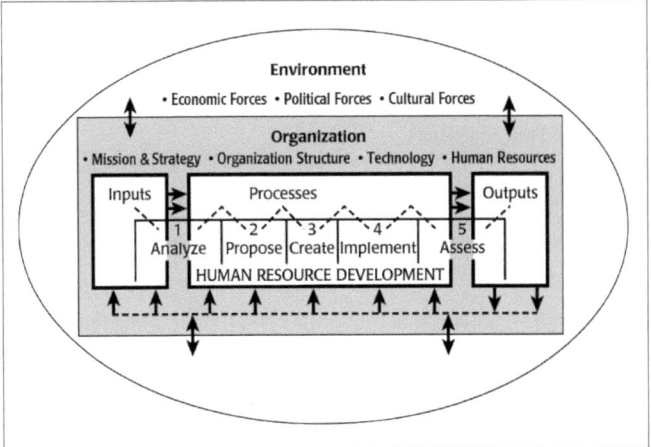

Figure 5: Human Resource Development within the Organization and Environment
Source: Swanson & Holton, 2001, p. 91.

Moreover, the author argues that humans change "… in concert with shifts in geographical, cultural, economic and social boundaries" (Lee, 2010, p. 528). To cope with such shifting boundaries, HRD includes both *organizational development* (OD) and *training and development* (T&D) which aim at improving performance on organizational, work process, group and individual levels (Swanson, 2001). The target of OD is to enhance performance through systematical implementation of organizational change. As a final definition, "T&D is the process of systematically developing expertise in individuals" (Swanson, 2001, p. 304). Altogether, beyond its effects on individuals and organizations by human capital formation, savings and investment, HRD can also benefit economic development (Zidan, 2001).

2.3 Research Status of HRD for Sustainability Endeavors

2.3.1 Critical Research Streams of HRD

First of all, a few specialist journals could be identified, including 'Human Resource Development International', 'Human Resource Development Review', 'International Journal of Training and Development', 'European Journal of Training and Development' and 'Journal of Human Resource and Sustainability Studies'. This note is owed to the fact that many of the experts introduced in this section are members of their editorial boards, granting them an impactful sphere. Accordingly, table 4 shows noteworthy experts within HRD research of interest. As a reference to the number of results presented, acknowledged authorities on sustainability like Elkington and Brundtland obtain 32,900 respectively 74,400 results. Evolving perspectives that have to be differentiated are strategic, critical and holistic HRD (Fenwick, 2005; Horwitz, 1999; Lee, 2007; McLean & McLean, 2001; Scully-Russ, 2012). In a *critical HRD* approach, Bierema and Callahan (2014) reject short-term economic performance as the driving force. Garavan and McGuire (2010) differentiate societal and global HRD while in a different approach of Sheehan, Garavan and Carbery (2014) four HRD concepts (sustainable, green, societal and socially conscious) are used. *Societal HRD* conceptions also plead for long-term profitability with a focus on the TBL (Garavan & McGuire, 2010). Additionally, *strategic HRD* focuses on the dependency on corporate competitive strategy (Horwitz, 1999) and *global HRD* takes the potential reach of globally operating HRD and learning functions of multinational corporations (MNCs) into account (Garavan & McGuire, 2010). As discussed earlier, Lee (2007, 2010) argues that *holistic HRD* underlies globalization and historic change.

Author (Results, Citations[1])	Theoretical Perspective
Fenwick, T. (907; -)	- Pleading for a greater engagement of HRD professionals in CSR.
Sheehan, M. (258; 2757)	- Despite its notable contribution to sustainability/CSR in theory and practice, HRD is something of a "black box", i.e. not sufficiently understood.
Bierema, L. (233; 1,987)	- Critical HRD (CHRD) rejects economic performance as driving force and stresses the humanistic roots of the field (socially conscious HRD). - Relating, Learning, Changing, and Organizing as the areas of HRD practice.
McLean, G. N. (519; -)	- Proposition of a global, expanded definition on HRD with constraint that ambiguity cannot be removed and HRD knowledge is in constant dialogue.
Lee, M. (829; 748)	- Adoption of a holistic view on HRD including climate, technological and population change and refusal to define HRD as a thing of stagnant being.
Garavan, T. (282; 4,790)	- Emphasis on societal HRD (SHRD) beyond short-term economic goals with its strong contribution to CSR, sustainability and ethics. - Identification of levels of barriers to implementation of CS in organizations and proposition of HRD intervention typology.

Note: [1] Both information retrieved from Google Scholar.
Table 4: Noteworthy Experts of Human Resource Development Research Field
Source: Own representation, retrieved on 22 May 2015.

Furthermore, a few major themes can be traced in HRD literature on sustainability. The first treats the above mentioned societal role and impact of HRD: The profession is criticized for disengaging with its roots in humanistic social science and its original mission of achieving well-being of people. In addition, HRD is described as an instrument of short-term profit maximization (Garavan & McGuire, 2010; Kuchinke, 2010). The second theme is related to the role of executives and senior managers in supporting sustainability and the aid of HRD to influence such key promoters, i.e. leadership development (Rimanoczy & Pearson, 2010; Waite, 2013). The third theme addresses instructional and training strategies that should be used to develop individuals sustainably (Kauffeld, Lorenzo & Weisweiler, 2012; Kira, Van Eijnatten & Balkin, 2010). One recommendation for developing sustainable human resources is to foster reflection, creativity and continuous individual learning within an organizational learning culture (Boud, Cressey & Docherty, 2006). Fourth, a stronger connection of sustainability-related training to ethics and CSR is supported by some authors (Ardichvili, 2013; Garavan & McGuire, 2010). Lastly, a growing body of literature treats strategies for embedding sustainability or CSR, CS and ethics in organizations (Fenwick & Bierema, 2008; Sheehan et al., 2014). According to Garavan and McGuire (2010), HRD can "... raise the awareness of employees and develop positive attitudes toward sustainability" (p. 489).

Regarding the research at hand, pertinent trends driving the field have to be highlighted. Specialist perspectives particularly relevant for this study are (1) demands for a holistic, yet societal conception of HRD; (2) instructional and learning strategies to embed sustainability; and (3) connection of sustainability-related training to ethics and CSR. The decisive ideas for training of ethics and CSR as stated in the third trend will be further clarified. As shown in figure 6, Garavan et al. (2010) classify HRD interventions according to the depth of intervention and to a focus on individual or organizational barriers of sustainability initiatives (Garavan et al., 2010). Consequently, the suggested HRD measures should be appropriate to conquer individual and organizational reluctance. Remarkably, referring to this study's guiding question of how HRD can influence employees – who are seen as key success factors (KSF) for sustainability strategies – appropriate interventions have to be directed at the entire organization and not only individuals. With regard to the empirical research conducted during this thesis firstly the integration of CSR or CS into HRD activities and secondly sustainability focused organizational learning have to be stressed (circled in Figure 6). According to the authors, an integration of CSR or CS with HRD only has surface level impact, whereas interventions that enable sustainability-focused learning result in more fundamental change for the organization (ibid.). To support the call for an overall integration of CSR or CS with HRD the authors refer to Fenwick and Bierema (2008) who state that "In any case, HRD needs to be involved in CSR conversations to ensure its integration with existing HRD education/ training programs in companies truly hoping to develop CSR" (p. 33). Moreover, organizational learning is useful in developing CSR and CS values and implicates active engagement, critical reflection, social validation and cultural interpretation (Garavan et al., 2010). Indeed, the authors acknowledge that "... some of the interventions identified in our typology can be cast as surface or deep depending on the organization" (p. 599). Obviously, variability along the two particular dimensions depending on the context is possible.

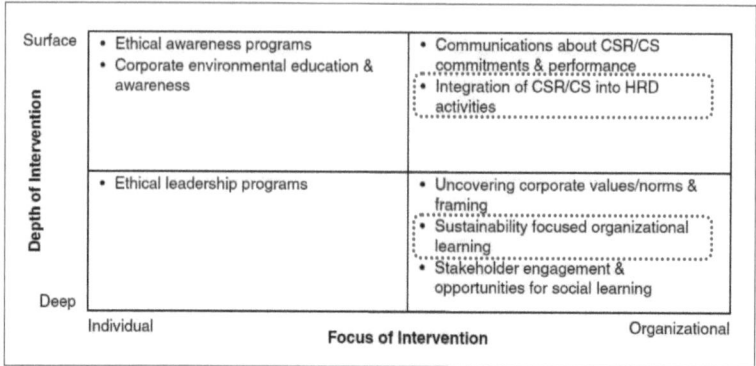

Figure 6: HRD Interventions to Address Corporate Sustainability Behavioral Barriers
Source: Garavan et al., 2010, p. 599.

The essential value of the foregoing is that theoretically HRD is believed to possess "... the knowledge and tools to change organizational behavior and ensure the integration of CSR/ CS into organizational processes and translate both into action" (Garavan et al., 2010, p. 606). The empirical study will determine if a gap exists between theoretical demands of HRD for sustainability aims and actual initiatives in practice.

2.3.2 Research Insights on HRD Practices for Sustainability

Intitial remarks concerning instructional strategies to embed sustainability and the connection of sustainability training to ethics and CSR were made above. Relating to the structure of the TBL, interdependencies of sustainability and employee behavior have been minded in empirical studies and theoretical reviews. In the following paragraph some interdependencies are discussed as they form a deeper understanding of the current state of research and the existing research gap which will be addressed in the study at hand. Additionally, Appendix A.1 lists the most relevant publications and their primary insights on the overall research question of HRD approaches for sustainability.

Concerning HRD for ecological sustainability, employee training can have a positive effect on the relationship between environmental attitude and companies' sustainability performance (Daily & Huang, 2001). Notably, some authors state that "... to the best of our knowledge, our study is the first to test the moderating effect of employee training" (Ji, Huang, Liu, Zhu & Cai, 2012, p. 3004). Young et al. (2013) also review the role of environmental programs in changing employee behavior and find environmental awareness, monetary incentives or management support and training as strong predictors. Furthermore, Scholz and Müller (2014) name green HR activities like green issues in job descriptions, in employer branding and training in green management. Several authors (Ardichvili & Jondle, 2009; Guerci, Radaelli, Siletti, Cirella & Shani, 2015; Hatcher & Aragon, 2000a, 2000b) analyze the role of HRD in developing ethical business cultures. They conclude that HRD needs to engage in activities like establishing a code of ethics and ethical training for employees (Ardichvili & Jondle, 2009). Mueller, Spiess, Hattrup and Lin-Hi (2012) find out that CSR positively influences employees' affective commitment to an organization. Thus, corporations can benefit from improving their social performance regarding both external stakeholders and their group of employees. The authors assess, that "This is even more relevant for companies operating in cultures higher in humane orientation, collectivism, and egalitarianism" (ibid., pp. 1195). Fenwick and Bierema (2008) confirm that integrated understandings and processes of organizational and human development, i.e. employee education and learning are vital for sufficient CSR commitment. Another relevant determinant of societal sustainability is assessed by Caliguri, Mencin and Jiang (2013) who discuss the influence of volunteer engagement. The authors state multiple benefits of volunteerism assignments that include meaningful projects, social support within NGOs, and opportunities for skill development (Caliguri et al., 2013). Global service learning has deep effects on cognitive, affective, and behavioral levels and helps participants develop socially responsible mindsets (Pless & Maak, 2011). Finally turning to economic sustainability, Kochan (2008) argues that HR professionals should become more analytical and able to document benefits of effective HR policies and practices to employees and firms. HR professionals need to be "... more analytical and able to justify suppport for progressive HR policies based on their demonstrated and documented bottom line results" (ibid,. p. 615). Furthermore, incentivizing middle managers toward the TBL is considered as economic sustainability program (Merriman & Sen, 2012).

It has been shown, that literature and empirical research concerning HRD interventions for sustainability focus on separate aspects. Comparing the information on the three aspects of sustainability, strong support is available for environmental training activities and social learning through corporate volunteering. Thus, how HRD can contribute the social as well as the economical and the environmental dimension is still underresearched. Therefore, the research approach of the study at hand is to look at all three dimensions of sustainability. Taken from the idea of a global mindset set out above, HRD approaches concerning all facets of a sustainability strategy will be considered. Finally, the undertaken research can make valuable contributions as it appears to be the first to analyze the practical status quo of employee training for sustainability within large corporations in Germany.

3 Empirical Research Methodology

This chapter describes the general qualitative research approach and thereafter the methodological choices that have been made for the present empirical research. The following chapter four contains the practical results.

3.1 Qualitative Research Paradigm

In order to gain practical insights into the research question at hand, *qualitative research* was chosen as methodology. Qualitative research addresses issues by inquiring about the interviewee's perspective, analyzing the data in an interpretative way and generalizing in a theoretical sense (Flick, 2015). One advantage of qualitative research compared to quantitative methods is that novel empirical facts are collected and a theory is developed in a non-standardized circular manner (ibid.). Instead of deriving hypotheses from theoretical frameworks and quantitatively testing them (deductive approach), this research makes use of inductive strategies. Hence, "… the research situation is designed more as a dialogue, in which probing, new aspects, and their own estimations find place" (Flick, 2015, p. 11).

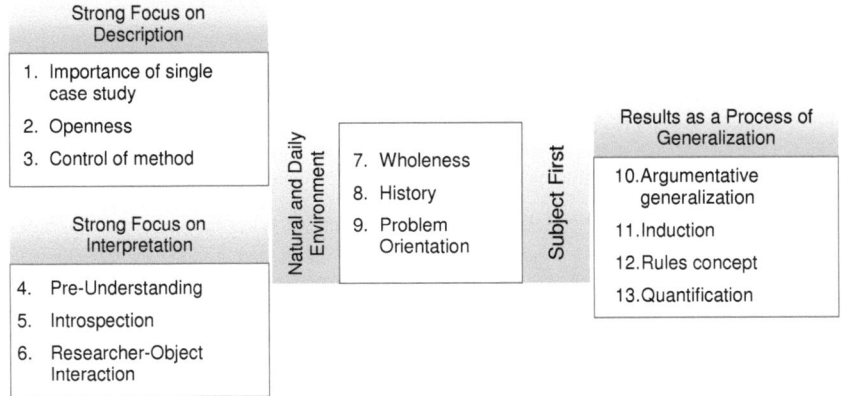

Figure 7: The Foundations and Pillars of Qualitative Thinking
Source: Translated from Mayring, 2002, p. 26.

The idea of qualitative thinking is represented in figure 7. These modular principles of qualitative reasoning should be understood hierarchically from left to right. As the final generalization process is addressed in detail later an explanation is omitted here. Only the most applicable pillars of those identified by Mayring (2002) will be highlighted. Regarding the focus on description it is essential for qualitative research to consider individual cases in an open but methodically controlled manner which provides an opportunity to make new findings (ibid.).

The focus on interpretation depicted in figure 7 is particularly important for the present study. Mayring (2002, pp. 24) demands for a treatment of prior knowledge in a *hermeneutic spiral*: Pre-understandings must be disclosed and gradually refined when divergent indications based on the research object occur (ibid.). The *qualitative content analysis* conducted further below has similarities with the hermeneutic spiral as preconceptions are modified through text evaluation. Moreover, the analysis of introspective data as an information source is admitted and research is seen as an interaction in which researcher and research object evolve (ibid.). To estimate the quality of qualitative social research, Mayring (ibid., pp. 144) formulates six generic quality criteria which are respected if applicable in the present study:

(1) *Process documentation* of methods, data generation and analysis;

(2) *Argumentative safeguarding* of interpretations;

(3) *Rule-governed* proceeding in order to systematize and secure data analysis;

(4) *Proximity to the research object*, through field research, exploring the environment of the examined individuals;

(5) *Communicative validation*, that is informant feedback as an ethical need to achieve mutual consent about the results between informant and researcher;

(6) *Triangulation* by comparing different procedures of analysis and the results against the background of the same research question.

Frequently, the target of qualitative studies is to generate a valid *grounded theory* which is a "... theory suited to its supposed uses" (Glaser & Strauss, 1967, p. 3). As can be seen in figure 8, within grounded theory the explorative process of inductive category formation is called *open coding* (Cho & Lee, 2014). Glaser and Strauss (1967) postulate that "[The researcher's job] is not to provide a perfect description of an area, but to develop a theory that accounts for much of the relevant behavior" (p. 30).

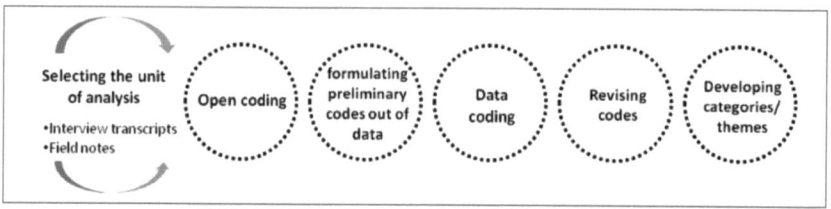

Figure 8: Procedure Used in an Inductive Approach to Qualitative Content Analysis
Source: Cho & Lee, 2014, p. 11.

However, the research outcome of the study at hand cannot be substantive theory. The aim is rather to apply qualitative content analysis which results in a structured, detailed description and evaluation of the empirical findings. In summary, the goal of this research is to describe the meaning of the gathered material and to develop categories or themes (see Chapter 3.2.5).

3.2 Empirical Method

3.2.1 Research Design

The empirical analysis in this thesis is based on primary data obtained through *explorative expert interviews*. Gläser and Laudel (2010) define expert interviews as reconstructive social studies with the objective of making knowledge of persons involved in particular situations or processes accessible. Notably, it is not the exposed status of an interviewee that distinguishes expert interviews in comparison to other research designs. The research target is decisive for the function of an interview and consequently the role of an interview partner arises (Gläser & Laudel, 2010). Bogner, Littig and Menz (2014) underline that unlike other forms of qualitative interviews, namely the problem-centered (Witzel, 1982), episodic or narrative interview (Flick, 2015; Hermanns, 1995), expert interviews do not have a preset methodological approach. Bogner and Menz (2009) suggest that expert interviews have three features which allow for the exploration, systematization and lastly theory-generation within a new research area. Consequently, aims of expert interviews are:

(1) *Orientation* in order to give a new field of study a thematic structure and to generate hypotheses,

(2) *Collection of context information* in order to complement insights from the application of other methods, and

(3) *Development of a typology or a theory* from reconstructing the knowledge of various experts (Bogner & Menz, 2009, pp. 46).

Despite the fact that expert interviews do not designate a specific methodological approach, Bogner et al. (2014) distinguish four functions that are listed in table 5. *Explorative expert interviews* give a first orientation in the field, sharpen the scientific awareness and generate hypotheses. The goal of *systematizing expert interviews* lies in a broad and comprehensive survey of expertise: The interview makes systematic information retrieval possible (ibid.). Based on this division, the approach of the present study is both information gathering and subsequently systematization of these, i.e. evolving from an explorative to a profound expert interview.

	Explorative	Profound
Informational	expert interview for explorative data collection	systematizing expert interview
Interpretive	expert interview for exploration of interpretations	theory-generating expert interview

Table 5: Forms of Expert Interviews
Source: Translated from Bogner et al., 2014, p. 23.

Experts are not only interviewed because of their rigid knowledge but first and foremost when their knowledge unfolds meaning through practical effectiveness and social impact (Bogner et al., 2014). Next to *reflexivity*, *consistency* and *certainty*, an important feature of expertise is practical effectiveness (ibid., p. 14). Pistrang and Barker (2012) declare inductive theory generation in underresearched, undertheorized areas as strength of qualitative approaches. Correspondingly, regarding the various experts interviewed, both *technical* and *process knowledge* is addressed. The first form relates to rules or application routines within a specific field, while process knowledge contains information on organizational constellations or actions. Lastly, the experts' subjective points of views, i.e. interpretive knowledge, are peripherally regarded since expert interviews should focus on the interviewees' expertise in a specific area (Flick, 2015).

Finally, within the discussion of expert interviews two aspects are central: On the one side the expert status depends on sought knowledge referring to the specific research interest. On the other side, a purely pragmatic determination of expert status according to the research interest is not adequate because it does not give any hints on where to find relevant experts (Meuser & Nagel, 2009). By implication, labeling a person as expert refers to an institutional-organizational attribution made beforehand in the respective field. The next chapter explains in detail how experts were selected.

3.2.2 Selection and Recruitment of Sample

In qualitative research two general directions of sampling can be distinguished: A priori and theoretical sampling. *Theoretical sampling* means that a sample is gradually supplemented on the basis of states of knowledge reached during the investigation (Mayer, 2004, p. 38). Since the expert interviews conducted for this study follow a concrete research question, the *a priori sampling method* with deliberate, reasoned criteria which are retained and not successively adjusted is used. Firstly, the companies selected for the qualitative inquiry were searched using the database Hoppenstedt provided by Bisnode Deutschland GmbH, which contains daily updated business data on the leading companies in Germany (Bisnode, 2015). Among the extensive options, the search was restricted to firms with over 4,000 employees within the federal state of North Rhine-Westphalia (NRW). To create a diverse sample all industries including chemical, electric utility or telecommunication industry were regarded. Thereby a broad cross-section of German industry was prepared. Furthermore, the widespread orientation was targeted to eliminate the risk of distinctive intra-sector practices which could not be transferred to other fields. Also, considering all industries would permit for recognition of pioneers or variances in the complex of themes. Which is more, a constraint to specific branches could interfere with the purpose of establishing a generalization through the evaluation and interpretation of findings. From the resulting list of 231 companies, those that met two criteria were selected:

(1) In accordance with cost, time and feasibility capabilities, the company has a branch in the greater Cologne-Bonn-Düsseldorf area, and

(2) The company has implemented a sustainability strategy.

For the most part, the filtered companies are members of the econsense forum[3], so that a specialization in the area of sustainable development is ensured per se (econsense, 2015). Otherwise information about a sustainability alignment was retrieved from the corporation's websites. Secondly, the individuals to be interviewed are not to be chosen randomly to construct a representative sample but according to their expertise on the topic (Flick, 2015). The expert status can be conferred by the researcher so that somebody is entitled expert through their role as respondent (Meuser & Nagel, 2009). Hence, the role of expert is no personal property or ability but an attribution (Bogner et al., 2014). Meuser and Nagel (2009) emphasize decoupling the terminus from a position in the social or professional status system. Furthermore, expertise gained through active participation in any problem-oriented function and not private experiences are at of central interest (Lamnek, 2010). However, separation of the two is hardly possible since experiences made outside the function potentially affect perceptions and behavior within the professional area of responsibility (Meuser & Nagel, 2009). To discern expert more precisely, peculiarities in knowledge and behavior that differ from common knowledge or everyday activities have to be considered (ibid.). *Specialists* have a limited working and skills range subject to control by supervisors or clients whereas experts have relative autonomy (Hitzler, 1994, pp. 25). The understanding of the expert role in the study at hand shall be emphasized: Experts are a unique medium to obtain information of interest, not

---

[3] Econsense is the Forum Sustainable Development of German Business e. V..

the object of exploration itself and they are considered to enhance their profiles due to the specific structure of their knowledge. Still, in pragmatic reality experts are recognized according to an exclusive status, enabling them for instance to describe internal processes and structures of companies (Gläser & Laudel, 2010). Lamnek (2010) stresses, that experts should not be chosen from the circle of personal acquaintances. Following these notions, persons with a suitable job title and description were approached mostly via the professional network platform XING which has around 8.8 million users in its core German labor market (2015). Otherwise, persons from company websites were contacted as gatekeepers. Lastly business acquaintances were asked to make contact with suitable, yet not personally known interviewees. Frequently, contacted people referred to and contacted colleagues with the right expertise if they did not possess expert knowledge in spite of their position title.

Altogether, reaching out to more than 70 persons garnered 12 interviews. For one thing, a manageable sample size agrees with the idea of qualitative thinking, i.e. a *qualitative sample* focuses on content-representation, not random sampling and statistical representation (Lamnek, 2010, p. 352; Mayer, 2004, p. 40). For another thing the research goal has to be reconciled with available resources (Helfferich, 2011). An overview of the type of corporation and the interviewees' job positions is provided in Appendix C.1.

3.2.3 Operationalization via the Interview Guideline

To conduct the interviews in a reasonable, reliable and objective manner, a *semi-structured interview guideline* was designed. As a preliminary point, a structured questionnaire is composed of definite, preordained questions (Ghosh & Chopra, 2003, p. 371). Semi-structured interview designs facilitate covering the intended scope but focus on subjective opinions of interviewees on an issue to some extent (Flick, 2015). In comparison to questionnaires it is allowed to alter formulations and to deviate from the sequence of questions (ibid.). *Open-ended questions* are questions that give respondents freedom to express their views (Ghosh & Chopra, 2003, pp. 371). From a scientific perspective, the question guideline holds a directive function: Unproductive topics are excluded and a narrow focus to the expertise of interest is applied (Meuser & Nagel, 2009). Effectively, each expert interview also involved individual queries and dynamic exchange. As a result, using an interview guide ensures consistent information for comparative purposes but also grants the interviewee flexibility to elaborate unique meanings or raise unanticipated issues (Bogner et al., 2014). Referring to the research topic, the semi-structured open dialogue is useful to find new facts through extensive studying of limited cases. To fulfill the premise of interview *validity*, some precautions have to be taken. All interview items applied in this study were created on the basis of the literature consulted in advance. Systematically, multiple questions were collected, reviewed, structured and subsumed in order to reduce, organize and cluster them content-wise with comprehensible wording.[4] The interviews are conducted in mother tongue (German) which is considered ideal since explanations are not restricted in virtue of a foreign language (Bogner et al., 2014). As a remark, the translation of categories within data analysis is an additional interpretation step which enhances the task of conceptual abstraction (see Appendix C.4).

At the start of each interview, the subject and purpose of investigation is explained and a guarantee of anonymity and audio recording of the conversation is given. The complete interview guideline can be found in Appendix B.1. Here, the most significant interview questions will be stressed. Aside from the introduction, which also clarifies the interviewee's job position, the guideline consists of three further sections. The first two parts ask for general descriptions of the firm's sustainability and HRD strategies or practices and their underlying concepts. In this sequence, an overall comprehension of the challenged study area – the influence and the impetus of HRD on sustainability strategies – is ascertained by the interviewer. In the focal third section, processes of collaboration and coordination, i.e. of HRD involvement in sustainability implementation are inquired about. Hence, respondents should outline their firm's sustainability priorities and the forms of engagement that the HRD unit or they personally undertake in promoting these priorities. In view of the research topic, questioning the help that is needed and provided from HRD in supporting sustainability strategies should extract valuable insights. Since specific teaching or training methods steered by the HRD department in implementing sustainability are a central research interest, the question 'Which kinds of HRD programs related to sustainability are carried out in your company?' is also pivotal.

3.2.4 Influence of the Interviewer

With regard to the quality and relevance of information collected through the interview, the perception of the interviewer by the experts is of particular importance. Also, the following clarifications refer to step two of the circumstances of origin within content analysis as described below. In the present case, the interviewer acts as *co-expert*, which effects a symmetrical dialogue on a high level of expertise (Bogner et al., 2014, pp. 49). It is the interviewer's responsibility to control the discourse so that interesting information is covered and serious digression from the topic is prevented. Mere exchange of ideas, shoptalk or too many counter

---

[4] Originally, the system is called SPSS and stands for "sammeln", "prüfen", "sortieren" and "subsumieren" which refers to gathering, examining, sorting and subsuming (Helferrich, 2011, pp. 182).

questions impedes efficient data collection (ibid.). According to Lamnek (2010), the interview should take place in an environment that is familiar to the respondents, that way artifacts are avoided. Furthermore, *reacting flexibly* to the respondents' needs and showing restraint, which implies *active listening* by the interviewer, are highlighted (ibid., p.320; p. 366). Lastly, steering the conversation on the basis of a semi-structured guide ensures thematic pre-structuring and more particularly mediates the competence of the interviewer (Bogner et al., 2014; Meuser & Nagel, 2009).

3.2.5 Analysis of Data

In this qualitative approach, the data analysis is conducted by the technique of *qualitative content analysis* rather than grounded theory coding (see Chapter 3.1). Content analysis aims at a "... systematic, objective and quantitative description of the manifest content of communication" (Ghosh & Chopra, 2003, p. 77). In line with the criterion of process documentation, the eleven steps of the qualitative content-analytical procedure as proposed by Mayring (2014, pp. 53) are presented in the following.

1. Definition of the Material

As this study produced data itself, the text material that is selected for the data analysis are interview transcripts. More specifically, the text material consists of 8 selected interviews of the overall population of 12 interviews. Two interviews were not analyzed since they did not yield sophisticated, precise expert knowledge. The other two interviews were excluded, because predefined sample criteria were not met: One interviewee is self-employed, the other one works in a medium-sized company outside the state of NRW. Transcripts are incomplete representations of their raw material (see step 3. Formal characteristics). Even when exact rules are applied transcripts always imply "... a loss of information, a focus on only some aspects of the spoken language" (Mayring, 2014, p. 45).

2. Analysis of the Circumstances of Origin

In a second step, it has to be explained, by whom and under which circumstances the material was produced (Mayring, 2010). In the present study, the semi-structured interviews were performed within a period of about six weeks with 12 participants in total. The interviews mostly took place in the working environment of the interviewee. The interview guideline was not send in advance, but in two cases participants requested a short briefing and possible question areas via email beforehand. Concerning the inquiry situation, an explanation of the research subject, the course of the interview and a note of both anonymity and audio recording formed the introduction. As stated above, the interview guideline was applied in a flexible manner. The duration of the interviews amounted to an average of M = 49 minutes (SD = 17.32 minutes).

3. Formal Characteristics of the Material

Since interviews focus on speech rather than visual channel they have to be audio recorded to secure detailed transcription before the analysis (Pistrang & Barker, 2012).[5] Concerning the transcription rules a focus was put on manifest not latent content, which is why para-linguistic and prosodic parameters (volume, intonation) were excluded. Mayring (2014) underlines that the level of transcription detail depends on the interest of evaluation and calls the economic procedure applied within this study a 'selective protocol'. "The researcher defines those parts of the (audio recorded) interview, which are relevant for the research question" (ibid., p. 45). In respect of the *transcription head* the specifications of Langer (2010, pp. 521) were applied: In each transcript the participants were assigned a coding (from A to H) while the letter I indicates the interviewer.

4. Direction of the Analysis

After having described the base material, the next step is to define what the specific line of inquiry should be. Following the content-analytical communication model, the analysis can either put the emotional, cognitive or motivational background of an interviewee into focus (Mayring, 2014). The chief aim in this study is to analyze the text for knowledge and experiences. For this reason, the chosen direction is to examine the cognitive background of the interviewee.

5. Theoretical Differentiation of Sub-Components of the Problem

According to Mayring's (2014, p. 59) content analysis definition, the procedure has to be *rule-bound* and the interpretation of text material has to be *theory-driven*. This is ensured by the fact that the analysis is based on the theoretical foundation presented in chapter 3. It is necessary to say that the theoretical orientation should ensure a framing perspective but does not indicate mere verification of theory – otherwise, it would not follow the intended inductive approach. Furthermore, only segments of the transcripts which are assigned to categories are interpreted.

---

[5] All interview transcripts are available for download on the server of the academic publishing house Josef Eul Verlag GmbH.

Segmentation rules are labeled units of analysis and serve the purpose of intersubjectivity[6] of the procedure (ibid., pp. 51). There are three types of units of analysis:

(1) Coding unit,

(2) Context unit, and

(3) Recording unit.

Coding units determine the minimum portion of text within one category while context units respectively stand for the maximum text components considered. The recording unit decides which text portions are evaluated sequentially with one system of categories (ibid.). In the present study, eight interviews (A-H) constitute the recording units and context units at once since the entire interview protocols but no further observation protocol or background information are analyzed. Clear semantic elements taken from the text material form coding units (see Appendix C.3).

6. Determination of Technique and Establishment of a concrete Procedural Model

At this point, the technique of analysis must be chosen. Mayring (2014, pp. 63) differentiates between three fundamental forms of interpreting: summary, explication and structuring. In the present study, the *summary technique* is chosen, which includes reducing and filtering out the essential aspects of the material. Furthermore, summarization and reduction make an *inductive category formation* possible (ibid.). Explication would not be appropriate since it demands contextual analysis. Thus, the tendency is exactly the reverse; text material in need of interpretation is enriched by other comprehensible information (ibid.). Structuring is used only for deductive category assignment (ibid.). According to the summary technique, the next steps of evaluation are determined.

7. Definition of Content Analytical Units

As the strategy undertaken to analyze the content is of inductive nature, analytical units were not predefined in a deductive way from theory.

8. Analytical Steps taken by means of the Category System

As can be seen in figure 9 a step-by-step model was used to summarize content and to form categories inductively. The overall principle is to determine a level of abstraction and to transform the text material by using so called macro-operators. During the first step, analytical

---

[6] Intersubjectivity of the procedure refers to the possibility for others to reconstruct or repeat the analysis (Mayring, 2014, p. 40).

units have to be generated. Subsequently, these coding units are rewritten into a descriptive short form, which is called 'paraphrasing'. In preparation for the first reduction, which eliminates repeated mentions, the level of abstraction has to be set and every paraphrase below this level is generalized. During the second stage of reduction, paraphrases that bear relations to one another are compressed into a single new statement (Mayring, 2014). Further interpretation rules applied to summarize can be found in Appendix C.2. Afterwards, when the category system as a synthesis of all new statements is definite, the final step is to ascertain if the collation represents the base material adequately. "All original paraphrases from the first stages of treatment must be included in the category system" (ibid., p. 67).

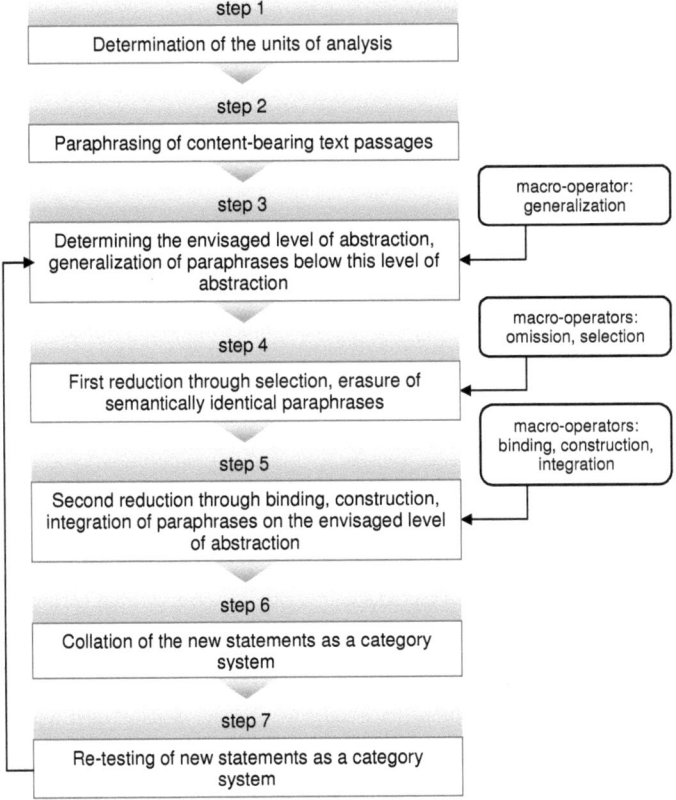

Figure 9: Step-by-Step Model of Summarizing Content Analysis
Source: Adapted from Mayring, 2014, p. 66.

9. Re-checking the Category System by applying it to Theory and Material

As already indicated in the final step of the summary technique, a reduction has to be verified, so that established categories are representative for the entire raw material (Mayring, 2014).

10. Interpretation of Results in Relation to the main Problem and Issue

A synopsis and interpretation of results is constituted in a structured manner from chapter four to seven.

11. Application of Content-Analytical Quality Criteria

Three central criteria usually determine the quality of research: *objectivity*, *reliability* and *validity* (Bortz & Döring, 2006, p. 195). However, the first two criteria of intersubjective reproduction and internal consistency are in conflict with the focus on individual expertise and single case analysis within qualitative research. Validity as third criterion indicates whether a test effectively measures what it claims to (ibid.). The above named classical criteria are considered unfit and imprecise for qualitative social research and consequently eight quality criteria for content analysis are postulated (Krippendorff, 1980, p. 158 as cited in Mayring, 2014, pp. 107). The five validity types for qualitative research are (1) semantic validity, (2) sampling validity, (3) correlational validity, (4) predictive validity, and (5) construct validity. *Semantic validity* is expressed through appropriate category definition, which is ensured through precise inductive analysis in the study at hand. *Sampling validity* is assured by thorough consideration of sample selection and recruitment. *Correlational validity* demands a comparison with external study results collected using a different method, but dealing with a similar inquiry (triangulation). In the present case, this cannot be reached since hardly any studies researching the same question but using different methods are available. Similarly, the *predictive validity* cannot be guaranteed because the actual implementation of impulses for action given at a later point in this work is not judgeable. Lastly, *construct validity* may be accepted on the basis of existing theories, models and studies presented earlier (ibid.). Furthermore, three reliability types are regarded: (1) stability, (2) reproducibility, and (3) accuracy (ibid.). Through repeated application of the same instrument of analysis to the material, *stability* can be secured. *Reproducibility* of empirical results is probable as the process of data evaluation is documented in very detailed and accurate fashion (inter-coder agreement). Stability and reproducibility function as preconditions for *accuracy* which "… refers to the extent to which the analysis conforms to a particular functional standard" (Mayring, 2014, p. 112). Overall, the results of the conducted data analysis can be regarded as meaningful on the basis of the examined quality criteria.

4 Research Results

Here, the results of the primary qualitative research are presented. The focus is put on the description of seven identified categories. A brief synopsis of results completes this chapter.

4.1 Overall Observations

While the emphasis is on the categories inductively formed from the transcripts which reflect the interview question topics, general convergent or divergent observations are briefly stated.

4.1.1 Insensitivity and Dissociation

When HRD managers of sustainability-committed firms were asked to participate in an interview for the study at hand, there was some confusion concerning the research question. Several persons suggested contacting colleagues that work in sustainability departments or similar functions. Others declined to participate on the grounds that they did not feel capable of making substantial, qualified contributions. Most emphasized their job function and educational background before or during the interview and pointed out that their knowledge and specialized input would be limited. These reactions might suggest both an organizational and awareness-related distance between the subjects of HRD and sustainability. Among the eight analyzed interviewees a lack of connection was reported between HRD and sustainability activities as well, which will be concretized in category 3 below. From a pragmatic point of view, responding managers seemed to show wariness about the research due to a lack of identification with the topic, but time constraints and the high volume of requests for assistance in university research had an influence as well.

4.1.2 Companies and their Environment

Even though the focus is upon each HRD managers' individual perspective of their role in promoting sustainability, the final sample of eight firms that participated shows noteworthy differences. The industries of the firms are deliberately quite diverse: Electric utility, retail and tourism, telecommunications, insurance, chemicals, logistics and automotive supply. Hence, products, services and customers of each firm vary significantly. Concerning *macroeconomic determinants*, several interviewees highlighted efficiency and savings pressure. In more detail, market pressure was explicitly addressed for the energy, insurance, logistics and automotive supply industry (A, 180-181, p. 6; D, 229-236, p. 6; G, 364-367, p. 10; H, 276-283, p. 7).[7] Secondly, *statutory regulations* and *legal obligations* were mentioned which en-

---

[7] For the presentation of results, references include the case letters A-H, lines and page numbers of the transcript documents.

force sustainability efforts on the one hand and mandatory training on the other hand (A, 199, p. 6; F, 52-58, p. 2; H, 3-12, p. 1). It stems from this fact, that sustainability is partially seen as a public relations practice (F, 271-275, p. 7). Lastly, as was detected in the interviewees' descriptions, these differences affect *organizational cultures* and *values*. In more detail, interviewees of a telecommunication and logistics firm named large company structures as well as cultures and macro-economic circumstances of foreign subsidiaries as barriers to form a uniform corporate culture (E, 373-382, p. 10; G, 299-308, p. 8). Moreover, for the automotive supplier the existing company culture was said to be incompatible with a holistic mindset of sustainability (H, 295-296, p. 8)

4.2 Inductive Category Presentation

In the following section, all seven inductively formed categories are described. The categories are presented to form a comprehensive picture (see Figure 10). Especially the second step of the content reduction available in Appendix C.3 can clarify the systematic forming of categories and sub-categories. As the topic evoked diverse opinions and firm-specific explanations, the categories both involve generalized themes and unique facts or statements.

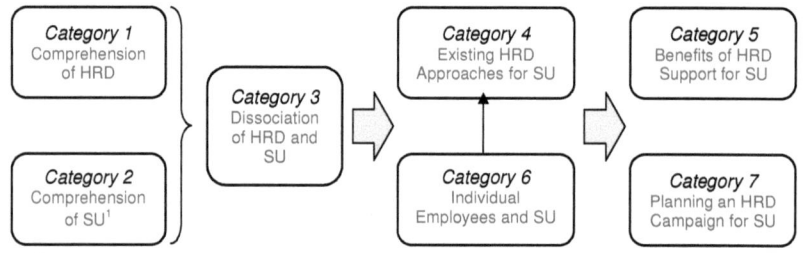

Note: [1] SU = sustainability.
Figure 10: Overview of the Inductive Categories
Source: Own representation.

4.2.1 Category 1: Comprehension of HRD

There is much agreement on the role of HRD among the eight experts interviewed. To begin with, strategic organizational development (B, 24-38, pp. 1) as well as development of individual competencies in a particular direction is a commonly held aim (incl. D, 26-31, p. 1; E, 421-428, p. 11). By implication, HRD is a broad field that requires present and future-oriented perspectives, i.e. it involves requirement planning and a concomitant strategy to attract and retain talents (B, 47-52, p. 2; D, 26-31, p. 1). In order to help employees to progress in their career, HRD defines global processes and provides them to executives (incl. F, 11-16, p. 1; H,

123-127, p. 4). While it is the managers' job to develop their employees, HRD professionals act as consultants and for instance monitor job profiles, onboarding plans or target agreements prepared by responsible superiors (H, 53-65, p. 2). Parallel to that, HRD usually holds talent reviews (H, 133-.140, p. 4).

> *„Wir als PE liefern diesen Prozess und auch Tools, Trainings, Coachings, 360° Feedback, arbeiten mit online Assessments, haben interne Trainer, die technische Schulungen machen, haben externe Trainer, die Soft Skill und Führungstrainings machen." (H, 141-143, p. 4)*
>
> [HRD provides processes, tools or coaching in cooperation with internal and external trainers.][8]

Concerning learning and training formats, it is consistent with the foregoing assertions that line managers are considered to be the actual developers of their employees. Indeed, a strong emphasis is put on learning on the job also for managers (F, 30-43, p. 2; H, 178-184, p. 5). Admittedly, the developmental intensity is conditioned by the type of job position (G, 2-8, p. 1). One interviewee describes the 70/20 Model, which stresses that 70% of development should be on the job, 20% near the job and only 10% classroom seminars (G, 155-164, pp. 4).

> *„Also wir haben von den Formaten alles, das was wir an Trainings machen versuchen wir eigentlich so wenig vortragsmäßig wie möglich zu machen." (H, 196-198, p. 5)*
>
> [Companies attempt to use lectures, i.e. classroom training formats as little as possible.]

While technical education is performed on-site by internal staff, the appropriate format for functional training is usually classroom teaching either through internal or external trainers. If colleagues with expertise are globally dispersed, video conferences are set up (H, 188-193, p. 5). For organizational change, independent external consultants with experience are preferred:

> *„Da sind natürlich oft auch externe Trainer sinnvoller, wenn es eine bestimmte Expertise ist, die wir so nicht haben, oder wo man sagt das ist gut, wenn da ein externer mit drauf ist. "*
> *(D, 51-53, p. 2)*
>
> [External change trainers with expertise and independent perspectives are often advisable.]

As a final remark, development ambitions can stem from an employee, supervisors or departmental needs and might target development of diverse competencies:

> *„Da ist unsere Aufgabe, unsere Verantwortung, bereichsspezifisch, unternehmensspezifisch, kulturspezifisch in Richtung fachlicher Weiterentwicklung, in Richtung methodischer und in Richtung persönlicher. Also adäquate individuelle und gruppen-, und bereichsbezogene Maßnahmen anzubieten. " (E, 423-428, p. 11)*
>
> [The task is to develop technical or personal competences of individuals, groups, departments or the entire company and its specific culture.]

---

[8] For the presentation of results, the essential message of inserted original statements of experts is prepared in a proper translation.

Indeed, HRD configurations in each firm vary and HRD managers carry different titles (see Appendix C.1). HR departments usually have complex architectures, especially in large companies which are accompanied by a considerable need for coordination (B, 45-47, p. 2; E, 358 -373, p. 9; G, 25-34, p. 1). Mostly, HRD is understood as a competence center and support function (A, 6-7, p. 1; C, 323-329, p. 8). That is to say HRD is seen as an internal service provider and generally a differentiation is made between strategic and operational talent management (D, 42-45, p. 2; F, 11-16, p. 1; G, 69-74, p. 2; H, 123-127, p. 4). Next to the fact that HRD internally sets up strategic processes, they cooperate with external training institutions (D, 51-55, p. 2; E, 388- 400, p. 10; G, 185-191, p. 5).

Concerning the measurement of HRD success, interviewees state that specially target planning and bonus agreement can steer the development of individuals and provide a control mechanism (H, 133-140, p. 4). Furthermore, career advancements are seen as a success indicator (A, 110, p. 4). Finally, employee surveys are frequently used to control success of HR-interventions (F, 181-185, p. 5).

> *„Ja, also der people survey das ist natürlich für uns so ein Messfaktor. Die Initiativen, die wir über das Jahr ergriffen haben, haben die auch genützt, gehen wir da in die richtige Richtung oder müssen wir das nochmal überdenken." (C, 230-234, p. 6)*
>
> [People surveys help to assess if initiatives are successful or if reconsideration is necessary.]

4.2.2 Category 2: Comprehension of Sustainability

HRD managers interviewed express different understandings of sustainability, ranging from philanthropic corporate responsibility to reducing energy consumption. In general conceptions sustainability is seen as a matter of finding a balance between diverse aims (A, 198, p. 6) and using all resources, including the human being cautiously in the long-term (B, 11-16, p. 1). Other experts see sustainability closely related to environmental protection, health and safety or as an indirect achievement of products and technologies (F, 189-194, p. 5; H, 3-12, p. 1; 42-46, pp. 1). The expert in the logistics firm believes social engagement to be enforced only selectively, while energy-saving is a deeply anchored concern within his company (G, 318-321, p. 8). Sustainability is also regarded as an issue of everyday work:

> *„Ich glaube, dass das Thema Nachhaltigkeit ein sehr lebendiges Thema aus dem aktiven Arbeitsalltag ist, was viel auch mit einer persönlichen Einstellung und Verhaltensorientierung zu tun hat." (F, 218-220, p. 6)*
>
> [Sustainability is a vivid topic in everyday work which especially concerns personal attitude and behavior orientation.]

Frequently, sustainability is understood as corporate responsibility with economic, ecological and social aims (D, 5-11, p. 1; E, 20-30, p. 1; 532-533, p. 13). Responsibility is said to be in the hands of the company and of employees at the same time (F, 220-222, p. 6). Furthermore, CR is perceived as closely related to topics of transformation and change (E, 69-74, pp. 2). Although most interviewees use the terms sustainability and corporate responsibility interchangeably, responsibility is applied more to individual persons:

> „Das was ich tue, das was wir tun, wird kontinuierlich hinterfragt und weiter ausgerichtet. Und dass man gleichzeitig, wenn das gut funktioniert auch einen sinnvollen Beitrag leisten kann."
>
> (E, 528-529, p. 13)
>
> [Our actions should be questioned continuously and further aligned. And if it works well, a meaningful contribution is made.]

With respect to HRD, one interviewee differentiates three levels of sustainability: The first one concerns sustainability as specific content of training. The second level implies sustainable training as such and the last level concerns sustainability of methods applied (B, 60-91, pp. 2). In some measure of agreement with this idea, another interviewee distinguishes between sustainability of HRD instruments and support of HRD in sustainability endeavors (D, 290-293, p. 7). Regarding the former view of sustainable HRD, several interviewees connect it to the challenges of handling demographic change and skills shortage (D, 11-15, p. 1; H, 242-266, pp. 6). Finally, as was highlighted that sustainability concerns individuals, talent management includes sustainability both of personal development and of the work situation (C, 51-53, p. 2).

Altogether, the interviewed experts make clear that reasons for sustainability and benefits of it involve all pillars of the TBL simultaneously (C, 151-161, p. 4; E, 219-224, p. 6). While several HRD managers expose that utilitarian, economic reasons and not mere goodwill initiated sustainability endeavors, they admit philanthropic values and benefits at the same time (D, 257-262, p. 7; E, 219-238, pp. 6). As a first point, sustainability strategies are often rationalized on the grounds of regulations, stress of competition, market pressure, demographic change and a priority on savings (incl. G, 247-248, p. 7; H, 289-301, p. 8). Nevertheless, personal interest is also identified as a driver (B, 207-212, p. 6; E, 300-309, p. 8) and positive effects on the organization and individual are named just as frequently (incl. B, 192-204, p. 6; C, 226-228, p. 6; D, 146-150, p. 4).

Sustainability configurations in each firm vary but the division is often organized as staff department directly linked to the executive board which certainly reflects the ascribed importance (F, 189-194, p. 5). In one telecommunications firm, the unusual case occurred that

CR, which is combined with the resorts transformation and change, was reorganized and integrated into the HR department (E, 13-19, p. 1). However, in subsidiaries and also in all other cases, sustainability or CR is not close to HR and the exact localization of the department is diverse.

Pertaining to the measurement of sustainability success, initiatives are merely indirectly controlled for through related questions within the employee survey. For instance through assessment of leadership or of employees' sustainable well-being:

> *„Es gibt viele Fragen in Sachen Gesundheit, es ist letztendlich auch eine indirekte Form von Vorgesetztenbeurteilung, weil es sehr viele Fragen gibt zu Führungskräften und so weiter."*
>
> *(E, 289-291, p. 8)*
>
> [Many questions concern health issues, which ultimately evaluate managers' actions indirectly.]

4.2.3 Category 3: Dissociation of HRD and Sustainability

As pointed out earlier, in most cases HRD and sustainability are perceived to be disconnected specialist and action fields (H, 48-49, p. 2). One of the interviewees brought up the fact that she had so far never received an assignment to conceptualize training on sustainability (F, 197-198, p. 5). Another interviewee supports this fact in arguing that HRD is not filtered on how sustainable it is:

> *„... es ist jetzt nicht so, dass Personalentwicklung, das was angeboten wird, dass das ausschließlich diesen Filter hat: ‚Inwieweit ist das nachhaltig?'."* *(E, 150-153, p. 5)*
>
> [Content of HRD measures is not controlled for inclusion of sustainability issues.]

Overall, HRD is not responsible for implementations with reference to sustainability and it is not considered a task of HRD to promote sustainability (G, 287-281; p. 8; H, 242-266, pp. 6).

> *„Was immer wichtig ist, ist es ein Problem vom Unternehmen nur so und so stark nachhaltig zu sein? Mal angenommen von 10 Punkten haben wir 3, und Sie fragen, warum haben wir nicht 10? [...] Aber warum steuern wir das nicht: Weil wir dafür nicht die Experten sind, weil das andere besser können."* *(H, 260-266, p. 7)*
>
> [First, it is questionable whether or not being sustainable to a limited extent poses a problem for the firm. Also, HRD professionals are not experts in promoting sustainability.]

In one case, the initially random interaction is said to have grown and the interviewee could discern existing direct and indirect bridges after putting some effort into exploring the sustainability-related activities of his firm (E, 147-150, p. 5). However, there is still little or no concrete professional interaction between sustainability and HRD professionals (F, 197-198, p. 5; G, 120-126, p. 4).

„Das ist absolut nicht unser Job, das sehe ich überhaupt nicht als unseren Job. Wir haben mit dem Thema Wirtschaftlichkeit bezüglich Humaner Ressourcen echt genug zu tun. Ich sehe keinen Vorteil darin, dass das Thema Umwelt von HR gesteuert wird, null. Wir sind nicht die Experten, die Ressourcen sind woanders, wir haben eine dicke EHS-Abteilung, die das know-how hat und...nein – ‚not our business‘ würde ich sagen." (H, 269-274, p. 7)

[It is absolutely not our job. We have enough to do with efficiently managing human resources. I do not see any advantage in having HR control environmental issues.]

Functional demands and guiding principles are decisive for the HRD strategy and internal assignments (E, 151-158, p. 5; F, 337-341, p. 8; H, 151-158, p. 4). Even though at different levels frameworks that create liabilities for employees exist and even though there are platforms or systems that request responsibility of all managers and employees to make their own contribution, the content is not mediated systematically and holistically.

„Aber um gleichzeitig ehrlich selbstkritisch zu sein: Dass es jemanden im Konzern gibt, der ihre Frage strategisch-konzeptionell besetzt im Sinne von Ganzheitlichkeit? Nein, das nicht."
(E, 342-344, p. 9)

[But to be honest and self-critical: nobody occupies this issue strategically, conceptually from a holistic perspective.]

4.2.4 Category 4: Existing HRD Approaches for Sustainability

All in all, there is no holistic sustainability training (incl. E, 167-182, p. 5; F, 197-198, p. 5; H, 269-274, p. 7). However, the following category describes several rudiments or training that is related to sustainability. As a prelude this quote makes clear why no holistic conceptual occupation of the sustainability topic through HRD exists so far:

„.... ich sehe es als eine unternehmerische Aufgabe und auch als eine Aufgabe von Personal- und Organisationsentwicklung an, die richtige Balance zu finden. Es nicht zu inflationieren, einen Sinnzusammenhang darzustellen, also wie sich Bausteine einfügen." (E, 471-474, p. 12)

[It is an entrepreneurial task and one of personnel and organizational development to find the right balance and not to inflate the topic but to ensure a meaningful context.]

The three-dimensional concept of ecological, economic and social aims functions as structural divisor for the subsequent deliberations.

Generally, all companies provide online learning opportunities. Next to e-learning that explain how the corporation acts upon sustainability or how it takes responsibility, several adjacent topics are available. Subjects named by the HRD experts include for instance compliance, diversity, health or ethical code of conduct (incl. C, 51-53, p. 2; D, 69-74, p. 2; G, 11-22, p. 1). Companies also include information about sustainability in onboarding events, trainee programs or executive and vocational training (incl. B, 103-108, p. 3; D, 98-108, p. 3).

Especially for environmental protection, safety at work and energy conservation, both web-based and classroom training are undertaken, which are partially even compulsory (C, 76-101, p. 3; H, 78-79, p. 3). Additionally, if statutory certifications are required, as in the chemical industry, there is mandatory environmental training which is led by authorities (F, 52-58, p. 2). With regard to economic sustainability, interviewees mostly name profitability of the company itself and efficient requirements planning of HRD (D, 61-64, p. 2; H, 242-266, pp. 6).

> „Dann das unternehmerisch Nachhaltige, also keine Gelder-Verschwendung." (D, 7-8, p. 1)
>
> [Commercial sustainability means no waste of money.]

Indirectly, profitability is said to be accomplished with highly qualified executives (H, 251-252, p. 7). Otherwise, concerning the economic sustainability of HRD, one interviewee states:

> „Ich glaube, dass wir durch die Art, durch das was wir tun, unsere Wettbewerbsfähigkeit stark zu-nimmt. Stichwort Demografie, dass wir unendlich viele Maßnahmen haben, um dem Demografie-Desaster und Fachkräftemangel zu begegnen, das zu lösen – das ist hochwirtschaftlich. "(E, 254-259, p. 7)
>
> [Our commercial conduct increases our competitiveness: We have an infinite number of measures to address the demographic disaster and shortage of skilled workers - which is highly economical.]

Concerning social sustainability, interviewees enumerate diverse social engagement initiatives (incl. A, 40-43, p. 2; C, 106-129, pp. 3; D, 109-114, p. 3; E, 81-94, p. 3). Lastly, counseling is available for many related topics, i.e. work-life balance, mental health, diversity and the like (incl. B, 113-120, p. 4; C, 76-101, p. 3). The majority of the above named seminars are controlled neither for participation nor for results (D, 268-270, p. 7; G, 25-34, pp. 1). One interviewee states that follow-ups of social initiatives with external agencies make future planning more sustainable:

> „Sodass wir uns kurz zusammensetzten: was war gut, was hat gut funktioniert, passte das für die Gruppe, sollten wir nächstes Jahr wieder so etwas Ähnliches machen." (D, 277-280, p. 7)
>
> [We briefly discuss what worked well and suited the group. Then we decide if something similar is appropriate for the next year.]

In a couple of interviews, very novel, innovative accomplishments regarding the subject matter were stated which will be particularized in the following paragraph. At the chemical company, the HRD competency model includes an item 'promoting sustainable solutions'. The generic competence description has to be specified for each employee in dialogue with his superior (F, 136-142, p. 4). However, it is a flexible choice among eight competences from the model for each target agreement.

> *„Also wir haben für jede Kompetenz, eben auch für diese die Ebene einmal ‚diese Kompetenz zei-*
> *gen bedeutet' aber auch ‚was bedeutet es diese Kompetenz unter dem Stichwort Führung aufzu-*
> *zeigen'. Das heißt als Führungskraft muss man ja einerseits Mitarbeiter befähigen, ein gewisses*
> *Verhalten an den Tag zu legen und andererseits hat man auch eine Vorbildfunktion mit seinem ei-*
> *genen Verhalten." (F, 127-131, p. 4)*
>
> [For each competency we define what showing it means but also what it means to demonstrate this
> competence as line manager.]

The insurance firm's trainee program includes a compulsory block for social engagement in their trainee program (D, 98-109, p. 3). At the retail company, sustainability is declared to be one of the values in the corporate principles. Therefore all managers have to address the topic at least once within the business year (B, 109-111, pp. 3). When asked about sustainability seminars, the HRD manager of the automotive supplier laid focus on so-called standardized work ergonomic movement, annual safety training, technical training on efficient technologies and basic introduction to environment, and health and safety during onboarding (H, 69-79, pp. 2).

One telecommunications firm shows best practice character as it is leading within the applied initiatives for corporate responsibility. Not only does the company provide diverse platforms like e-learning, training and social engagement opportunities for all employees to make their own contribution. These platforms are also framed at different levels, for instance through a professional corporate volunteering department (E, 101-122, pp. 3).The group also uses a series of standardized KPIs to measure and control their instruments across all three pillars of sustainability. In particular, one KPI of social sustainability relates to employees: The 'Employee Satisfaction CR'. This KPI assesses how well employees identify themselves and how satisfied they are with the companies' CR activities (E, 273-283, pp. 7). Next to that, top-down and bottom-up mechanisms in the form of employee survey and idea systems enable all members to explicate what social and ecological areas the company should get involved in (E, 265-268, p. 7). Taken as a whole, the definition of specific processes and KPIs reflects serious engagement with the topic.

Evidently, most companies are subject to industry factors which influence training topics and forms (see Chapter 4.1). Under the premise of achieving a sustainable mindset, the character of HRD interventions to promote sustainability or corporate responsibility among employees should to be stressed. To present further expert input and fulfill the need of conciseness at the same time, the rest of the category is described with compact listing. First, to achieve sustainability awareness and behavioral competence the following HRD formats are applicable:

> *Awareness*: E-learning, info event, corporate and managers' communication,

> *Competence*: Social engagement, workshop, target planning and bonus agreements.

Concerning the configuration of training according to the character of the topic these features have to be regarded:

> Classify between *self-competence* and *professional skill*,

> Ensure specific *relationship* to *working sphere*,

> Treat subject in an *integrative manner*,

> Apply a *mix of methods*,

> Ensure *reference points* to employee for high involvement.

4.2.5 Category 5: Benefits of HRD Support for Sustainability

Regarding internal success of HRD activities for sustainability, functional results are claimed to be visible (E, 512, p. 13). In the long run, companies are believed to prosper if their employees are doing well (B, 143-144, p. 4; C, 226-228, p. 6). This goes in line with greater employee loyalty and retention (D, 257-262, p. 7). However, the time lag of effects on organizations was stressed:

> *„Es tritt in einem Zeitversatz von 1-2 Jahren ein, dass man dann auf einmal auch in dem Unternehmen besser wird und diesen Mehrwert erkennt." (B, 145-146, p. 5)*
>
> [Added value and improvements are recognizable with a time lag of 1-2 years.]

Social engagement is considered useful both for personal and team development and for society (D, 146-150, p. 4). One interviewee critically outlines the suitable handling:

> *„Aber nicht aus dieser moralischen Ecke, sondern wirklich nach dem Motto ‚Ja, ist uns auch wichtig als Teil der Unternehmenskultur', aber das dann verknüpfen mit einer Kompetenzentwicklung, einem Mehrwert und auch mit einer Wirtschaftlichkeit."*
>
> *(H, 447-450, p. 11)*
>
> [Social engagement cannot be compelled out of moral considerations but must be part of the corporate culture and effectuate skills development, added value and profitability.]

Turning to external impact for companies, several interviewees appreciate the positive effect on employer image, and in contested industries a strong focus on external visibility is stressed (D, 215-218, p. 6; F, 271-275, p. 7). In support of that, one HRD manager names recruitment marketing as a reason (G, 239-243, p. 7) and one HRD manager cites employer branding as a clear benefit of social sustainability (H, 430, p. 11).

4.2.6 Category 6: Individual Employees and Sustainability

Generally, sustainability and particularly corporate responsibility are commonly characterized as individual topics. While the former refers to how sustainable individuals are with themselves, the latter includes a call for altruistic responsibility by each employee (B, 11-16, p. 1; E, 432-439, p. 11).

> *„Also ressourcenschonend könnte man sagen. Neben gesellschaftlichen Themen auch persönliche Themen, also Nachhaltigkeit betrifft ja auch die Person."* (B, 11-12,. p. 1)
>
> [Resource-friendly I would say. And in addition to social issues also personal issues, since sustainability does indeed relate to the individual.]

On the opposite side, working experience determines if sustainability and related subjects are known or unknown to employees, too (C, 197-203, p. 5). As employees need to get in touch with specific sustainability strategies in order to have an interest, it was mentioned that the further away from the headquarters the less awareness is likely (G, 323-334, p. 9). Arguing from the position that responsibility is a personal attitude, many interviewees demand responsible management by executives and leading by example (D, 74-81, pp. 2; E, 532-533, p. 13).

> *„Das heißt als Führungskraft muss man ja einerseits Mitarbeiter befähigen, ein gewisses Verhalten an den Tag zu legen und andererseits hat man auch eine Vorbildfunktion mit seinem eigenen Verhalten."* (F, 129-131, p. 4)
>
> [Executives should be role models and also empower employees to show a certain behavior.]

In consequence, the conviction that personal interest and commitment of executives as role models promote sustainability prevails (B, 146-161, pp. 4; D, 173-179; p. 5; E; 300-322, p. 8; F, 129-131, p. 4). Likewise, explicit significance of sustainability issues for the executive board steers the pursuit and pervasion of them (E, 467-470, p. 12; F, 189-194, p. 5).

> *„.... die sehr individuelle Wichtigkeit, die diese Themen für den Vorstand haben. Wenn wir einen Vorstand haben, der sagt mir sind soziale oder Umweltthemen wichtig, dann wird er die auch weiter treiben und auch nicht nur um sie verkaufen zu können. Da ist sehr entscheidend, weil so eine Kultur von oben geprägt wird."* (D, 249-254, pp. 6)
>
> [The individual importance these issues have for the executive board. It is very crucial because culture is influenced from the top.]
>
> *„Führungsverantwortung ist wirklich verantwortliches Handeln. Verantwortliches Handeln gegenüber Individuen, gegenüber Unternehmen und gegenüber der Gesellschaft auch."*
> (E, 530-531, p. 13)
>
> [Managerial responsibility really is responsible behavior: Responsible action towards individuals, companies and the society as well.]

4.2.7 Category 7: Planning an HRD Campaign for Sustainability

The overarching research question was how HRD as an organizational function can ensure that sustainable behavior will be part of all members of the company, assuming that HRD activities are relevant for sustainability.

As already mentioned, several interviewees perceive a holistic HRD campaign for sustainability to be unrealistic and very unusual (F, 275-282, p. 7; E, 338-346, p. 9). Furthermore, one participant questions if a major campaign would be sensible or necessary (F, 289-298, p. 7). Furthermore, it is accentuated that HRD would neither be the preferred channel to implement such a campaign nor provide direct added value (F, 220-222, p. 6).

> *„Wenn ich versuche das umzusetzen, was Sie geschildert haben, also eine Kampagne 'Wie kann jeder Einzelne durch sein Verhalten - nach dem Motto viele kleine Menschen, viele kleine Schritte gehen', das wäre für unser Unternehmen ein ganz neues Aufhängen von Nachhaltigkeit. Das wäre für uns sehr ungewohnt."* (F, 275-279, p. 7)
>
> [A campaign on 'How can each individual's behavior have an impact?' would be a very unusual, completely new positioning of the sustainability issue for our company.]

This assertion stems from the fact that a sustainability campaign is viewed more as a concern of information brokering, not concrete behavioral change or development managed by HRD (F, 222-229, p. 6). Indeed, raising awareness about the subject matter is believed to be possible, while the suitable format is believed to be information and discussion-driven (F, 331-333; 357-368, pp. 8). Due to the focus on appealing enlightenment among the entire staff, a campaign for sustainability or corporate responsibility is firmly classified as a task of corporate communication or the sustainability department itself (F, 331-333, p. 8; H, 269-274, p. 7).

Under condition of the aforementioned missing functional responsibility, some propositions on the conceptualization of a holistic campaign are put forward. First, on a meta level an HRD campaign for sustainability should be conveyed in an overall context. It cannot be comprised of a multitude of single, independent measures (F, 239-255, p. 6). A precondition for this is a discussion of fit and a specific determination of sustainability goals within the corporate strategy:

> *„... wir haben es weder als eine Strategieformulierung oder in unserem Führungsverständnis verankert. Bevor das passiert, muss die strategische Diskussion und die Passungsdiskussion stattgefunden haben, bis hin zu einer Vorstandsebene."* (E, 480-484, p. 12)
>
> [We have neither anchored it in a strategy formulation nor in our leadership values. A discussion of fit would be necessary beforehand.]

What is more, anchoring sustainability or CR in company values and a competency model for employees can influence positively (B, 109-111, pp. 3; F, 121-125, p. 4).

With regard to organizational factors, the fit with an individual company culture has to be respected. Moreover, large corporations might prove to be too frayed for a uniform, global corporate culture as team, group, department or national subsidiary cultures may predominate (E, 256-261, p. 7; G, 299-308, p. 8). The interviewee of the automotive supplier stresses that within their firm, such a campaign would create irritation and that limited staff support would be probable (H, 295-296, p. 8). Thus, cultures have to be considered as barriers on an organizational and individual level: The successful corporation-wide diffusion might be hindered by organizational structures and prevailing cultures. Furthermore, dominant individual mindsets, cultural imprints and knowledge about, awareness for or attitudes towards sustainability have to be considered. A specialist for HR development at the chemical firm explains it the following way:

> *„Das ist auch schon eine unternehmenskulturelle Frage, da stellt sich die Frage ‚Wie können wir als PE das unterstützen‘, da glaube ich sind klassische Trainingsformate nicht das Richtige. Weil ein Training ist immer noch dieses ‚Andere erzählen einem, wie etwas laufen oder nicht laufen kann‘. Sondern da muss es eher darum gehen, Menschen zu befähigen, Freiraum zu geben sich darüber Gedanken zu machen und die Entscheidungen für das eigene Leben auch treffen zu können." (F, 313-321, p. 8)*

> [I do not believe classic training formats are appropriate because they depend on lecturing others. We should rather enable people, provide freedom to think and decide for themselves.]

In line with this notion of providing freedom and empowering people to think for themselves, the HRD manager at the automotive supplier stresses that indoctrination of adults would not be appropriate and dogmatism has to be avoided (H, 452-453, p. 11). As an additional remark, this manager points out that values of HRD measures need to be fundamental values of humanity (H, 328-345, pp. 8). This conception reflects the appreciation of HRD professionals as coaches and not teachers, which was clarified in category 1. Developing the prospective campaign further, possible formats to mediate the topic and essential criteria were inquired about. To ensure employee behavior that goes beyond the scope of awareness, it is determined that active participation in the form of workshops and tasks responding to personal dimensions of motivation are needed (H, 382-388, p. 10), i.e. aesthetic, altruistic, economic, individualistic, political, regulatory and theoretical motivators (Spranger, 1928). Furthermore, a link of tasks in training to the actual work environment must be given, i.e. the considerations of actions for a stronger commitment to sustainability must relate directly to the personal sphere of work (H, 399-409, p. 10).

As interim summary it can be said, that experts skeptically commentate on the meaningfulness of adopting a holistic sustainability mindset. Previous comments made clear that HRD managers see great possibilities for personal growth and self-improvement of employees through social engagement. Social projects to discover unused potential are considered to relate to the core purpose of HRD (H, 306-316, p. 8). Moreover, employees' and teams' progress as result of an involvement in social projects is appraised (D, 146-150, p. 4). However, social engagement should not happen under duress, because corporate responsibility is contingent upon personal conviction. The following quote mirrors the settled conviction of one manager against proactive support of social projects through HRD:

> *„Ist das nicht belehrend? Ist das nicht unglaublich übergriffig, wenn ein Unternehmen definiert, dass sich Trainees sozial engagieren müssen? Also die Möglichkeit zu geben, ja. Oder gut ein Familienunternehmen kann sagen, dass ist Teil von unserer Corporate Identity. Aber ich halte auch nichts davon, dass Leute solche Dinge tun, weil sie es tun müssen. Das geht dann nicht – um sentimental zu werden – ins Herz, ,Was nicht im Herz ist, ist nicht im Kopf.'" (H, 433-437, p. 11)*
>
> [Is is not instructive and encroaching when a company defines that trainees must be socially engaged? Giving the opportunity or declaring it a part of the corporate identity is acceptable. But engagement should not be enforced – what is not in the heart is never in the head.]

As grasping the potential configuration of a systematic HRD intervention for a responsible, sustainable mindset and deliberate behavior of employees is a pivotal interest of this empirical research, the main facets identified from the opinions of eight experts are summarized:

➢ Ideally *no compulsory* participation,

➢ Short *lecture sequence for general awareness*,

➢ Subsequent *active workshop* and flexible alignment with *individual motivators*,

➢ *Direct link* of topics to work environment,

➢ *True fit* with company culture,

➢ Conveyance in convincing, *coherent context*.

4.3 Summary of Empirical Findings

Here, the empirical findings will be discussed in a cursory manner to lay the foundation for the critical review and discussion of findings provided in the subsequent chapter.

As pointed out at the beginning of this chapter, HRD managers' functions and personal conceptions tend to remain disconnected from sustainability initiatives, even if the companies profess such a commitment. The conduct for sustainability and a linkage to HRD appears to depend on the industry and to be decided by unique organizational structures, products and culture. Within these large corporations sustainability is focused on environmental and social activities. Sustainability is concerned less with behavior of employees but more on external visible activity and is designed without the integrative participation of the HRD unit. Furthermore, HRD professionals felt more connection to the idea of responsibility and of sustainable working environments. Generally, HRD provides employees with learning and promotion opportunities and views these activities as helping to support a company strategy. Thus, there was little evident notion of sustainability in the interviewees' sense of HRD except for HRD as an element of a sustainable HR strategy. However, employee development is already extended to promoting policies in compliance, ethics, mutual respect, safety, health, and a discrimination-free and diverse work environment. Moreover, all companies provide e-learning on sustainability-related topics, corporate volunteering opportunities and frequently directives for energy savings and environmental protection are communicated.

Accordingly, the key findings of the seven inductive categories are summarized as follows:

(1) Much agreement on the role of *HRD as service provider*,

(2) *Varied comprehensions of sustainability* including philanthropic responsibility,

(3) *Perceived dissociation* of HRD and sustainability outweighs,

(4) Existing HRD measures are primarily *e-learning for related topics*,

(5) *Employer Branding* is seen as significant benefit,

(6) *Personal interest and commitment* are powerful drivers,

(7) Major campaign must be *thoroughly conceptualized and planned*.

5 Critical Review and Guidance

This thesis examines the degree to which HRD is involved in shaping employee behavior concerning sustainability strategies. As the major finding of the empirical study above shows, this is not yet the case. The resulting overall implication is that chances of success of the sustainability strategy are low and the long-term competitive advantage (CA) of the companies will suffer. Thus, this chapter critically reviews the empirical findings, provides a pathway for academia and practical measures to increase the contribution to sustainability.

5.1 Advice for Theoretical Approach

First, the study at hand has to be placed in the broader picture of *organizational change*. As *time lags* of change are mentioned within one interview (B, 145-146, p. 5), it is quite possible for the subject of HRD approaches for sustainability to permeate in the future. Moreover, this assessment is probable as several interviewees believe the importance of sustainability and responsibility will be intensified (incl. A, 180-181, p. 6; G, 364-367, p. 10). It also became clear that shifts in individual values have prompted an organizational focus on the well-being of employees (C, 151-161, p. 4). Within this tendency, many companies strive for a strong attention to health, respect, safety, work-life balance and the like (C, 51-53, p. 2; D, 69-74, p. 2; G, 11-22, p. 1). It follows from these empirical facts that the proposal to integrate the topic in the theoretical context of organizational change is apparent. Beyond that, a comparison with the organizational enforcement of themes which are estimated to be related to holistic sustainability, i.e. compliance, health or work-life balance presents an outlook on the possible development of the explored sustainability mindset.

5.1.1 Integration in the Context of Organizational Change

In an earlier chapter, three core theories that stand as the basis of HRD, T&D, and OD were identified: psychological, system, and economic theories. As explained, the target of OD is to enhance performance through systematical implementation of organizational change (Swanson & Holton, 2001). The classic change model of 'unfreezing, moving, and refreezing' is attributed to Lewin (1951). Swanson and Holton (2001, p. 273) define OD as a five-phase process that essentially defines and consequently solves a problem: (1) analyze, (2) diagnose, (3) plan, (4) implement, and (5) evaluate. When considering the empirical findings, the topic at hand clearly classifies as *transformational change* issue, as it demands a strong paradigm-shift of organizing and performing work which is not incremental (French, Bell & Zawacki, 1999, p. vii). Moreover, especially according to characteristics identified by Cummings and

Worley (2001), HRD approaches to promote sustainability can be classed within transformational change. Explicitly, transformational change is triggered by environmental and internal disruptions; needs to be driven by senior executives and line management; requires a substantial learning process, and results in a revolution of the organizational system according to a new paradigm (Cummings & Worley, 2001).

A *culture* is about a group's shared norms and values, which shapes how that group understands a situation and acts upon it (Schein 1990, p. 111). MacKenzie, Garavan and Carbery (2011) propose that HRD interventions to promote sustainability and CSR should be accompanied by efforts to create ethical corporate cultures. As indicated by one interviewee (C, 197-203, p. 5), organizational culture is also shaped by employees' individual mindsets and habits. Ardichvili (2013) proposes an interaction model which jointly considers the role of individual characteristics, organizational culture and ethical behavior. This relational model links multiple determinants that form organizational culture, which is understood as "... constantly changing power configurations, resulting from interactions among individuals" (Ardichvili, 2013, p. 465). Figure 11 shows how the interaction that is argued to lead to ethical behavior is shaped by individual dispositions, human capital, moral virtue and habitus. Moreover, organizational practices including HRD, culture and external factors are decisive for ethical decision making. One decisive point which becomes apparent in this interactional model is that differentiated activities for individual and organizational mindsets are needed. By implication, HRD can provide sustainability-related training for employees who will not immediately change dispositions but "... provide a fertile ground for such changes" (Ardichvili, 2013, p. 466). This model supports the significance of organizational culture as key generative mechanism while ethical behavior depends to a large extent on individual's moral virtue (ibid.).

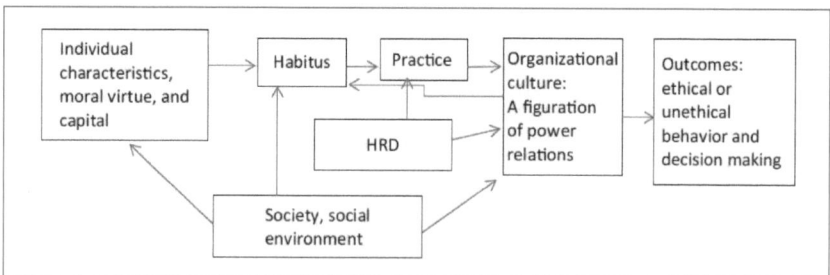

Figure 11: Emergence of Organizational Culture of Ethics, CSR, and CS
Source: Ardichvili, 2013, p. 465.

Awareness can be raised by training and education programs, but development of an ethical, responsible organizational culture is a result of long-term change efforts and requires redesign of processes, routines, mission and values (Liebowitz, 2010; Sroufe, Liebowitz & Sivasubramaniam, 2010).

In summary, a transformation according to the study at hand concerns a company's vision, i.e. beliefs, principles and mission. As a result of targeted interventions, *cognitive change* in individual members could be achieved (Porras & Silvers, 1991, p. 53). Furthermore, the success of change efforts relies heavily on an organization's ability to develop new competencies and mindsets among executives and managers (Rimanoczy & Pearson, 2010). Thus, the importance in change efforts is to develop an organizational culture which embraces the sustainability paradigm. The HRD staff is likely to be the one professionally trained to change the attitudes and behaviors of executives, managers, and employees. However, it is not sufficient if only HRD systems are modified, i.e. single training cannot develop sustainability mindsets. In an overall strategic approach, change management effort to create the new sustainability-oriented work behavior needs to be employed.

5.1.2 Evolution of Adjacent Corporate Standards

Just as the reported corporate standards of work-life balance or health (incl. B, 113-120, p. 4; C, 76-101, p. 3) flank the pillar of social sustainability, anti-corruption compliance is one aspect of economic sustainability (H, 98-110, p. 3) and energy savings are one feature of ecological sustainability (G, 318-321, p. 8). Liebowitz (2010) evaluates that increasingly staff considers environmental goals, and appreciates receiving training: "Employees should have access to workshops and conferences on 'back wheel' technical, ecologically-friendly (eco-friendly) topics, such as recycling, green building materials, energy conservation, and waste reduction" (p. 52). Boudreau and Ramstad (2005) assess that compliance and social accountability are topics already integrated in HR programs. When assessing the future enforcement of a sustainability mindset, it is interesting to reflect the evolution of some separate facets. Generally, *compliance* means conforming to laws and policies like sustainability-related regulations (Baumgartner & Ebner, 2010). Furthermore, besides legal standards, corporate codes of conduct can for instance concern corrupt practices, human rights or ethical behavior (Aguinis, 2011). Among the reasons to improve *work-life balance* of employees, globalization, demographic change, and modern technology are frequently named (Von Kettler, 2010). Corporate health management with the intention of enabling employees to increase control over their health goes back to principles of the 1986 Ottawa Charter for Health Promotion of the World

Health Organization (WHO). Climate change, global warming and environmental protection are frequently discussed social and political issues. Early debates occurred in 1992 during the United Conference on Environment and Development in Rio (United Nations). In the so-called 1997 Kyoto Protocol first binding indications for greenhouse gas emission were developed (United Nations). Specific policies have proven to cause stricter obedience of sustainability issues by organizations and its members. Still, considering the time it took for instilling environmental or health protection and compliance into the minds of corporate members, it is clear that such evolution is of a gradual kind (Sroufe et al., 2010). However, the question remains: *Why is change implementation for a holistic sustainability mindset different from previous cultural change?* Neither organizational change nor programs concerning parts of sustainability policies are new topics (Fernández, Junquera & Ordiz, 2003). Although organizations must adapt to sustainability demands, the answer seems to be that in practice, diffusing a holistic mindset is very complex: Getting all members of an organization committed to work in an ethically responsible and economically sustainable fashion, with thoughts of the environment in their minds when making any strategic decisions as well as in their daily work is a high ambition. As mentioned, changing a culture takes time (Bluestone, 2011), which is something that is likely to be true for the planned type of cultural change as well. As individual, organizational and external reasons for sustainability will pertain in the future, the necessity to ensure pro-sustainability behavior among employees is likely to become more intense. Finally, the likelihood of a widespread adoption of sustainability mindsets among employees can be projected in analogy to Bluestone's (2011) notion: "Cultural change is evolution, not revolution" (p. 21).

5.1.3 Establishment of a Holistic Framework

To propose a suitable conceptual model that copes with the interdisciplinary and all affected subjects, an illustrative framework which takes insights gained through the empirical study into account was established. The framework considers HRD as an independent variable which directly influences the dependent variable of sustainability or CR endeavors' success and is mediated by pro-sustainability and responsible behavior of employees. A *moderator* affects the direction and strength of a direct relationship between the independent and dependent variable, while a *mediator* transmits the effect in a causal sequence (MacKinnon, Coxe & Baraldi, 2012, p. 2). In a simple model the predictor causes the mediator which then causes the dependent variable (see Figure 12). The purpose of this model is to clarify the different ways in which variables may account for peoples' behavior (Baron & Kenny, 1986).

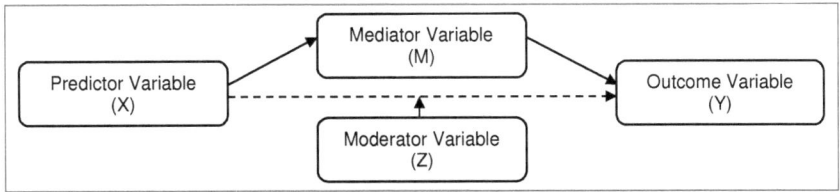

Figure 12: Diagram of Direct, Moderator and Mediator Effects
Source: Own representation based on Baron & Kenny, 1986, p. 1176.

Following this, the broad causal system below that includes both a mediator and moderators is a constructive suggestion of variables, which should be considered to better implement HRD efforts for sustainability (see Figure 13). The model of determinants for employee pro-sustainability and responsible behavior is based on the conducted research. It shows factors mentioned by the experts that evidently demonstrate strong influence on such behavior. While HRD and the altered employee behavior will have desired impact on external sustainability matters which do not concern the organization itself – for instance community engagement programs have an impact on society – these relationships are not shown in the diagram, since they are not central to the argument advanced in this thesis.

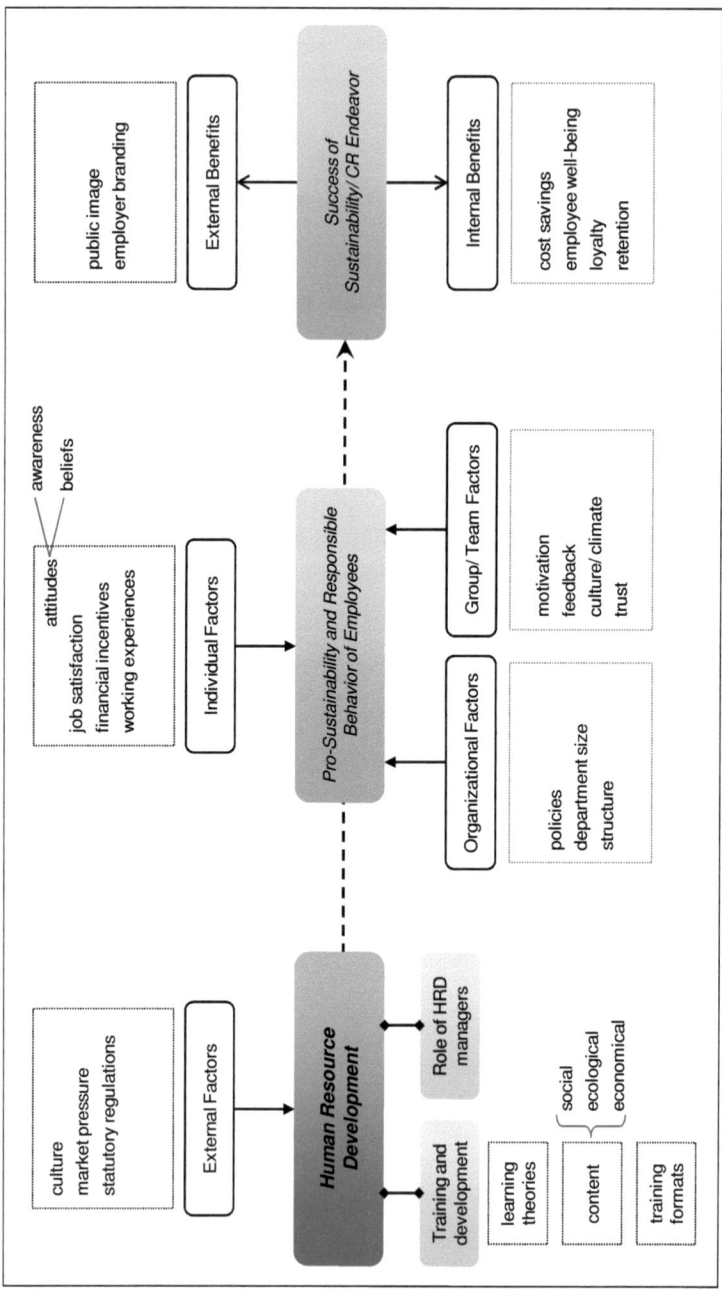

Figure 13: Process Framework of Determinants for Employee Pro-Sustainability Behavior
Source: Own representation.

5.2   Guidance for Practical Action

As explained before, the implication following from the research results is that the chances of success of the sustainability strategy and the long-term CA of the company are at risk. Thus, this section guides HRD professionals in how to address the issue more and how to increase their proactive influence.

5.2.1 Understanding Reasons for Resistance to CS in Organizations

This thesis argues that HRD can and should make an important contribution to sustainability. However, as firms appear to be most focused on their business roles (Pundt, Martins, Horsmann & Nerdinger, 2007), barriers to the adoption of sustainability strategies on an individual, organizational and institutional level have to be taken into account (Garavan et al., 2010). Barriers are clustered into psychological and structural categories concerning the organizational and institutional barriers. The latter include macro rules and regulations (Garavan et al., 2010). In more detail, employee-level barriers are distinguished into issues "… arising from CSR/CS knowledge and awareness, CSR/CS fit and motivation, perceived organizational support, attitudes toward CSR/CS, perceived social action, egocentrism, and positive illusions, perceptions of organizational justice" (Garavan et al., 2010, p. 589). Transferring these notions to the research question at hand, the lack of internal capacity or knowledge should be addressed by HRD professionals. Furthermore, the authors name organizational-level barriers including culture, structures and organizational inertia. Lastly, institutional barriers are said to stem from regulatory or normative forces and cognitive influences (ibid.). An overall failure of widespread adoption of sustainability initiatives is also ascertained by Sroufe et al. (2010). The main obstacles on the pathway to sustainability are:

(1) Lack of commitment and buy-in,

(2) Lack of resources,

(3) Cultural and institutional resistance to change (ibid., p. 39).

Another obstacle that hinders organizations from engaging in sustainability is the difficulty of measuring its effects (SHRM, 2011, p. 66). Besides obstacles of accounting for cost of launching and maintaining sustainability, 35% of surveyed organizations ($n = 369$) state that the difficulty of measuring return on investment (ROI) is preventing them from implementing a sustainability plan. The readiness to change and reasons for resistance have to be minded especially in order to capture employee motivation and commitment to get involved in sustainability initiatives.

5.2.2 Expansion of HRD Engagement towards Sustainability

In practice, HRD professionals may often be caught by functional requirements of departments and organizational demands emphasizing performance and profit. On the other hand, sustainability coordinators tend to have backgrounds in technical, environmental, safety, or scientific areas (Woodward, 2008). Many sustainability authorities have expressed a frustration that their organization has not progressed enough (Walker, 2007). Certainly, HRD specialists possess the competencies to change attitudes and behavior to focus more on sustainability (Harmon, Fairfield & Wirtenberg, 2010). Attention has to be paid to a critical comment: HRD professionals should not and cannot be the only ones to bear the responsibility for a change in sustainability mindsets. HRD initiatives represent just one influencing factor and must be accompanied by other aligned organizational components. This thought goes in line with the above notion on transformational change and with *social systems theory*, which requires a joint consideration and adjustment of all concerning factors (Luhmann, 1984). For instance referring to HR functions, Liebowitz (2010) discusses that concomitant changes in recruitment, selection, onboarding of employees or performance evaluations are inevitable. Selection and hiring decisions should take individual's knowledge and attitude towards ethics and responsibility into account (Ardichvili, 2013). Then, new employees who already possess the desired moral virtue and habitus can act as *change agents*.

In this paragraph, prospective steps that could be taken by HRD professionals to focus employee learning more on sustainability will be noted. HRD specialists should first of all familiarize themselves with the principles of sustainability and CR, and *rethink their roles* in furthering sustainable objectives. They should also *identify key stakeholders* and involve them in policy development. Lastly, HRD professionals need to employ *processes of organizational change* and *employee learning* (Fenwick & Bierema, 2008). Regarding the first recommendation, HRD professionals could participate in organization's cross-functional task forces or sustainability councils so that exchange is stimulated. Also, HRD concerns could be included in CSR or CS audits and reports. Furthermore, HRD representatives should advise during the creation of processes for sustainability or design implementation plans themselves. Concerning key stakeholders, HRD professionals should involve primary stakeholders in policy development and obtain senior management support. Consequently, HRD should offer leadership development workshops to help managers train their skills or behavioral competencies in managing change and sustainability endeavors (Ardichvili, 2013).

Discourse: Transformational Learning and Employee Empowerment

Since employees are considered KSF for sustainability strategies, one remark has to be made. Transformational change at the organizational level needs to be accompanied by transformational change at the individual level "... through some process of critically challenging and changing internal cognitive structures" (Swanson & Holton, 2001, p. 171). For the designated mindset, double and triple-loop learning (Argyris, 1977; Jensen, 2005) which requires employees to alter their mental scheme in a fundamental way is needed. HRD initiatives can prevent possible employee misunderstanding and resistance by involving these parties. Employee engagement is highly influenced by self-efficacy, e.g. through participation in the establishment and design of actions or the opportunity to demonstrate opinion via suggestion schemes (Sukserm & Takahashi, 2012). In a joint thought, power injustices resulting from HRD activities including only few stakeholders may be prevented (Ardichvili, 2013; Garavan, 1995; Gollan, 2006). Furthermore, motivation, trust building, communication and accountability are proven strategies for HRD to deal with the principal–agent dilemma (Swanson, 2001).

5.2.3 Conceptualization of a Competency Model for a Sustainability Mindset

As explained above, single HRD measures cannot establish a sustainability mindset. The conceptualization of a holistic campaign was considered in previous propositions (see Chapter 4.2.7). One of the challenges in operationalizing sustainability lies in transferring the abstract term into shared meanings. As a tool to form the shared mindset within organizational change and employee learning, a competency model was drafted (see Figure 14). The model includes four stages of changing employee behavior starting from *unconscious incompetence* with the aim of sustainability becoming an *unconscious competence* mindset for everyday operations (Oerter & Montada, 2008). The central element in this model is the definition of the desired competence both for general employee behavior and for leadership behavior. A liable competence model is a pivotal basis on which HRD professionals can establish suitable initiatives for sustainability. Realistically, HRD professionals might have limitations to assess the dispositions of employees and to decide who should participate in training sessions on which level of discourse or complexity of content (Ardichvili, 2013). However, the idea behind this competence model is to define yearly development goals for each employee, to select individual training formats and to control for success according to such target settings. Employees who perform their job well should be rewarded and mutual feedback is key to motivate employees for a change process (Fernández et al., 2003). In conclusion, HRD professionals should ensure that competency frameworks include statements of CSR, CS and ethics behavior. Needless to say, such individual development has to be accompanied by an overall strategic vision and organizational change.

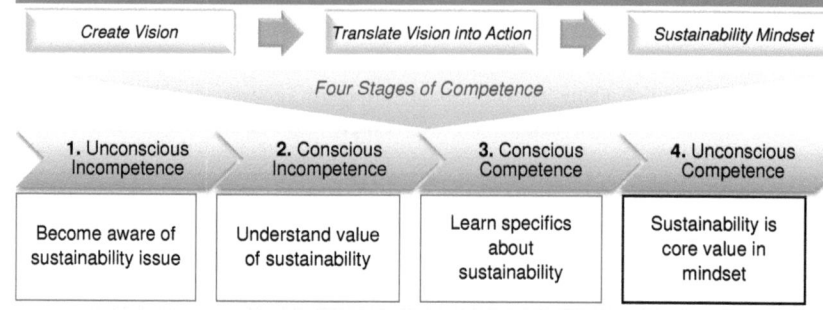

Phases and Components of a Sustainability Initiative from an HRD Perspective

Create Vision	Translate Vision into Action	Sustainability Mindset

Four Stages of Competence

1. Unconscious Incompetence	2. Conscious Incompetence	3. Conscious Competence	4. Unconscious Competence
Become aware of sustainability issue	Understand value of sustainability	Learn specifics about sustainability	Sustainability is core value in mindset

Sustainability Mindset, Behavior and Decision Making of all Company Members

Showing this competence means...
- Understands and is interested in commitment to sustainability
- Thinks and plans ahead to achieve long-term corporate goals
- Searches for durable solutions internally and externally and takes responsibility for their implementation

Leading with this competence means...
- Promotes and ensures a working environment that stimulates wellbeing, health and safety of the team
- Detects long-term opportunities and risks for the company and its stakeholders
- Meets and promotes decisions that require an immediate investment in the sense of long-term benefits

Required Character of HRD/ T&D Interventions

- Mix of Methods: Experiential and active learning, simulations

- Mix of Formats: E-learning, info or onboarding event, corporate and managers' communication, social engagement, workshop, target planning and bonus agreements, award and recognition, certifications

Propositions for Involvement according to the TBL of Sustainability

Environmental	Social	Economical
- Promote energy saving - Conserve resources - Reduce pollution - ...	- Corporate Volunteering - Health & Work-Life Balance - Code of Conduct - ...	- Compliance - Fair Trade - Sustainable investments - ...

Figure 14: Competence Model for Sustainability Mindset
Source: Own representation.

Adjacently to the competence model, these are some important recommendations of tools and learning principles HRD professionals should respect:

> *Integration* of CS and CSR with existing HRD education and training programs (Fenwick & Bierema, 2008).

> The long-term vision for change has to include *short-term goals* with reachable steps leading to achieving the vision (Kotter, 2007).

> A documented change plan that justifies the need for change, i.e. an *implementation plan* is necessary (Andre, 2013, p. 43).

> *Policies* are rules for the codes of conduct. They should contain and communicate the values and core ideals of the organization (Fernández et al., 2003, p 644).

> HRD activities are measured in *CS or CSR audits* of effectiveness and included in *CSR reports* (Garavan et al., 2010).

> HRD professionals know how to *design assessments* and audit tools for "… processes such as changing behaviors (learning) and long-term CSR outcomes" (Fenwick & Bierema, 2008, p. 33).

> *Coherent, consistent systems* and processes related to sustainability initiatives, e.g. short-term financial incentives are not likely to engage employees but undermine intrinsic motivation (Frey & Jegen, 2001).

> Experiential and *active learning*, as well as simulations are considered most appropriate (Haugh & Talwar, 2010).

> Foster *reflection, creativity*, continuous learning and an organizational learning culture (Boud et al., 2006).

6 Discussion

This chapter draws conclusions from the theoretical and practical research conducted above. After presenting the research contributions, the implications of the findings are put forward. In a final section, research limitations and suggestions for open research questions are given.

6.1 Theoretical and Practical Research Contributions

As was shown, scientific research and specialized literature relevant for the theoretical discussion of the subject stem from diverse perspectives. The combination of these distinct research fields was explored in a detailed, structured manner. During the literature review it was demonstrated that whereas HRD and especially sustainability have been widely addressed as separate issues, the joint area of HRD approaches to sustainability has only just begun to receive academic attention. An attempt to close this research gap was made using the combined analysis of these often distinct research fields. Cooper explains that "The research synthesist hopes to present the state of knowledge concerning the relation(s) of interest and to highlight important issues that research has left unresolved" (1998, p. 3). Following this, and since the treatment of the research issue represents a young interface, the preparation of the structured literature review and the exposition of the current state of research laid the foundation to conduct the empirical research. Major themes within HRD literature and a number of HRD interventions among all three pillars of sustainability were introduced. The most relevant conclusions from the literature analysis involve the striking demand in academia for greater recognition of HRD's role in promoting sustainability and the theoretical qualification of some HRD interventions. Furthermore, within the previous chapter the study was embedded into organizational change and a holistic framework was established. With regard to the identified gap of a suitable theoretical model, the proposed framework enriches the existing research field.

This section highlights the contributions for the identified practical research gap. The undertaken research appears to be the first to analyze the practical status quo of employee training for sustainability within large corporations in Germany. Even if limited in scope, the eight analyzed expert interviews conducted in large companies within the federal state of NRW point to several issues that are important in beginning a deeper examination of HRD's potential involvement in sustainability initiatives. The observations made in this study show that although large companies have not embraced sustainability fully as a triple bottom line, HRD practices do uphold human values and the common good. It was ascertained, that companies put emphases on ethics, staff well-being, respect, diversity and responsibility. Altogether, quite a few HRD initiatives were named which do advance a sustainability agenda and improve its integration in everyday organizational practice. This thesis contributes to the existing research field by adding primary qualitative research that extends previous findings through the collection of new facts on the research field. Finally, guidance for HRD was provided, including the conceptualization of a competency model. Thus, clear approaches to raise the influence on employees with regard to sustainability endeavors were given.

6.2 Theoretical and Practical Research Implications

The final implications for academic research and for HRD managers resulting from theoretical and practical findings and the novel conceptualizations of chapter 5 will be presented here.

The combined theoretical examination of the two research fields within this thesis is still rare. Therefore, the literature review of existing studies enhanced the approach of parallel consideration of the subject matter. Overall, a continuative analysis is advisable in further research. More precisely, this thesis should foster profound interdisciplinary research which focuses on the intersection of HRD initiatives and sustainability or corporate responsibility. Moreover, the model established in the previous chapter is seen as impetus for further framework development rather than as a complete, final proposition. In more detail, single relations of variables as well as the entire framework and moderating or mediating effects should be evaluated, revised and studied. Furthermore, the presented framework could be integrated with other theories or critical experiments already conduced to explain particular psychological, behavioral or organizational interaction effects.

It has frequently been highlighted that stronger involvement of HRD in sustainability issues is necessary, as employees have to support company-wide endeavors. The results of this research indicate that HRD currently does not appear to sufficiently prioritize training employees for sustainable behavior. Thereby, HRD professionals do not fully exploit their potential in making a positive impact on the corporate sustainability (CS) strategy. Suggested directions partially drawn from the evidence of how HRD should engage in sustainability were presented. The guidance given for HRD on recognizing reasons for resistance and thereafter expanding their engagement towards sustainability aims should stimulate HRD managers. In particular, the prepared competency model should encourage and facilitate HRD professionals to actively increase their impact on sustainability strategies. Thereby, the implied recommendation to strengthen the sustainability efforts of HRD in order to ensure long-term corporate success was supported by explicit practical guidance.

6.3   Limitations and Suggestions for Further Research

This section will explain methodological and practical limitations of the study at hand and will then point out research questions yet to be explored within the overall context of the subject matter.

6.3.1 Limitations of the Study

Overall, the accusation of qualitative methodology being unscientific does not hold since the explicit empirical orientation on the present social world realizes trustworthy, valid results (Lamnek, 2010). However, the applied qualitative method has limitations concerning sampling, interviewing and data analysis (Flick, 2015). Lamnek (2010) underlines that it should be guaranteed to interrogate actors that can provide the relevant information. But selecting interviewees with reference to organizational structures and their professional status does not ensure identifying the right person. As stated earlier, expert knowledge is not contingent on a particular job position but can be achieved in any institutionalized active function (Meuser & Nagel, 2009). Additionally, drawing conclusions about expertise according to hierarchical ranks is misleading, as experts are often found in second or third level functions, where decision-making options are prepared. Wrongly addressing a person as expert despite a priori sampling is called the *iceberg effect* (Lamnek, 2010, p. 657). Due to the difficulty of reaching the right experts; the inability to guarantee versed knowledge and considering the scope of this thesis there is an inherent need for limitation. That is, HRD professionals had to be selected according to suitable job positions and ideally based on a higher career level. Notably, some contacted persons made reference to colleagues more experienced in the topic and two interviews which did not yield precise expert knowledge were excluded (see Chapter 3.2.5). One feature of experts is their action-orientation which naturally signifies actors in senior positions that are ascribed a greater level of prestige and influence (Bogner et al., 2014). Thus, the identification of experts according to their job titles, and years of work and leadership experience via the network XING can still be assessed as scientifically sound. Expert interviews are regarded as susceptible to interaction effects (Lamnek, 2010). Bogner et al. (2014) argue that interaction is the natural constituent of interviews and must not be perceived as impairing effect. Amongst all hindering interactions that can occur, only the ones which might have conceivably occurred during this study are brought up. If the researcher, who is viewed as co-expert, poses rhetorical questions and influences the responses of the expert this is called the *feedback effect* (Lamnek, 2010, p. 657). Additionally, while an interview guide promises thematic competence on the part of the researcher as co-expert and induces fruitful exchange (Meuser & Nagel, 2009), too much familiarity carries the risk of assuming agreement and of exploring the topic insufficiently (Lamnek, 2010). Furthermore, the effects of *status and gender relations* between expert and co-expert have to be considered (Meuser & Nagel, 2009, p. 475). Even if the interviewer's status impression is positively influenced by the perception as a competent interlocutor, young female researchers within a male-dominated field can be impacted unfavorably (Meuser & Nagel, 2009).

To verify interpretative outcomes, internal and external validity can be examined (Bortz & Döring, 2006). While *internal validity* means consent among interpreters, *external validity* implies the capability to transfer idiographic insights to greater populations (ibid., pp. 334; ibid., p. 335). The methodological approach determined by the scope of this thesis does neither suffice for the confirmation of universally valid empirical facts nor for the deduction of substantive theory. It did however collect much useful, systematized information which present the current perspective of HRD professionals. More specifically, a clear advantage of this empirical study is that it provides a reflection of the operational status quo concerning the research question within representative companies. In accordance with the chain of qualitative thought, a large amount of novel empirical facts was collected (see Appendix C.3 and C.4).

Furthermore, this stream of research faces the constraint of measuring CS since "... the economic value of more sustainable business strategies is a lot more elusive, since it only materializes in the long-term" (Salzmann, Ionescu-Somers & Steger, 2005, p. 33). Banerjee (2011) differentiates the difficulty of assessing sustainability outcomes: "There are measurable indicators for economic and environmental dimensions of sustainability, but social sustainability is a much more complex issue" (p. 720). Besides measuring the success of sustainability alone, clearly determining and predicting the success of training on employee behavior and the succeeding effect on sustainability is an ambitious task. The inability to prove a priori added value of HRD interventions for sustainability resulted in some interviewee's incomprehension for the significance of the issue.

In all examined companies, the HRD departments do not have a training approach to fully satisfy all elements of the TBL, so that the discussion with HRD professionals had to be characterized by hypothetical reflections and ideas to some extent. However, due to the questionable a priori added value, some participants showed less conceptual or strategic interest in building possible future scenarios. Their focus was rather on narratively particularizing their current working area and on finding bridges concerning the inquiry between topics of business practice they are involved in or influenced by. Indeed, by doing so sustainability was not necessarily understood in the holistic way aimed for. Realistically, peripheral themes like health, compliance or work-life balance were linked to HRD while the appreciation and discussion of the imagined broad mindset covering the entire TBL was restricted by rather pragmatic, solution-oriented thought and views.

Admittedly, due to the novelty of the subject and the current lack of a concept for HRD interventions to foster a mindset for CS strategies, challenges occurred within the interviews. Little experience on how to implement an integrated HRD approach for a holistic sustainability mindset exist. Additionally, organizational change and system theory have insufficiently addressed the request to establish a culture that is infused with a mindset of sustainability. In consequence, introducing and proposing holistic, educationally grounded HRD measures to the interviewees and asking for their expert opinion was not an option. However, in alliance with the contingency concept, even if clear theoretical rationales would exist, they could not ensure the enforcement of a widespread sustainability mindset and its measurable benefits in all business contexts. Indeed, the primary aim of exploring present HRD processes and methods for sustainable practices was achieved.

6.3.2 Suggestions for Further Research

It has become clear during this research that further theoretical and empirical research is needed to build on the existing explorations of the study area. The theoretical interaction of HRD and sustainability and their effective practical synergies are still underresearched. The research fields that should be scrutinized can be allocated to the following four elements:

(1) *Companies and industries* investigated,

(2) *Persons* interviewed,

(3) *Content* inquired,

(4) *Methodology* applied.

To begin with, further companies within each industry should be explored, on the one side to identify similarities and divergences between industries: On the other side this could be valuable to contrast innovative industry champions against latecomers who have not dealt with the issue at all. Accordingly, industry champions should be investigated in depth in order to describe a best practice example that other firms can use as a benchmark to launch tested and effective processes. For instance, within this study one telecommunications firm proved to be leading in HRD initiatives for sustainability and could be studied extensively. Indeed, it is not plausible that the inclusion of small and medium-sized enterprises (SME) would be very productive. Especially smaller companies should only be approached if they claim sustainability to integrated into their business activities in order to understand how the topic is seen and treated in smaller organizational structures. However, it is to be expected that HRD and sustainability, but especially their interdisciplinary collaboration, might be less professionalized. Of course, extending the considered geographic region, for instance to the whole of Germany would ensure that potential regional differences are taken into account. Lastly, regarding companies that are sustainable in their entire business sense, like Ulrich Walter GmbH/ Lebensbaum or GEPA mbH - The Fair Trade Company, would result in empirical findings on how sustainability is purposefully anchored in the minds of their employees.

> Question: How does HRD involvement in sustainability or CR vary by industry, size, regional location and business sense of firms?

Turning to the actors interviewed, research could include various other experts and affected individuals. First, it would render further informative content to assess the unique perspective of sustainability managers. As pointed out by most of the participants in this study, sustainability managers could provide in depth knowledge that HRD professionals do not possess. From an organizational and conversational point of view it would also be fruitful to interview both experts jointly. Furthermore, as the role of the executive board commitment is striking, questioning its perspective would generate contents on an elevated strategic level. As was established during the empirical research, most companies distinguish between central HR functions which work strategically and affiliated service departments which execute operationally. In another approach it would thus be useful to interview multiple HR and HRD-professionals. Associated with this, operative personnel developers, i.e. trainers, should be consulted. In-house training as well as commercial training providers and self-employed coaches could possibly explain educational grounds and propose specific training methods from their work experience. Lastly, questioning employees of diverse career levels and positions which may or may not involve themselves in sustainability issues and potentially participate in relevant training should be interviewed. Including external authorities would provide supplementary discoveries.

> Question: How does the comprehension of HRD involvement in sustainability or CR vary according to the interviewed person?

> Question: Is the HRD unit viewed as full partner by the sustainability or CSR departments and do the latter know how to include HRD specialists in the design and incorporation of sustainability and CR initiatives?

Regarding content, if more enterprises are taken into account, the analysis could differentiate concrete sustainability strategies, i.e. a stronger focus on one of the pillars which supposedly tends to go in alliance with an industry. That is, companies like the electric utility or chemical firm proved to focus on ecological sustainability and cost savings. In addition, corporate responsibility was highlighted by most HRD professionals in connection with health or work-life balance. It could be interesting for future research to segregate the broad definition of sustainability as a mindset and to contrast the comprehension of corporate responsibility. SHRM (2011, p. 9) describes a three phase process for implementing sustainability: *compliance*, *integration* and *transformation*. It would be valuable to analyze a correlation between phases of sustainability implementation and HRD initiatives, while the identification of a particular phase must be thoroughly verified. The focus on one facet of sustainability could then be set according to the expertise of interviewees.

As for the methodological choice, both a mixed approach and a quantitative questionnaire can compile complementary information. For instance, a quantitative questionnaire could be applied in two phases, using knowledge gained during the first interrogation to strategize on launching specific measures and controlling for their effects. In such a long-term study, the effects of training can be measured by comparing the treatment group to a control group. Furthermore, both in further qualitative or mixed approaches, integrating other background information on companies like sustainability reports or employee surveys can be fruitful. Since feasibility issues have to be dealt with for the suggested broader research on HRD practices of sustainability or CR in large firms, stand-alone studies which consider any of the specified propositions could contribute much practical insight.

All propositions for further research are connected to the exploratory study reported here, which focused on *what* the status of business practice is in encouraging sustainability through HRD activities. From a critical point of view, it became clear that neither academia nor business managers are not extremely familiar with the research field. Thus, it would be useful to add a new dimension which moves away from the question of *whether or not* HRD is presently engaged in sustainability, CR or CSR towards the question of *how* this might be accomplished. This challenge was already thoroughly minded in chapter 5, which provides specific guidance for theory and practice. Similarly, a second critical inquiry approach could be to ask what a plan or process for personnel training would be like. Such research should approach either educational theorists, practical educational experts, for instance self-employed trainers, or both. Lastly, as executives were frequently mentioned as the strongest enablers of employee engagement, leadership development for a sustainability mindset could be studied further.

The result of this twofold research would be to gather additional recommendations for HRD professionals on how to implement such a process and ideally the formulation of a learning plan.

> Question: Can campaigns and processes of change strategies aimed at creating and maintaining e.g. a focus on health or compliance issues be transferred to the pursuit of broader sustainability goals?

To resume, the study at hand can be assessed as one of the exploratory pilots within the research field which is in clear need of further and broader studies and the inclusion of diverse perspectives.

7 Conclusion and Outlook

This final chapter summarizes the collected primary and secondary insights. Finally, a recommendation why companies should face the challenge of implementing HRD interventions for sustainability is given.

7.1 Interface of HRD and Sustainability

Overall, it is obvious that in some HRD and sustainability literature and practice a movement towards an integration of the two issues is evolving. A number of recent articles argue that HR departments can make significant positive contributions toward implementing sustainability in their organizations. Remarkably, thus far the two areas addressed in this research have not been investigated jointly in German firms. This thesis addresses this need by looking at how HRD experts in large organizations perceive and handle the subject. More than 70 persons were contacted, which effectuated 12 interviews. Qualitative data of eight expert interviews was analyzed with the *summary technique* set out by Mayring, which includes reducing and filtering out the essential aspects of the material. Furthermore, summarization and reduction made the formation of *seven inductive categories* possible. Generally, the interview transcripts were examined on how organizations deploy HRD activities to support the success of sustainability strategies. Within the seventh inductive category, important remarks on developing an *HRD campaign for sustainability* were explained. As a summary of the empirical findings concerning the guiding questions, figure 15 shows all inductive categories and their respective central insights. Furthermore, within the discussion a *holistic framework* was proposed which should be seen as a next step in theoretical model development. Likewise, the framework is a constructive suggestion of variables, which should be considered to better implement HRD efforts for sustainability in practice. Finally, the *competency model* conceptualized for a corporate sustainability (CS) mindset serves as concrete guidance for the actions of HRD professionals. The center of attention in this thesis was given to these guiding research questions on the integration of HRD approaches and sustainability:

> ➢ *Question 1:* Which forms of HRD are used to support sustainability strategies?

> ➢ *Question 2:* How effective are HRD interventions and which factors have an influence on transfer into practice?

> ➢ *Question 3:* Are results of training measured and if so, how? Is internal or market-related performance enhanced after an HRD intervention for sustainability?

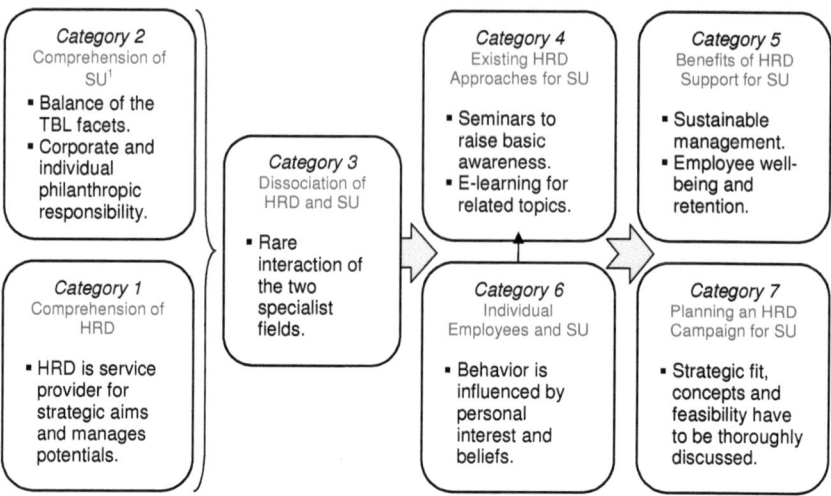

Note: [1] SU = sustainability.

Figure 15: Empirical Research Results within Inductive Categories
Source: Own representation.

Regarding these questions, there appears to be some consensus among business firms that their organizations need to integrate economic, social, and environmental dimensions of sustainability. However, empirical data showed that HRD professionals have been minimally involved in the transformation of their companies towards sustainability. As explained, all companies provide e-learning and social learning opportunities and diverse directives are communicated. In essence, these means of supporting sustainability strategies do not necessarily meet the core of HRD: Most tools raise awareness for the issue, none of the companies worked actively on establishing a sustainability mindset culture. Consequently, the effectiveness of HRD interventions cannot yet be accurately measured. However, tendencies can be assessed by regarding employee survey questions which are indirectly linked, and target agreements can steer supportive behaviors. Further empirical studies should explore the role of HRD activities in making organizations sustainable.

7.2   Strategic Perspective and Future Outlook

In this thesis, it was argued that employees are regarded as critical success factor and HRD as training enabler for sustainability strategies. Empirical research showed that HRD managers today do not fully comprehend their role in such a way and are rarely involved in corresponding organizational change. In business strategy, sustainability has generally meant ensuring survival of companies and sustaining long-term performance. However, in the long run a satisfaction of all three dimensions of the TBL should be achieved because a single focus on economic sustainability can only persist in the short run (Dyllick & Hockerts, 2002). *Environmental impacts* are becoming an important concern for businesses. Pressures from both external and internal stakeholders are forcing MNCs that are not operating sustainably to re-think their strategy and operations (Vithessonthi, 2009). Companies are also required to measure their *social impact* to be more responsible and accountable for their business opera-tions (Epstein & Yuthas, 2014). Though any company's main goal is to make a profit, of in-creasing importance is how the company treats its employees, how it benefits the community where it is located, and how the company helps sustain the environment. Ultimately, in im-plementing sustainable practices, the culture must change to support these practices (Fernández et al., 2003; Griffiths, Dunphy & Benn, 2005).

In 2010, the results of a survey presented in figure 16 show which sustainability issues Ger-man companies find important (on a scale from 1 = 'not at all' to 5 = 'very'). As can be seen, energy consumption, emissions, and education and training are issues of sustainability that are highly important to German firms ($n = 112$). Nevertheless, all other themes are of great signif-icance for the respondents as well. Thus, many companies have indeed recognized the need to consider sustainability. The Sustainability Code is a benchmark for sustainability manage-ment in Germany. Currently, its application is voluntary: In response to the Code's 20 non-financial parameters, companies submit a summary declaration of the undertaken measures relating to the environment, society, employees, human rights, anti-corruption and diversity (German Council for Sustainable Development, 2015). Recently however, the European Commission (2014) has issued a directive which makes disclosure of non-financial and diver-sity information binding for companies with over 500 employees as of 2017.[9] The Sustaina-bility Code can be applied to report performance annually: "It focuses on public-interest enti-ties that are listed on the stock exchange or issue bonds, as well as financial service providers such as banks and insurance companies" (p. 30). This *reporting obligation* can be seen as a strong impetus for sustainability. Another survey by Ernst & Young (2012, p. 16; $n = 272$) concerning the top three stakeholder groups in driving their company's sustainability initia-tives, ranked employees second (cited by 22% of respondents), behind customers (37%) and ahead of shareholders (15%), NGOs (7%) and policymakers (7%). Considering this and the future reporting obligation, increasing employee support will be necessary for the success of CS endeavors.

---

[9] Directive 2014/95/EU holds for companies of public interest with over 500 employees and a balance sheet total over 20 million Euros or a net turnover over 40 million Euros (EU Commission, 2014).

Figure 16: Importance of Sustainability Issues for German Companies
Source: Schaltegger, Windolph & Harms, 2010, p. 43.

According to a 2015 Gallup poll, only 15% of employees in Germany are truly engaged at their workplace, which causes immense financial damage on companies (*n* = 2,212). Employee engagement is critical as those most committed to their organizations put in 57% more effort on the job – and are 87% less likely to resign – than employees who consider themselves disengaged (Corporate Leadership Council, 2004, pp. 6; *n* = 50,000). Besides other determining factors, *employee engagement* is also influenced by the company's commitment to sustainability and CSR: More than two-thirds of survey respondents prefer to work for socially responsible companies (Nielsen, 2014, p. 3; *n* = 30,000). The survey also found that half of respondents who are responsive to sustainability actions are millennials (49%), followed by generation X (age 35-49) respondents (25%) and baby boomer (age 50-64) respondents (12%) (Nielsen, 2014, p. 7; *n* = 30,000). According to Meister and Willyerd (2010, p. 1) millennials are "… the most socially conscious generation since the 1960s". Another poll supports that "Millennial and Generation X employees were more likely than Baby Boomers to report their organization's commitment to CSR as 'very important' job satisfaction contributor" (SHRM, 2015, p. 26; *n* = 600). To clarify, employees who engage in the company's sustainability and CSR initiatives will have increases in their overall engagement rate, as there is a growing importance by the workforce of the future to have meaningful jobs. As the overall engagement rates are generally low in German companies, sustainability and CSR initiatives are a way of improving engagement. Employees lay great emphasis on varied activities, training opportunities and indeed on the company's image as well as the social commitment (Lünendonk & Orizon, 2013; *n* = 2,072). By implication, employees appreciate companies to have sustainability programs and to provide quality training and learning opportunities which will positively influence their commitment and engagement on the job (Rupp, Ganapathi, Aguilera & Williams, 2006). The survey findings show additional benefits for engaging in sustainable practices: Attracting top talent, and improving employee engagement and retention.

Altogether, several necessities and reasons for requesting organizational and especially HRD initiative to improve sustainability approaches of companies were described. At this point, the sustainability movement cannot be considered a passing trend. In view of the steadily increasing complexity and globalization of the world economy, sustainability constitutes a common topic for increasing the value of a company. Companies increasingly seem to operate according to the idea of shared value introduced by Porter and Kramer in 2011. Taken from the organizational change perspective and interviewees' statements, sustainability will become even more important in the future. The awareness of sustainability issues calls for a paradigm shift in corporate mindsets. Fenwick and Bierema postulate that "HRD potentially offers important voice, expertise and services to achieve the fullest development of CSR" (2008, p. 34). Despite the growing sense of responsibility and sustainability, the challenge remains how to instill the discipline to incorporate sustainability in employees' everyday operations in a way that ultimately influences outcomes, i.e. direct cost savings from operational efficiencies or potential revenue increases from enhancing the corporate image as well as safeguarding the firm's long-term prosperity. When an organization decides to become more aware of how its practices are affecting the environment, society and economy, HRD activities can be used as a strategic asset in ensuring success in sustainability endeavors. The strategic vision is to achieve changes in overall employee attitude and behavior. This has to be accompanied by long-term changes in organizational culture and values and consequently organizational routines and processes.

Since employee support is a key success factor for sustainability performance, HRD professionals need to get involved and fulfill the task of creating a strategic learning plan focused on employee engagement and education.

Appendix

For the purpose of better presentation, the complete Appendix is available for download at the following link. In addition, the full interview transcripts are also available for download: https://www.eul-verlag.de/pdf-wz/9783844104523_Appendix.zip.

Appendix A: Review of Literature

A.1 Most Relevant Publications Identified during the Systematic Literature Review

No.	Title, (Journal)	Author (Year)	Count of Google Scholar Citations	Abbreviated Abstract
1	Corporate social responsibility: issues for human resource development professionals (*International Journal of Training and Development*)	Fenwick, T., Bierema, L. (2008)	114	"[…] the evidence shows that their engagement tends to focus on employee learning and promotion, employee ownership of development, and employee safety and respect. Overall, however, HRD appeared to be only marginally involved or interested in the firms' CSR activities."
2	Human resource development and society: human resource development's role in embedding corporate social responsibility, sustainability, and ethics in organizations (*Advances in Developing Human Resources*)	Garavan, T. N., McGuire, D. (2010)	62	"It [HRD] is criticized for moving away from its mission to advocate humanistic values in organizations […]. This article argues that societal HRD (SHRD) can make an important and long-lasting contribution to CSR, sustainability, and ethics through its capacity to question a continual focus by organizations on efficiency and performance."
3	Sustainability, corporate social responsibility and HRD (*European Journal of Training and Development*)	Sheehan, M., Garavan, T. N., Carbery, R. (2014)	-	"The role that HRD plays in contributing to sustainability and CSR in organisations is not well understood. […] However, we propose that a focus on sustainability and CSR will serve to advance the field of HRD and contribute to enhancing practices within organisations."
4	The role of HRD in CSR, sustainability and ethics: A relational model (*Human Resource Development Review*)	Ardichvili, A. (2013)	11	"The model suggests that CSR, CS, and ethics are parts of the same organizational subsystem […]. HRD can influence this system by engaging in culture change efforts, ethics and CS-/CSR-related education and training on all levels of the organization, and raising awareness of isues of power".
5	Human resource development as an element of corporate social responsibility (*Asia Pacific Journal of Human Resources*)	Wilcox, T. (2006)	37	"These issues arise in part from a shifting of the regulatory ground from the achievement of 'social good' to 'economic good'[…]. Some of the areas in which an organization's social and ethical responsibliity can encompass HRD practices are explored […]."
6	HR's role in building a sustainable enterprise: Insights from some of the world's best companies (*Human Resource Planning*)	Wirtenberg, J., Harmon, J., Russell, W. G., Fairfield, K. D. (2007)	67	"[…] specific HR-related actions to help develop these qualities: inculcating sustainability-oriented values, helping to elicit senior management support for making sustainability central to business strategy."

No.	Title, (Journal)	Author (Year)	Count of Google Scholar Citations	Abbreviated Abstract
7	Role of HR in the new world of sustainability (Industrial and Commercial Training)	Rimanoczy, I., Pearson, T. (2010)	24	"The purpose of the paper is to assess the strategic role that the human resource department (HRD) can play in the development and implementation of an organization's sustainability program. [...] such programs require change in organizational culture, which in turn demands new leadership competencies, behaviors and mindsets.'"
8	Human resource development and sustainablity: beyond sustainable organizations (Human Resource Development International)	Scully-Russ, E. (2012)	5	"It is argued here that if HRD scholars and practitioners are more deliberate in their relationship with sustainability, they will encounter new and powerful conceptual and ethical frameworks to address the long standing tension in the field."
9	The effects of employee training on the relationship between environmental attitudes and firms' performance in sustainable development (The International Journal of Human Resource Management)	Ji, L., Huang, J., Liu, Z., Zhu, H., Cai, Z. (2012)	12	"With better employee training, a firm's correct environmental attitude should be more likely to help improve its performance in sustainable development. Moreover, [...] employee training may also have a positive direct effect on firms' performance in sustainable development".
10	The impact of human resource practices and corporate sustainability on organizational ethical climates: An employee perspective (Journal of Business Ethics)	Guerci, M., Radaelli, G., Siletti, E., Cirella, S., Shani, A. B. R. (2015)	1	"[...] the perceptions of the company's employees in terms of corporate sustainablity moderate these relationships, by reinforcing the positive relationships of ability-enhancing and motivation-enhancing HRM practices in terms of benevolent and principled ethical climates [...]".
11	Extending corporate social responsibility research to the human resource management and organizational behavior domains: A look to the future (Personnel Psychology)	Morgeson, F. P., Aguinis, H., Waldman, D. A., Siegel, D. S. (2013)	23	"We propose that a focus on HR/OB will improve our understanding and the antecedents and consequences of CSR and also benefit HR/OB in terms of bridging the science-practice and micro-macro gaps."
12	The central role of human resource management in the search for sustainable organizations (The International Journal of Human Resource Management)	Jabbour, C. J. C., Santos, F.C. A. (2008)	112	"The relationship between human resources and organizational sustainability, which is based on economical, social and environmental performance, involves some important aspects concerning management such as innovation, cultural diversity and the environment."
13	The role of HR in achieving a sustainability culture (Journal of Sustainable Development)	Liebowitz, J. (2010)	24	"[...] it is recommended that an organization's Sustainability Coordinator work more closely with the organization's Human Resource executive."

No.	Title, (Journal)	Author (Year)	Count of Google Scholar Citations	Abbreviated Abstract
14	Building sustainable organizations: The human factor *(Academy of Management Perspectives)*	Pfeffer, J. (2010)	284	"[...] outlines a research agenda for investigating the links between social sustainability and organizational effectiveness as well as the role of ideology in understanding the relative neglect of the human factor in sustainability research."
15	Changing behavior: Successful environmental programmes in the workplace *(Business Strategy and the Environment)*	Young, W., Davis, M., McNeill, I., M., Malhotra, B., Russell, S., Unsworth, K., Clegg, C., W. (2013)	9	"[...] the strongest predictors are environmental awareness, performance feedback, financial incentives, environmental infrastructure, management support and training. [...] attitude change is not necessarily a pre-requisite for behaviour change in the workplace."
16	Self-efficacy as a mediator of the relationships between learning and ethical behavior from HRD in CSR activity *(Asia-Pacific Journal of Business Administration)*	Sukserm, T., Takahashi, Y. (2012)	3	"[...] companies should pormote and encourage employees in acutal learning of such kinds of CSR activity in order to develop confidence."
17	Conceptualizing the behavioral barriers to CSR and CS in organizations: A typology of HRD interventions *(Advances in Developing Human Resources)*	Garavan, T., N., Heraty, N., Rock, A., Dalton, E. (2010)	30	"HRD has a major role to play in changing employee behavior and organizational values [...]. This article discusses a typology of HRD interventions that may be used to address barriers to the implementation of CSR/ CS initiatives."
18	The effects of CSR on employees's affective commitment: A cross-cultural investigation *(Journal of Applied Psychology)*	Mueller, K., Spiess, S.-O., Hattrup, K., Lin-Hi, N. (2012)	25	"In particular, perceptions of CSR were more positively related to AC in cultures higher in humane orientation, institutional collectivism, ingroup collectivism, and future orientation and in cultures lower in power distance."
19	Leadership's influence on innovation and sustainability: A review of the literature and implications for HRD *(European Journal of Training and Development)*	Waite, A., M. (2013)	4	"This article is among the first to highlight leadership as a connection between innovation and sustainability and provides a valuable platform for HRD scholars and practitioners interested in enhancing leadership capacity and development in these areas."

Appendix B: Empirical Research - Operationalization

B.1 Guideline Applied during Expert Interview

Personal and Company information.

Name _____   Male ☐   Female ☐
Company_____
Position _____
    Position responsibilities:
Department _____
Corporate sustainability department_____

Part 1: Defining Key Terms and Linking the Idea of Sustainability to Human Resource Development.

The interviewee will describe his/her concept of sustainability and HRD.

1. Please describe your understanding of (corporate) sustainability.

2. Please explain what HRD means to you.

If necessary, the interviewer will give a definition of sustainability.

> **Triple-Bottom Line- Concept of Sustainability**
> "The right to development must be fulfilled so as to equitably meet developmental and envi-
> ronmental needs of present and future generations."
> (Elkington, 1994)

    ▫ Would you like to add supplementary ideas to your prior answers now?

Part 2: Briefly Recognizing Sustainability Strategies in the Respective Company.

1. What are (strategic) activities associated with sustainability in your company?

    ▫ Does your company follow a corporate sustainability strategy?
    ▫ How many employees are involved in actions surrounding sustainability?
    ▫ Which sustainability strategies are prioritized in your company?

2. Was a sustainability report established and objectives determined, how were they met?

    ▫ How is sustainability measured or controlled for?
    ▫ Do you track whether employees or other stakeholders/public read the report and
       provide feedback? Do you measure it (what percentage reads it)?
    ▫ What insights have you gained from the last report?

Part 3: Focusing on HRD practices in Detail.

1. What help is needed from HRD in which areas of implementing sustainability strategies?

2. Which kinds of HRD programs related to sustainability are carried out in your company?

   ▫ Content of these teaching and training activities? Form of training? Duration?
   ▫ Participants?

3. What are problems faced by HR departments when implementing development methods with reference to sustainability?

4. How could these obstacles be overcome?

5. What are concrete results of HRD approaches to sustainability?

   ▫ Are results measured? Is behavior to support sustainability strategies assessed?
   ▫ If so, how? Not necessarily in a quantitative way, but can changes be observed?

6. Which is the influence of employees on sustainability strategies?

7. Would you characterize employees as a key success factors for sustainability strategies/the company a whole? If so, why?

Part 4: Look to the Future and Personal Note.

1. What is the importance of a sustainability strategy and what is the importance of HRD?

2. What are events, trends, developments driving the field?

3. What are some of your proudest achievements?
   What are some of your persistent challenges?

4. What kinds of projects do you have planned for the future?
   What kinds of changes are you planning to implement?

Appendix C: Empirical Research - Results

C.1 Overview of the Interviews

Case	Job Title	Industry of Company	No. of Employees[1]
A	Head of CoE "People Development" Cluster Deutschland	Electric utility	59,784
B	Senior Experte Personalentwicklung	Retail and Tourism	327,548
C	HR Business Partner Central Europe	Telecommunications	14,000
D	Expert Management Development & Talent Management	Insurance	14,518
E	Senior Business Advisor	Telecommunications	228,248
F	Specialist HR Development	Chemicals	113,292
G	Senior Experte	Logistics	493,207
H	Specialist HR Development EU & SA	Automotive Supplier	5,500

Note: [1] *Information retrieved from Bisnode/ Hoppenstedt on 09 May 2015.*

C.2 Interpretation Rules for Summary in Content-Analysis

S1: Paraphrasing

S1.1 Cut all the text components which are not content-bearing or only minimally so, such as embellishing, repetitive, or explanatory expressions.

S1.2 Transpose the content-bearing parts of the text on to a uniform stylistic level.

S1.3 Transform them into a grammatically abbreviated form.

S2: Generalization to the required level of abstraction

S2.1 Generalize the referents of the paraphrases to the defined level of abstraction, so that the old referents are implied in the newly formulated ones.

S2.2 Generalize the sentence kernels (predicates) in the same way.

S2.3 Leave those paraphrases standing which are above the intended level of abstraction.

S2.4 In cases of doubt make use of theoretical preconceptions.

S3: First reduction

S3.1 Cut semantically identical paraphrases within units of evaluation.

S3.2 Cut paraphrases which are not felt to add substantially to the content on the new level of abstraction.

S3.3 Adopt the paraphrases which continue to be thought of as vitally content-bearing (selection).

S3.4 Resolve cases of doubt with the aid of theoretical preconceptions.

S4: Second reduction

S4.1 Combine paraphrases with identical or similar referents and similar statements to form one paraphrase (binding).

S4.2 Combine paraphrases with several statements on the same referent into one (construction/integration).

S4.3 Combine paraphrases with identical or similar referents and differing statements into one paraphrase (construction/integration).

C.3 Inductive Forming of Categories Step 1

Schritt 1: Paraphrasierung und Kategorienbildung

Fall	Nr.	Zeile (n)	Paraphrase	Generalisierung		Reduktion
A	1	6 – 7	wir sehen uns in der Personalentwicklung als Kompetenzcenter	Personalentwicklung als Kompetenzcenter	K1	**K 1 Verständnis von Personalentwicklung**
A	2	7 – 11	wir befähigen Führungskräfte, Mitarbeiter zu entwickeln	Führungskräfte befähigen, ihre Mitarbeiter zu entwickeln	K1	· Kompetenzcenter
A	3	18 – 32	Nachhaltigkeit bedeutet hier Potenzialeinschätzung: Qualifikation von Führungskräften im Prozess	Nachhaltigkeit in der Führungskräfte Entwicklung	K2	· Führungskräfte zur Mitarbeiterentwicklung befähigen · berufliche Erstausbildung
A	4	40 – 43	Gesellschaftliches Engagement durch Projekte: "Companius", "Mitarbeiter machen Schule"	gesellschaftliche Verantwortung des Konzerns durch soziales Engagement	K2.1	· technische Weiterbildung durch interne Mitarbeiter · Führungskräfte sollen sich im Job entwickeln
A	5	46	Nachhaltigkeitsabteilung steuert interne Aufklärung	für Nachhaltigkeitsthemen intern ist nur die spezifische Abteilung zuständig	K2.2	· Aufstieg von Mitarbeitern als Erfolgsmessung der Entwicklungsmaßnahme · Maßnahmen aufgrund des Marktdrucks zurückfahren
A	6	49 – 50	zu Feedback zum Nachhaltigkeitsbericht wird man aufgefordert aber kein Nachhalten, ob er gelesen wird	keine Überprüfung ob Nachhaltigkeit-Report gelesen wird, Feedback ist gewünscht	K2.2	
A	7	59 – 61	Mitarbeitermotivationsindex wird alles 2 Jahre erhoben durch 12 Fragen	Erhebung Mitarbeitermotivation alle 2 Jahre		**K 2 Verständnis von Nachhaltigkeit** · Potenzialeinschätzung und Führungskräfteentwicklung
A	8	66 – 71	Ausbildung ist klassische Personalentwicklung, jemand lernt im Unternehmen die praktischen Inhalte	klassische Personalentwicklung beinhaltet die Berufsausbildung	K1	· eine Balance finden · nicht aus der ethischen Orientierung der Nachhaltigkeit selbst getrieben
A	9	71 – 75	im Personalmarketing ist unsere Strategie Trainees nach dem Programm einzustellen, außerdem stellen wir Kontakte zu Exzellenz Universitäten her und geben Stipendien	Personalmarketing Strategie fokussiert das Trainee-Programm und Kontakte zu Exzellenz Universitäten		**K 2.1 Soziale Nachhaltigkeit**
A	10	83 – 89	gesetzlich vorgeschriebene technische Weiterbildungen zu 80% durch eigene Mitarbeiter durchführen lassen	technische Weiterbildungen durch interne Mitarbeiter	K1	· soziale Projekte als Zeichen der gesellschaftlichen Verantwortung
A	11	98 – 104	Führungskräfte sollen selbst schauen nach "Entwicklung im Job"	proaktives "Training on the Job" aus Eigeninitiative der FK	K1	**K 2.2 Organisation**
A	12	110	wir gucken wer sich zur Führungskraft entwickelt hat	Führungskraft-Aufstieg als Erfolgsmessung	K1	· spezifische Abteilung für alle Themen
A	13	118 – 119	zu Anfang eines Trainee Programms gibt es ein Info-Seminar	Infoveranstaltung für Trainees beinhaltet Nachhaltigkeitsthemen	K3.2	· keine Überprüfung, ob Nachhaltigkeitsbericht gelesen wird, Feedback ist erwünscht · Nachhaltigkeit im Stab organisiert
A	14	143 – 144	man hat erkannt, dass Nachhaltigkeitsthemen auch die Arbeitsqualität verbessern	ein Mehrwert von Nachhaltigkeit ist verbesserte Arbeitsqualität	K3.1	**K 3 Schnittstelle Personalentwicklung und Nachhaltigkeit**
A	15	145 – 146	in einem Zeitversatz von 1-2 Jahren erkennt man im Unternehmen den Mehrwert	organisationale Wirkung dauert 1-2 Jahre	K3.1	**K 3.1 Nutzenaspekte**
A	16	154 – 155	in Technik Trainings sind immer Umweltaspekte enthalten	nachhaltige Themen in Trainings nur bei konkretem Bezug	K3.2	· ein Mehrwert ist verbesserte Arbeitsqualität · Wirkung im Zeitversatz von 1-2 Jahren erkennbar
A	17	163 – 164	umfassende Lehr- und Lernmaßnahmen nur wenn ein Vorstand erkennt, dass es im Sinne der Außen- und auch Innenwirkung wichtig ist	bei Unterstützung des Vorstandes, hoher Außen- und Innenwirkung sind ganzheitliche Nachhaltigkeitsmaßnahmen möglich	K3.2	**K 3.2 Veranstaltungen**
A	18	168 – 169	Thema Nachhaltigkeit hat keine Vergänglichkeit, gerade in der Energiebranche	in Energiebranche bleibt Nachhaltigkeit ein Thema		· Infoveranstaltung für Trainees beinhaltet Nachhaltigkeitsthemen · nachhaltige Themen bei Trainings nur mit konkretem

				PE-Maßnahmen		Bezug
A	19	180 – 181	aufgrund des Marktdruckes wird viel zurückgefahren	PE-Maßnahmen unterliegen Investitionsüberlegungen und Marktdruck	K1	• umfassende Lehr- und Lernmaßnahmen nur wenn ein Vorstand erkennt, dass es im Sinne der Außen- und Innenwirkung wichtig ist
A	20	198	Nachhaltigkeit bedeutet eine vernünftige Balance zu finden	Nachhaltigkeit heißt eine Balance zu finden	K2	
A	21	199	man macht das nicht aus der Nachhaltigkeit getrieben	hinter Nachhaltigkeit steht nicht eine ethische Überzeugung als Treiber	K2	
A	22	202	Nachhaltigkeit ist eine Stabstelle	Nachhaltigkeit im Stab organisiert	K2	
B	23	2 – 10	ich sehe Nachhaltigkeit weit gefasst und langfristig nur im Umgang mit der Natur, sondern auch mit allen Ressourcen wie auch dem Menschen.	Nachhaltigkeit bedeutet ganzheitlicher, langfristiger, schonender Umgang mit allen Ressourcen, auch dem Menschen.	K2	**K 1 Verständnis von Personalentwicklung** • PE weitgreifend verstanden • bedarf eines Ist- und Zukunftblicks • Kompetenzaufbau bei Mitarbeitern • Organisationsentwicklung in eine bestimmte Richtung • Recruiting zählt dazu • Onboarding und Ausbildung sind Teil der PE • Trainings werden durch interne Kollegen gegeben • Standardpräsentationen kommen aus der Zentrale • Führungskräfte vermitteln selbst gewisse Themenkomplexe • nur in Ausnahmefällen externe Trainer
B	24	11 – 16	Nachhaltigkeit betrifft auch die Person, wie nachhaltig bin ich mit mir persönlich	persönliche Nachhaltigkeit des Einzelnen	K2.1	
B	25	19 – 24	Personalentwicklung ist der gesamte Themenkomplex, die richtigen Mitarbeiter zum richtigen Zeitpunkt am richtigen Ort zu haben; das bedeutet Ist- und Zukunftsblick	PE weitgreifend über den gesamten MA-Zyklus und mit einem Ist-und Zukunftsblick	K1	
B	26	24 – 38	klassische PE-Denke ist, Menschen zu entwickeln, Kompetenzen aufzubauen durch Seminare und das Unternehmen zu entwickeln	PE ist Kompetenzaufbau bei Mitarbeitern und Organisationsentwicklun g in eine bestimmte Richtung	K1	
B	27	40 – 43	"Change" als zentraler Begriff, Veränderung von Menschen, Strukturen, der kollektiven Kultur oder DNA	PE ist ein strategisches Thema in dem es zentral um Veränderung ("Change") geht	K1	
B	28	45 – 47	bei kleineren Firmen ist Personal eine "one man show", je größer die Firma desto mehr Bereiche	Personal-Bereiche in Abhängigkeit von der Größe der Firma	K1.1	**K 1.1 Organisation** • je größer die Firma, desto mehr Bereiche im Personal
B	29	47 – 52	interne Rekrutierung und externes Rekrutierung gehören zur PE	Recruiting zählt zur Personalentwicklung	K1	
B	30	55 – 57	Ausbildung ist für mich Teil der PE, aber auch das "Onboarding" müssen wir betrachten	berufliche Erstausbildung und "onboarding" als Teil der PE	K1	**K 1.3 Nachhaltigkeit durch Personalentwicklung**
B	31	60 – 62	das klassische Schulen kann Nachhaltigkeit zum Inhalt haben, durch Fachthemen wie Arbeitssicherheit, Gesundheitsmanagement, wertorientierte Führung, gewaltfreie Kommunikation	Nachhaltigkeit als ganzheitliches Konzept Ebene 1 - Nachhaltigkeit als Inhalt in Fachthemen: Arbeitssicherheit und Gesundheit	K2	• Nachhaltigkeit für jeden Mitarbeiter strukturell verankert durch Jahreszielplanung, Bonusvereinbarungen • Nachhaltigkeit integriert in Führungskräfteentwicklung und Ausbildung • Nachhaltigkeit in Firmenwerten enthalten und daher "Muss"-Schulungsthema • für Mitarbeiter, die einzelne Nachhaltigkeitsthemen betreuen spezielle Schulungen
B	32	64 – 75	Ausbildung unter der PE und Organisationsentwicklung selbst nachhaltig gestalten, strukturell, Rahmenbedingungen	Ebene 2 - strukturelle Nachhaltigkeit der PE durch Seminarzeiten, Ort, Ausgestaltung	K2	
B	33	75 – 91	bei einem Seminar durch Pausengestaltung ("Bio-Pausen"), Feedback, die Haltung des Trainers methodisch nachhaltig sein	Ebene 3 - methodische Nachhaltigkeit in der Durchführung (Meta-Ebene)	K2	• Teilnahme an Schulungen in Abhängigkeit von Position, höhere Frequenz bei FK
B	34	93 – 95	Nachhaltigkeit hat vier Säulen, Mitarbeiter ist eine davon genauso wie Kunde, Umwelt und Klima - als Lebensmitteleinzelhändler ist das klar	Nachhaltigkeit hat vier Säulen insbesondere den Mitarbeiter	K2.1	• auf niedrigen Hierarchieebenen kommen nur Richtlinien an • keine Nachhaltigkeitsschulung für alle Mitarbeiter außer Compliance
B	35	96 – 102	Nachhaltigkeit durch PE in Moderation von Jahreszielplanung, Bonusvereinbarungen (enthalten auf allen Ebenen), strategische Workshops	Implementierung durch PE: strukturell verankerte Nachhaltigkeit durch Jahreszielplanung, Bonusvereinbarungen, Strategie-Workshops	K1.2	• hinter der Umsetzung von Nachhaltigkeit steckt persönliches Interesse der Führungskräfte
B	36	103 – 108	das was die Firma macht ist tatsächlich Lehrstoff in der Ausbildung oder Führungskräfteentwicklung z.B. Arbeitssicherheit, rechtliche Aspekte, Hygiene	Nachhaltigkeitsthemen integriert in FK-Entwicklung und Ausbildung	K1.3	• Auszubildende werden für soziales Engagement von der

B					
B	37	109 – 111	das Firmen-Leitbild hat Nachhaltigkeit als einen Punkt integriert	Nachhaltigkeit ist in den Firmenwerten enthalten, daher auch MUSS-Schulungsthema	K1.3
B	38	113 – 120	zudem gibt es noch Schulungen für Mitarbeiter in speziellen Nachhaltigkeitsbereichen wie "Energiemanager" oder interne Berater zu Themen Sucht, Insolvenz, Scheidung, Tod	zusätzlich zu breit gesehenem Leitbild gibt es für Mitarbeiter, die einzelne Nachhaltigkeitsthemen betreuen, Schulungen	K1.3
B	39	123 – 133	Teilnahme an Schulungen von Positionen abhängig, FK werden häufiger geschult und haben Meetings wo das Thema anschlägt; bei vielen Mitarbeitern kommen nur Richtlinien an	Teilnahme abhängig von Position, höhere Frequenz für FK auch durch Meetings; auf niedriger Hierarchieebene kommen nur Richtlinien an	K1.3
B	40	135 – 144	es gibt keine Schulung, die alle FK machen, außer ein Compliance E-Learning, wenn man es als Nachhaltigkeitsthema sieht; in den Märkten ist Arbeitssicherheit eine Standardschulung	es gibt keine Nachhaltigkeit-Schulung für alle FK oder Mitarbeiter; ausschließlich Compliance für FK und Arbeitssicherheit im Lagerbereich von Märkten	K1.3
B	41	146 – 161	nationale Vorgabe in der Jahreszielplanung sagt, alle FK thematisieren das Thema Nachhaltigkeit im Jahr 2015, es muss allerdings nur einmal thematisiert werden	hinter der Umsetzung von Nachhaltigkeitsthemen steckt persönliches Engagement der FK	K1.3
B	42	175 – 189	Gesundheitsmanagement ist im Personalbereich angesiedelt, da kann ich einen Kollegen bitten Themen vorzustellen; die Standard-Präsentation zur nationalen Vorgabe kommt aus der Zentrale; bestimmte Themenkomplexe mache ich selbst aufgrund meiner beruflichen Erfahrung und Ausbildung	Trainings werden durch interne Kollegen, Standardpräsentationen aus der Zentrale, oder selbst aufgesetzte Präsentationen der FK vermittelt, nur in Ausnahme externe Trainer	K1
B	43	192 – 204	die wichtigsten Themen sind Gesundheit der Mitarbeiter, um Langzeitkrankheit zu vermeiden, das ist aber schwer messbar, und Thema Umwelt, wie z.B. Bioprodukte, Fair-Trade, Regionalität	die größten Hebel der Nachhaltigkeit bestehen in Bezug auf Gesundheit der Mitarbeiter und Umwelt	K2.2
B	44	207 – 212	in der Masse ist Nachhaltigkeit eher ein lästiges Thema, ich gehöre zu denen, die sich engagieren, es ist Aufwand und man sieht den Nutzen nicht direkt	persönliches Engagement als Treiber von Nachhaltigkeitsthemen	K2.1
B	45	216 – 220	Mitarbeiter in Nachhaltigkeit sitzen teilweise auf "verlorenen Posten"	nicht alle Themen sind umsetzbar und manche Nachhaltigkeitspositionen sind "verlorene Posten"	
B	46	228 – 239	Hauptargument ist ein kapitalistischer Ansatz kein Gutmenschentum; habe ich Mitarbeiter, die nachhaltig leben und wirtschaften, wirtschaftet das ganze UN besser; ökologisch weniger Schaden für die Umwelt, Investition der Konzerne in Regionen	Nachhaltigkeit aus rein kapitalistischen Aspekten kein Gutmenschentum	K2.2
B	47	247 – 252	Themen der Nachhaltigkeit werden noch stärker kommen aus drei Gründen, gesetzliche Regulierungen, gesteigerte Notwendigkeit und Umdenken bzw. Werteveränderung	Nachhaltigkeit wird stärker kommen aufgrund von Regulierungen, Notwendigkeit, Werteveränderung der Mitarbeiter	K2
B	48	256 – 259	viele sehen das Thema als PR-Maßnahme oder Beimisch, die werden aber durch den demografischen Wandel feststellen dass die alte Denke nicht funktioniert	häufig wird Nachhaltigkeit als PR-Maßnahme gesehen, demografische Wandel kann dies ändern	K2

- Arbeit freigestellt
- Lernen durch häufige Wiederholungen des Themas
- Jahresziele für jeden Mitarbeiter und Commitment aus dem Vorstand erhöhen den Erfolg
- Nachhaltigkeit integrativ, nicht als Randthema behandeln

K 2 Verständnis von Nachhaltigkeit

- ganzheitlicher, langfristiger schonender Umgang mit allen Ressourcen, auch dem Mensch
- Ebene 1: Nachhaltigkeit als Inhalt in Fachthemen
- Ebene 2: Nachhaltigkeit der Trainings
- Ebene 3: methodische Nachhaltigkeit in der Durchführung
- wird stärker kommen aufgrund von Regulierungen, erhöhter Notwendigkeit, Werteveränderung bei Mitarbeitern
- der demografische Wandel zwingt zum Umdenken

<ins>K 2.1 Nachhaltigkeit des Menschen</ins>

- Nachhaltigkeit betrifft auch die Person
- der Mitarbeiter stellt eine Säule dar
- persönliches Engagement und Interesse als Treiber

<ins>K 2.2 Kosten-Nutzen Abwägungen</ins>

- größter Hebel in Bezug auf Gesundheit der Mitarbeiter und Umwelt
- Kontinuität in der Investition notwendig
- rein utilitaristische, wirtschaftliche Gründe kein Gutmenschentum
- alle vier Säulen gleichstark fördern, im Verhältnis sind PE-Maßnahmen günstig

B	49	263 – 272	die strikte Trennung von Beruf und Privat ist durch Flexibilisierung der Arbeitswelt und Technologisierung verändert, das kann Lebenszeit schenken für Mitarbeiter in der Verwaltung	Aufhebung der Trennung von Beruf und Privat durch Technologisierung; Flexibilisierung der Arbeitswelt hat positive Seiten		
B	50	278 – 282	Auszubildende in der Verwaltung haben 30 Stunden von der Arbeitszeit für soziale Arbeit, das wird aktiv gefördert	Auszubildenden wird für gesellschaftliches, soziales Engagement Arbeitszeit freigestellt	K1.3	
B	51	285	PE-Maßnahmen über Nachhaltigkeit um es auf der Agenda zu haben, häufige Wiederholungen, so lernt der Mensch	Thema Nachhaltigkeit muss häufig wiederholt werden, so lernt der Mensch	K1.3	
B	52	290 – 297	Vorstand hat Jahresziele definiert für alle Mitarbeiter mit dem Thema Nachhaltigkeit	Commitment durch das Top-Management Board und Definition von Nachhaltigkeitszielen für jeden Mitarbeiter erhöhen den Erfolg	K1.3	
B	53	293 – 297	manchmal ist weniger mehr, man kann weniger sagen und tun, aber lieber kontinuierlich als hinterher keine Ressourcen oder Geld mehr	Kontinuität ist in der Investition auf das Thema Nachhaltigkeit maßgeblich, sowohl inhaltlich als auch monetär	K2.2	
B	54	302 – 309	wichtig ist, wenn man vier Säulen hat, dann behandelt man alle gleich, es werden viele Millionen investiert	alle vier Säulen sollen gleichstark gefördert werden. Im Verhältnis sind Seminare und E-Learnings günstig	K2.2	
B	55	314 – 324	viele sehen Nachhaltigkeit als Randthema, es ist eine Parallelwelt, die meisten gehen sehr beschränkt in kleinen Einheiten darauf ein; das "big picture", das große Ganze ist aber wichtig, auch wenn es strukturell getrennt ist	Nachhaltigkeit sollte integrativ nicht am Rande behandelt werden um das große Ganze zu sehen, doch es wird häufig als Randthema auf kleinen Einheiten beschränkt	K1.3	
C	56	28 – 46	HR Business Partner bedienen sich als strategische Partner des Directors der Center of Expertise; das Center of Expertise beschäftigt sich mit diversen Themen, HR BP sind verantwortlich für eine BU und passen globale Systeme an	HR Business Partner sind Generalisten und decken alle Themen ab, sie bedienen sich dabei dem Center of Expertise		**K 1 Verständnis von Personalentwicklung** · Talentmanagement beinhaltet Nachhaltigkeit bezüglich der persönlichen Entwicklung und der Arbeitssituation
C	57	51 – 53	Nachhaltigkeit bezüglich der persönlichen Entwicklung und der Arbeitssituation, z.B. Work-Life Balance, Sport sind unter dem Thema "Talent" vereint	Talentmanagement beinhaltet Nachhaltigkeit bezüglich der persönlichen Entwicklung und der derzeitigen Arbeitssituation	K1	· Entwicklungsprogramme angepasst an Zielgruppe (Karrierestufe), Eintrittsvoraussetzungen und Fokus · kein ganzheitliches Training zu Nachhaltigkeit
C	58	60 – 72	Entwicklungsprogramme sind verschieden je nach Zielgruppen (in Abhängigkeit von der Karrierestufe für Trainees, FK, Mitarbeiter), Eintrittsvoraussetzungen, Fokus	Talent-Entwicklung angepasst an Zielgruppe (Karrierestufe), Eintrittsvoraussetzungen und Fokus (Fachkarriere oder "people manager")	K1	· Anlaufstellen für diverse angrenzende Themen · deutliches Werteverständnis, das gelebt wird · Lernen von Themen hängt von Format der Vermittlung, Spannungsfaktor und Häufigkeit der Wiederholungen ab
C	59	76 – 101	es gibt kein ganzheitliches Training für die Führungslinie zum Thema Nachhaltigkeit; Werte wie Diversity, Sport, Ernährung, Mental Healthiness, Life-Work-Balance, Arbeitssicherheit werden vertreten	kein ganzheitliches Training zu Nachhaltigkeit für Führungskräfte, dafür Anlaufstellen für diverse Themen und Leben von Werten	K1	· Mitarbeiterbefragung als Kontrolle des Erfolgs von Initiativen · Trainings-Angebot ist nicht gleich Nutzung, Eigenleistung der Mitarbeiter ist gefordert
C	60	106 – 129	auf die einzelnen Säulen der Nachhaltigkeit bezogen gibt es viele Themen, z.B. Umwelt (paperless office), soziales Engagement auch mithilfe von moderner Telekommunikation	Nachhaltigkeit wird durch diverse Themen repräsentiert		· Kompetenzen in Fach und Führung unterteilt · Formate sind online und offline · HR als unterstützender

C		Lines			
C	61	132 – 143	es wird ständig kommuniziert, was gemacht wird, durch Newsletter, Geschäftsbericht, "soft reportings"	durch zahlreiche interne Kommunikation werden Themen, Engagement transparent	K2
C	62	151 – 161	Gründe für Nachhaltigkeitsbestreben kann man nicht trennen, im UN verdient man Geld und muss produktiv sein, die moderne HR-Welt hat aber gelernt, dass man gute MA nur halten kann, wenn man auf sie eingeht	Nachhaltigkeit aufgrund des Wettbewerbsdrucks und wegen des Mehrwertes für die Menschen und das Unternehmen	K2
C	63	162 – 172	je diverser ein Team, desto effizienter, kreativer, man muss Diversity leben, zulassen und das Maximale herausholen	die Mitarbeiterstruktur und UN-Werte sollten Diversity betonen für den Erfolg	
C	64	172 – 181	jeder Mensch hat persönliche Herausforderungen im Leben, ein Arbeitgeber kann viel für das Wohlbefinden tun	Arbeitgeber sollten viel dafür tun, dass sich Mitarbeiter wohlfühlen	
C	65	191 – 193	viele Themen, die behandelt werden, z.B. Arbeitsschutz fallen im weitesten Sinne unter den Begriff Nachhaltigkeit	periphere Themen der Nachhaltigkeit werden häufig erklärt	
C	66	194 – 196	es gibt Unterschiede in der Vermittlung, etwas das man am Anfang im Intranet lesen muss wird nicht unbedingt gelebt, es ist nicht spannend für Mitarbeiter, wenn es nicht aus HR-Perspektive auf der Agenda steht, wird es nicht wiederholt	ob Themen der Nachhaltigkeit gelernt werden hängt von Format der Vermittlung, einem Spannungsfaktor und Häufigkeit der Wiederholung ab	K1
C	67	197 – 203	individuelle Erfahrungen prägen Mitarbeiter, etwas kann als selbstverständlich angesehen werden	berufliche Vorerfahrungen der Mitarbeiter prägen, sodass Themen bekannt, selbstverständlich oder neuartig sein können	K3
C	68	203 – 217	durch die UN-Größe ist die Möglichkeit gegeben, sich mit Themen intensiv zu beschäftigen, das ist in kleineren Unternehmen nicht so	Unternehmensgröße ermöglicht intensive Beschäftigung mit Themen	K4
C	69	226 – 228	es bringt Unternehmen nach vorne, wenn sich Mitarbeiter wohl fühlen, unabhängig von der Frage was zuerst kommt	Unternehmen sind erfolgreich wenn es den Mitarbeitern wohlgeht	K4
C	70	230 – 234	als Messfaktor dient die jährliche Mitarbeiterbefragung um Erfolg von Initiativen und deren Richtung zu prüfen, ggf. zu überdenken	jährliche Mitarbeiterbefragung als Kontrolle des Erfolgs ergriffener Initiativen	K1
C	71	235 – 250	es bedarf der Eigenleistung der Mitarbeiter, angebotene Talentprogramme auch anzunehmen, auch sie müssen etwas investieren und Angebote nutzen	Programme anbieten heißt nicht, dass Mitarbeiter die Trainings annehmen, außerdem ist Eigenleistung notwendig	K1
C	72	252 – 263	es kann zwischen functional business und leadership skills gewählt werden; bei den einen geht es um Fachkompetenzen bei dem anderen eher Präsentation, Projektmanagement, Organisation	Kompetenzen werden ich Fach- und Führungskompetenzen unterteilt zu denen es passende Trainings gibt	K1
C	73	264 – 266	neben den online basierten gibt es auch face2face Trainings, die mehrere Tage gehen mit Kollegen aus unterschiedlichen Ländern	Formate der Trainings sind online und offline, also persönliche Trainings, Workshop, Simulation	K1
C	74	274 – 287	Vermischung von Privatleben und Arbeitsleben wird mit Sicherheit noch mehr werden, wobei Art des UN, Alter, Familienstand und sozialer Umkreis sowie Arbeitszeiten moderierend wirken	zunehmende Vermischung von Privat- und Arbeitsleben unter Berücksichtigung von moderierenden Faktoren	
C	75	288 – 301	Flexibilisierung der Arbeitswelt schafft ständige Erreichbarkeit, das kann ein gesundheitliches Risiko darstellen	ständiger Kontakt zur Arbeitswelt stellt ein gesundheitliches Risiko dar	K2

Unternehmensbereich

K 2 Verständnis von Nachhaltigkeit

- durch häufige interne Kommunikation werden Themen und soziales Engagement transportiert
- Gründe für Nachhaltigkeit kann man nicht trennen
- Nachhaltigkeit aufgrund des Wettbewerbsdrucks
- ständiger Kontakt zur Arbeitswelt (24/7 Erreichbarkeit) ist Gesundheitsrisiko

K 3 Aspekte der Mitarbeiter

- berufliche Vorerfahrungen prägen
- Themen sind bekannt, selbstverständlich oder neuartig

K 4 Aspekte des Unternehmens

- Unternehmensgröße ermöglicht intensive Beschäftigung mit Themen
- Unternehmen erfolgreich, wenn es Mitarbeitern wohlergeht

C	76	306 – 318	nicht jede Industrie und jedes UN kann dieselben Schwerpunkte setzen, dies ist eine sehr schnelles UN innerhalb einer sehr schnellen Industrie und "leading by example" z.b. bezüglich Diversity	thematische Schwerpunkte hängen von Industrien und Unternehmen ab, jedes UN hat andere Ziele und Strategien trotzdem zeichnen sich Trends ab	K4
C	77	323 – 329	HR ist ein unterstützender Bereich, der nicht an vorderster Front arbeitet	HR ist ein unterstützender Bereich	K1
D	78	5 – 11	Nachhaltigkeit besteht aus drei Aspekten: ökologisch nachhaltig zu agieren, sodass es der Umwelt zu Gute kommt oder sie möglichst wenig beeinträchtigt wird; unternehmerisch nachhaltig i.s.v. keine Gelder-Verschwendung; den dritten Aspekt kann man nochmal splitten in die soziale Seite und die interne Seite der Mitarbeiter	Nachhaltigkeit besteht aus drei Säulen, Umwelt, Wirtschaft und Soziales, wobei die letzte in die soziale Seite und Mitarbeiterebene unterteilt wird	K2
D	79	11 – 15	auf der internen Mitarbeiterebene sind demografischer Wandel und dadurch nachhaltige interne Personalpolitik wichtige Themen	demografischer Wandel bedingt nachhaltige Steuerung von Personalentscheidungen	K2
D	80	16 – 22	die menschliche Säule bedeutet wie kann man sich unabhängig vom Geschäft sozial engagieren, und was kann man anbieten innerhalb und außerhalb der eigenen Branche	menschliches soziales Engagement hat eine aktive Facette, zudem können im sozialen Bereich Angebote gestellt werden die inner- und außerhalb der Branche des UN liegen	K2
D	81	26 – 31	eine konkrete Personalstrategie, bzw. Entwicklungsstrategie zählt zu PE, darauf bezogen wie Talente langfristig eingestellt, gehalten werden	zur PE zählt eine Entwicklungsstrategie um Talente zu gewinnen und zu halten (Bedarfsplanung)	K1
D	82	32 – 41	es wird zwischen Personal und Management/Talent-entwicklung unterschieden, erstere betrifft Mitarbeiter, letztere Führungskräfte und besondere "Talente"	Unterscheidung zwischen Personal- und Management/Talententwicklung	K1
D	83	42 – 45	wir sind eher strategisch, gucken was für Programme brauchen wir, um MA besonders zu fördern	Management Development und Talent Management sind strategisch ausgerichtet	K1
D	84	39 – 55	Personalentwicklung selbst arbeiten aktiver, sind diejenigen die Trainings geben, je nach Thema sind auch externe Trainer sinnvoller, die eine Expertise mitbringen	Personalentwickler selbst arbeiten aktiv, geben Trainings	K1
D	85	51 – 55	gerade bei Veränderungsprozesse, man fast immer hat in den diversen Konzernunternehmen, DL-Gesellschaften sinnvoll sein externe Trainer mit neuen Ansätzen	Veränderungsprozesse können durch externe Trainer z.B. mit "change management"-Seminaren teilweise besser unterstützt werden	K1
D	86	57 – 59	PE heißt Leute identifizieren, die wir besonders fördern müssen oder wollen, die sich auch selbst einbringen möchten und die mittel- bis langfristig in höheren Positionen gesehen werden	PE bedeutet MA die möchten, zu fördern um perspektivischen Aufstieg zu ermöglichen	K1
D	87	61 – 64	in Hinblick auf Personalstrategie sollte man einen Talentpool mit Leuten auf unterschiedlichen Ebenen haben, die in kritische Positionen nachrücken können	Personalstrategie bedeutet, für zukünftige Bedarfe einen Talentpool zu haben	K1
D	88	69 – 74	auf Mitarbeiterebene gibt es zu Themen Arbeitsschutz, Datensicherheit und Ethischer Codex Online Schulungen die bei Neueinstieg in den ersten Monaten verpflichtend sind	jeder Mitarbeiter muss zu gewissen Themen die an Nachhaltigkeit angrenzen Online Schulungen absolvieren	K1.1

K 1 Verständnis von Personalentwicklung

- Entwicklungsstrategie, um Talente zu gewinnen und halten
- Bedarfsplanung
- Unterscheidung Talent/Managemententwicklung und Personalentwicklung
- Management und Talent Development sind strategisch aktiv, geben Trainings
- Personalentwickler arbeiten aktiv, geben Trainings
- Veränderungsprozesse, Change Management besser durch externe Trainer
- MA fördern, um höhere Positionen zu erreichen
- Personalstrategie bedeutet Talentpool für zukünftige Bedarfe haben

K 1.1 Nachhaltigkeit durch Personalentwicklung

- jeder Mitarbeiter muss zu angrenzenden Themen online Schulungen absolvieren
- verantwortungsvolle Führung, Vorleben und Kommunikation von Nachhaltigkeit
- soziales Engagement fester Bestandteil des Trainee Programms
- Motivation durch den Vorgesetzten wirkt positiv
- soziales Engagement ist gute Tat für die Gesellschaft und ein Lernfeld, Chance zur Teamentwicklung
- Führungskräfte für Verantwortung sensibilisieren
- bei Neueinstellung Passung zur Kultur, Werten
- Führungskräfte vermitteln eher nachhaltige Alltagsthemen
- Ergebnisse von Nachhaltigkeit-Schulungen nicht kontrolliert
- Trainings selbst können durch "follow-up", Feedback nachhaltig sein

K 1.2 Organisation und Austausch

- Vernetzung mit Kollegen die demografischen Wandel thematisieren
- individuelle Wichtigkeit für

D					
D	89	74 – 81	für Führungskräfte ist es weiter aufgehangen, ein ganz wichtiger Punkt ist verantwortungsvolle Führung, es spielt auch mit rein, dass MA bestimmte Dinge mitgegeben werden	verantwortungsvolle Führung ist ein ganz wichtiger Punkt, FK sollen Nachhaltigkeit kommunizieren und vorleben	K1.1
D	90	82 – 84	damit eine FK Nachhaltigkeit kommunizieren und vorleben kann gibt es spezifische Module "Wie führe ich überhaupt?"	in Trainings für neu in der Führungsrolle gestartete Manager zählt mit ein Teil Verantwortung	K1.1
D	91	85 – 97	unter Verantwortung sind der "Zukunftfond" und eine Nachhaltigkeitsverantwortliche organisiert, die auch in Vorträgen Inhalte vermitteln	Kommunikation der Nachhaltigkeitsbeauftragten und des "Zukunftsfonds" wird genutzt, um FK zu zeigen was Verantwortung und Nachhaltigkeit bedeutet	K1.1
D	92	98 – 108	im Trainee Programm gibt es den Baustein "Service Learning", der soziales Engagement im Umfang von 20-30 Stunden während der 18 Monate vorsieht und einen Freiwilligentag	soziales Engagement ist fester Baustein im Trainee-Programm	K1.1
D	93	109 – 114	auch für alle anderen Mitarbeiter wird soziales Engagement durch den Zukunftsfondleiter angeboten	soziales Engagement wird auch für alle Mitarbeiter gefördert und angeboten	K2
D	94	120 – 127	offiziell sollen Werte gelebt werden, ob das in allen Ländern der Fall ist, ist fraglich auch wenn sie von Oben kommuniziert werden	selbst wenn Werte von Oben kommuniziert werden ist schwer abzuschätzen inwieweit sie überall in der Gruppe gelebt werden	K1.1
D	95	128 – 132	der Zuspruch durch den Abteilungsleiter, der Interesse zeigt ist für Freiwilligentage förderlich	Motivation durch den Vorgesetzten wirkt sich positiv auf Engagement der Mitarbeiter aus	K1.1
D	96	133 – 146	ein großer Teil der Mitarbeiter nimmt die Angebote sich sozial zu engagieren gerne an, auch die Trainees	Angebote für soziales Engagement werden gerne (freiwillig) wahrgenommen	K1.1
D	97	146 – 150	zudem ist es eine gute Möglichkeit, sich als Team zu entwickeln, es ist immer ein Geben und Nehmen	neben der Tat für die Gesellschaft nimmt man viel aus sozialem Engagement mit, es ist eine gute Chance ein Team zu entwickeln	K1.1
D	98	162 – 171	der Austausch zwischen Personalabteilung und Zukunftsfond ist viel enger als mit der Nachhaltigkeitsbeauftragten, dies liegt in den Themen begründet wie z.B. demografischer Wandel, zudem ist die Person vom Hintergrund Personaler	die Vernetzung ist stärker mit Personen, die nachhaltige Themen vorantreiben und zudem einen HR-Hintergrund haben	K1.2
D	99	173 – 179	Führungskräfte haben eine große Verantwortung, unglaublichen Einfluss etwas vorzuleben und eine Kultur aufzubauen, ein Bewusstsein zu schaffen in eine bestimmte Richtung zu denken und sich zu engagieren	wie Themen gelebt werden hängt stark von Einzelpersonen, insbesondere Führungskräften ab	K1.1
D	100	180 – 187	Führungskräfte müssen sensibilisiert werden und man kann bei Neueinstellungen darauf achten Leute einzustellen, die eine Kultur mittragen und leben	Führungskräfte für Verantwortung sensibilisieren und bei Neueinstellung der Kultur passende Leute wählen	K1.1
D	101	190 – 195	über die menschliche, soziale Säule - den Zukunftfond - wird häufig im Intranet kommuniziert oder an das Personalteam geschickt	über Themen des Zukunftsfonds werden häufig Neuigkeiten kommuniziert	K2
D	102	199 – 210	bei Umweltthemen gibt es sehr deutliche Regeln, die auch offiziell die Umwelt schonen, sicherlich aber auch eine Kosteneinsparung bedeuten	für Umweltschonung sehr deutliche Regeln, allerdings durch Kosteneinsparung bestimmt	K2

Vorstand entscheidet über Verfolgung von Themen, Durchsetzung einer Kultur

K 2 Verständnis von Nachhaltigkeit

- drei Säulen, dritter Aspekt in soziale Säule und interne Seite der Mitarbeiter geteilt
- demografischer Wandel bedingt nachhaltige Personalentscheidungen
- Menschliche Säule bezogen auf Engagement in- und außerhalb der Branche
- soziales Engagement für alle Mitarbeiter angeboten, gefördert
- Neuigkeiten über soziales Engagement, Zukunftsthemen häufig kommuniziert
- Umweltschonung deutliche Regeln, durch Kosten bestimmt
- Nachhaltigkeit kann auf PE-Instrumente oder die Unterstützung durch PE bezogen sein

2.1 Nutzen

- fördert attraktives Arbeitgeberimage, dient aber auch Nachhaltigkeit selbst Nachhaltigkeitsthemen gehen mit Mitarbeiterbindung einher

2.2 Wirtschaftlichkeit

- aufgrund des Wettbewerbs Druck in der Branche
- Situation fordert Einsparungen, hat höchste Priorität
- Nachhaltigkeit darf nicht wirtschaftlichen Erfolg mindern
- für nachhaltiges Wirtschaften reicht intrinsische Motivation nicht

D	103	215 – 218	echte Nachhaltigkeitsbestreben gehen mit Mehrwert der Attraktivität einher, bisher wird die Unterstützung von sozialem Engagement wenig werblich als Aushängeschild benutzt	Nachhaltigkeitsbestreben fördert ein attraktives Arbeitgeberimage aber dienen auch der Nachhaltigkeit selbst	K2.1
D	104	220 – 227	Umweltthemen sind immer auch ein Einsparthema, aber das passt schön zusammen man hat dann beides; bei sozialen Themen ist es keine Positionierung, der Vorstand ist sehr sozial	soziale Themen werden durch den Vorstand vorangetrieben wohingegen Umweltschonung häufig durch Einsparungen bedingt ist	
D	105	229 – 236	Versicherungsbranche konnte bisher großzügig wirtschaften, gesamte Produktpalette anbieten der Wettbewerb wird härter, Niedrigzinsversprechen deshalb muss man in Zukunft gucken wo man wirtschaftlich arbeiten kann	Versicherungen müssen durch Wettbewerb zukünftig noch wirtschaftlicher sein	
D	106	246 – 248	wir sind gerade in der Situation, dass wir extrem einsparen an vielen Stellen, da sind jetzt andere Prioritäten	Versicherungen müssen derzeit extrem einsparen, daher andere Prioritäten	K2.2
D	107	249 – 254	individuelle Wichtigkeit, die Themen für den Vorstand haben entscheidet, wie sie voran getrieben werden, eine Kultur wird von oben geprägt	individuelle Wichtigkeit durch Vorstand entscheidet über Verfolgung nachhaltiger Themen und Durchsetzung einer Kultur	K1.2
D	108	257 – 262	es ist ein Zusammenspiel eine win-win Situation, soziales Engagement, Umweltschutz ist gut, wenn Mitarbeiter angezogen und gebunden werden und die Umwelt geschützt wird	Nachhaltigkeitsthemen wie soziales Engagement, Umweltschonung gehen mit Mitarbeiterbindung einher	K2.1
D	109	268 – 270	es wird wenig kontrolliert bezüglich der Erfolge von Maßnahmen außer kontrollierbare Regelungen	die Ergebnisse von Schulungen mit Nachhaltigkeitsthemen werden nicht kontrolliert	K1
D	110	272 – 281	bei dem Freiwilligentag gibt es oft ein "follow-up" Feedback mit den Institutionen oder mit Freiwilligenagenturen, bei den Einzelengagements die freiwillig sind eher nicht	im Anschluss an den Freiwilligentag Feedback-Runde was gut funktioniert hat	K1
D	111	283 – 284	man kann auch sagen, Trainings sind nachhaltig wenn man nachhält und ein "follow-up" macht	Trainings selbst können nachhaltig sein durch Erfolgskontrolle	K1
D	112	290 – 293	Nachhaltigkeit kann sehr vielschichtig verstanden werden, daher ist die Frage geht es um nachhaltige PE-Instrumente die für langfristigen Erfolg sorgen oder geht es letztendlich darum wie unterstützen wir von PE-Seite	Nachhaltigkeit kann auf PE-Instrumente oder die Unterstützung durch PE bezogen sein	K2
D	113	298 – 299	Nachhaltigkeit gerne, solange es nicht den wirtschaftlichen Erfolg schmälert	Nachhaltigkeit darf nicht den wirtschaftlichen Erfolg mindern	K2.2
D	114	302 – 308	in der Versicherungsbranche konnte man es sich bisher leisten über solche Themen nachzudenken und den Gewinn zu steigern, jetzt müssen neue Herausforderungen bewältigt werden	Versicherungen können es sich vielleicht zukünftig nicht mehr leisten, nachhaltige Themen zu behandeln	K2.2
D	115	315 – 316	es sollte eine politische Entlohnung geben für nachhaltiges Wirtschaften denn die Leute sind sich selbst nicht Motivator genug	politische Entlohnung für nachhaltiges Wirtschaften, intrinsische Motivation nicht genügt	K2.2
D	116	337 – 345	Führungskräfte haben durch das Alltagsgeschäft keine Zeit sich mit Themen zu beschäftigen, vermitteln eher kleine Alltagssachen an Mitarbeiter als konzeptionell große Schulungen aufzusetzen, weil das mehr Arbeit bedeutet	Führungskräfte geben ihren Mitarbeitern eher nachhaltige Alltagsthemen mit, weil das Tagesgeschäft die Zeit beschränkt	K1.1

D	117	346 – 351	was kann man überhaupt vermitteln außer der Alltagssachen, eventuell stärker Umweltthemen, direkt Prozesse verbessern	was man vermitteln kann ist fraglich		
E	118	4 – 19	Nachhaltigkeit ist in der Personalentwicklung kein zentrales Filterkriterium aber es gibt mittelbare und unmittelbare Schnittmengen	zwischen PE und Nachhaltigkeit gibt es zahlreiche mittelbare und unmittelbare Schnittmengen	K3	**K 1 Verständnis von Personalentwicklung**
E	119	13 – 19	der CR Bereich ist aufbauorganisatorisch im Vorstandsbereich Personal aufgehangen und beinhaltet die Bereiche "Responsibility", "Transformation" und "neue Lernformen"	Corporate Responsibility ist im Personalbereich organisiert, die Bereiche "Responsibility", "Transformation" und "neue Lernformen" zählen dazu	K2.2	· HR-Bereiche in Konzernen unübersichtlich, Architektur vielschichtig, erheblicher Abstimmungsbedarf · Diskrepanz zwischen globalen Vorgaben für HRD und Bedürfnissen der Ländergesellschaften
E	120	20 – 30	Corporate Responsibility meint die wirtschaftliche, unternehmerische und gesellschaftliche Verantwortung sowohl national als auch international	unter CR wird wirtschaftliche, unternehmerische und gesellschaftliche Verantwortung verstanden	K2	· eigener Trainingsanbieter intern · externe Kooperation mit Trainingsinstitutionen · Bildungsanspruch aus Person selbst, seiner FK oder Bedarf von Fachbereichen
E	121	46 – 55	der Impuls das Thema zu besetzen kam aus einer gesellschaftspolitischen Verantwortung heraus, zudem gibt es beim Thema Einkauf und Energieverbrauch Verantwortlichkeiten, die das UN hat	Impuls CR zu besetzen aus gesellschaftspolitischer Verantwortung und Verantwortlichkeiten in Bezug auf Einkauf, Energieverbrauch	K2	· Weiterentwicklung fachlicher, methodischer, persönlicher Kompetenzen · Führung ist verantwortliches Handeln
E	122	69 – 74	die Verortung im Personalbereich ist durch die Kombination von CR und Transformation/ Change begründet, das Thema CR ist wesentlich breiter als nur sozial, beinhaltet viele Dimensionen die in Sachen mind-change, mind-set, enabling der Mitarbeiter betrachtet werden sollen	CR führt weiter als CSR, ist eng verknüpf mit Transformation/ Change und findet sachlogisch seinen Platz im Personalbereich	K2.2	**K 1.1 Nachhaltigkeit durch Personalentwicklung** · ehrenamtliches Engagement einsehbar
E	123	81 – 94	im "Ehrenamts Mosaik" kann man alle Kollegen finden, die ein Projekt unterstützt haben, so wird es getrackt da Projektname, -beschreibung, Motivation und Link zu der jeweiligen Organisation enthalten	das ehrenamtliche Engagement der Kollegen kann man im Intranet einsehen	K1.1	· Angebote/Gesuche und Erfahrungsberichte zu sozialen Projekten · abhängig von Interesse der Führungskräfte
E	124	96 – 100	zudem kann man unter Engagement Angebote/ Gesuche, Erfahrungsberichte und abgeschlossene Projekte einsehen	im Intranet kann man zusätzlich Angebote/Gesuche mit Erfahrungsberichten, abgeschlossenen Projekten einsehen	K1.1	· FK implizit angehalten, Verantwortung zu leben · um Thema bei MA zu platzieren, muss es immer Bezugspunkt geben · überfachliche Herleitung durch ethischen Anspruch nur wenn Bezug gegeben
E	125	101 – 122	Corporate Volunteering meint dass entweder einzelne Mitarbeiter oder auch ganze Bereiche, Organisationseinheiten Projekte unterstützen, CR macht ein Scanning/Vorsortierung/ Review der Projekte und berät intern	"Corporate Volunteering" Projekte werden von ganzen Bereichen/ Organisationseinheiten durchgeführt, dabei werden die Projekte von der CR Abteilung professionell überwacht	K1.2	**K 1.2 Organisation und Austausch** · "Corporate Volunteering" professionell durch CR Abteilung überwacht, beraten · CR Abteilung als Scharnier Top-Down und Bottom-Up Mechanismen, um Engagement zu fördern
E	126	109 – 133	der Link ist, dass sowohl PE als auch CR involviert sind, beide Seiten haben gemerkt es gibt einen riesigen Bedarf und es wurde ein Rahmen geschaffen, damit das was gut gemeint ist auch gut gemacht wird, das hat mittlerweile eine Professionalität und Qualität	Corporate Volunteering wurde der erkannten wichtigen Verbindung von PE mit sozialen Maßnahmen ein Rahmen gegeben, der Qualität absichert	K3	
E	127	137 – 140	der Engagement/Corporate Volunteering Bereich fungiert wie ein Scharnier, die beraten, denn oft kommen Mitarbeiter mit Ideen aber so werden sie gefiltert	die CR Abteilung fungiert als Scharnier um im ehrenamtlichen Engagement intern zu beraten	K1.2	**K 2 Verständnis von Nachhaltigkeit** · CR ist wirtschaftliche, unternehmerische, gesellschaftliche Verantwortung
E	128	147 – 150	früher war die Interaktion eher zufällig, durch die organisatorische Einheit und dass entschieden wurde "mindset-change" und "enabling" gehören dazu bestehen nun viele Brücken	die anfänglich zufällige Interaktion ist gewachsen, zwischen CR und PE bestehen nun viele Brücken	K3	Impuls CR zu besetzen aus Verantwortlichkeiten im Einkauf, Energie, Gesellschaft Dreiklang von Kosten, Umwelt, Gesellschaft

E	Nr.	Zeilen			K
E	129	151 – 158	es ist nicht so, dass die PE-Angebote den Filter haben "inwieweit ist das nachhaltig", da spielen unterschiedliche Kriterien eine Rolle, auch spezifische fachliche Bedarfe oder in der FK-Entwicklung das Konzernleitbild	PE-Angebote nicht generell durch das Kriterium "wie nachhaltig" gefiltert, vielmehr spielen fachliche Bedarfe oder das Konzernleitbild eine Rolle	K3
E	130	167 – 182	Inhalte über Nachhaltigkeit sind nicht in Vollständigkeit und Systematik vorgegeben, es gibt einzelne Verknüpfungen beim "onboarding" Programm, beim Trainee Programm oder in berufsbegleitenden Studiengängen ist das Thema als elementarer Baustein enthalten	Inhalte über Nachhaltigkeit werden nicht in Vollständigkeit, Systematik vermittelt, finden sich aber als Bestandteil in Informationsüberblicken wieder	K3
E	131	186 – 199	wenn man sich näher mit dem Thema beschäftigt, wird deutlich, dass aus vielen unterschiedlichen Quellen etwas kommt und iterativ dann etwas entsteht	das Thema Nachhaltigkeit stammt aus unterschiedlichen Quellen und iterativ entsteht eine Summe an Initiativen	K3
E	132	201 – 211	mein Punkt ist, dass es eine Vielzahl an Einzelinitiativen gibt	es gibt viele Einzelinitiativen mit nachhaltigem Bezug	K3
E	133	219 – 238	Nachhaltigkeit ist zweiseitig, der Arbeitgeber wird nach Außen als gesellschaftlich verantwortlich dargestellt und Energieeinsparungen führen zu Kostensenkungen das wiederum unterstützt Nachhaltigkeit Richtung Umwelt und Gesellschaft	Nachhaltigkeit zwei Seiten, die wirtschaftliche und die philanthropische, die wirtschaftliche Nachhaltigkeit wirkt sie sich positiv auf Kosten aus, daher steht die UN als gesellschaftlich verantwortlicher AG dar und unterstützt Richtung Umwelt und Gesellschaft	K2.1
E	134	219 – 224	ideal ist der Dreiklang zwischen Kosteneinsparungen, Umwelt und Gesellschaft in Bezug auf Nachhaltigkeit wobei häufig größere Investitionen vorangehen	einem ausgeglichenen Dreiklang von Kosten, Umwelt und Gesellschaft gehen häufig höhere Investitionen voran	K2
E	135	242 – 246	Umsetzungen von Nachhaltigkeitsansätzen sind ein iterativer Prozess, dabei dienen nationale und internationale Zertifizierungen als Gütesiegel und Verträge als wirksames Steuerungsinstrument	Nachhaltigkeitsbestrebungen können nur längerfristig iterativ umgesetzt werden, dabei können Zertifizierungen und Verträge als Steuerungsinstrument dienen	K2
E	136	250 – 254	kritisch und schwierig ist häufig die Umsetzung, gerade auch bei Beteiligungen im Ausland	kritisch und schwierig ist häufig die Umsetzung	K2
E	137	256 – 261	bleibt ein schwieriges, kontroverses Thema weil nicht sämtliche deutsche Standards (gewerkschaftlich, betrieblich, mitbestimmungs-, arbeitsrechtlich) auch als Maßstab in andere Länder eingebracht werden können	deutsche Standards können nicht als Maßstab in ausländischen Beteiligungen übernommen werden	K2.2
E	138	265 – 268	durch eine top-down Umfrage können Mitarbeiter sagen wo sie sich mehr Engagement wünschen, bottom-up können Mitarbeiter ehrenamtliches Engagement bekannt machen und andere motivieren	aus verschiedenen Richtungen, top-down und bottom-up kann Engagement für Nachhaltigkeitsthemen gefördert werden	K1.2
E	139	273 – 283	eine Bewertung des Erfolgs ist immer eine Frage der Perspektive, das ist viel oder wenig, Ernsthaftigkeit kann man an der Entwicklung von konkreten KPIs abmessen, denn das ist gerade bei qualitativen Messungen schwierig	Bewertung des Erfolgs ist eine Frage der Perspektive, gerade qualitative Messungen sind kritisch aber die Entwicklung von KPIs signalisiert Ernsthaftigkeit	K4

- zunächst hohe Investitionen
- Bestrebungen nur längerfristig, iterativ
- Umsetzung häufig schwierig
- Hinterfragen des Tuns, kontinuierliche Verbesserung und sinnvoller Beitrag

K 2.1 Verantwortung

- philanthropische und wirtschaftliche Verantwortung von MA gefordert
- Führungskräfte haben Verantwortung

K 2.2 Organisation

- CR im Personalbereich, "Responsibility, Transformation, neue Lernformen"
- CR eng verknüpft mit Transformation, Change
- deutsche Standards können nicht in Ländergesellschaften gelten
- Verortung von CR ist divers, nicht unbedingt nahe an HR/HRD

K 3 Schnittstelle Personalentwicklung und Nachhaltigkeit

- mittelbare und unmittelbare Brücken
- "Corporate Volunteering" gibt der Verbindung einen professionellen Rahmen
- anfänglich zufällige Interaktion ist gewachsen
- PE wird nicht über "wie nachhaltig" gefiltert, fachliche Bedarfe und Konzernleitbild bestimmen
- Inhalte über Nachhaltigkeit nicht vollständig, systematisch vermittelt
- viele Einzelinitiativen
- keine Besetzung des Themas, strategisch-konzeptionelle Betreuung
- für Verankerung in Strategie Passungsdiskussion voranstellen
- Vorstandsebene muss Thema tragen

E	140	284 – 295	Akzeptanz für ein Thema und Beschäftigung damit ist auch durch Mitarbeiterbefragung ablesbar, die response rate und kritische Rückmeldungen sind u.a. Schlüsselfaktoren, daraus zieht man viele Schlüsse was besser werden muss	die Mitarbeiterbefragung liefert viele Indizien zur Verbesserung	K4
E	141	300 – 309	viel hängt davon ab, wer befragt wird, jeder hat einen unterschiedlichen Fokus und Blick, ich persönlich bin für das Thema aufmerksam, sensibilisiert und fördere den intensiven Austausch und habe einen "best practice exchange" angestoßen	wie stark das Thema gefördert wird hängt stark von individuellen Führungskräften und deren Interesse ab	K1.1
E	142	311 – 322	CR ist sehr unterschiedlich aufgehangen, teilweise in den HR Organisationen, nahe an HRD dran, teilweise als Stab direkt beim CEO oder an die Communication angebunden	die Verortung von CR in der Organisationshierarchie ist sehr divers und nicht zwingenderweise nahe an HR oder HRD	K2.2
E	143	338 – 346	nach intensiver Auseinandersetzung kann bewiesen werden, dass es faktisch schon konkrete Brücken zwischen den Themen gibt, die aber nicht eingängig, ohne Anstrengung wahrnehmbar sind, gleichzeitig muss selbstkritisch festgehalten werden dass es niemanden im Konzern gibt, der sich mit der Frage strategisch-konzeptionell im Sinne von Ganzheitlichkeit auseinandersetzt	nach längerer Überlegung feststellbar, dass es Brücken zwischen den beiden Bereichen gibt aber keine Besetzung des Themas für eine strategisch-konzeptionell ganzheitliche Betreuung	K3
E	144	347 – 354	im Konzernleitbild steht für die Führung nichts explizit über responsibility oder sustainability als Baustein, implizit aber doch über Themen wie Work-Life Balance, die FK hat eine Verantwortung was die WLB, die Gesundheit der Mitarbeiter angeht, sie sind role models und gleichzeitig Berater, Begleiter der MA	FK haben keine expliziten guiding principles aber implizit ist Verantwortung für MA als Vorbild, Berater und Begleiter eindeutig	K1.1
E	145	355 – 358	bezüglich Training und Entwicklung sind auch bausteinhaft Bezüge erkennbar, über verschiedene Themen ist Sustainability in den PE-Bereich eingebunden	Nachhaltigkeit ist im PE-Bereich bausteinhaft eingebunden	K1.1
E	146	358 – 373	strukturell gesehen sind HR Bereiche bei einem großen UN mit vielen MA weltweit sehr zerfasert in Konzernzentrale (Personal- u. Organisationsentwicklung, Performance Development, CR, Transformational Change) d.h. globale Verantwortung und nationale Competence Center, Vorstandsbereich Europa, jeweils eine HR-und HRD Organisation in den Ländern	strukturell gesehen sind HR-Bereiche in großen Konzernen unübersichtlich, die Architektur vielschichtig, damit geht erheblicher Abstimmungsbedarf einher	K1
E	147	373 – 381	einzelne Ländergesellschaften äußern eigene Kultur, Historie, Ausbildungssysteme, Bildungsstruktur, Demografie und dementsprechend andere Bedürfnisse, möchten viele Freiheitsgrade wohingegen globales HQ den definierten Konzernrahmen in allen Ländern umsetzen will	Diskrepanz zwischen den globalen Vorgaben für den HRD Bereich und Bedürfnissen einzelner Ländergesellschaften	K1
E	148	381 – 387	als FK in der Vermittlerrolle muss man informiert sein, aktiver Sparringspartner der Kollegen im globalen Competence Center sein und gleichzeitig für die Länder, aktiv antizipativ Einfluss nehmen und gutes Stakeholder Management	eine FK kann nicht alle Ansprüche der PE-Organisationseinheiten zufriedenstellen, muss aber als Sparringspartner fungieren und detailliert über Anforderungen informiert sein	

K 4 Bewertung des Erfolgs
- Frage der Perspektive, was ist viel
- Entwicklung von KPIs zeigt Ernsthaftigkeit
- Mitarbeiterbefragung liefert Indizien
- fachliche Ergebnisse erkennbar

E	149	388 – 400	innerhalb der Trainingsorganisation (Bildungsanbieter) gibt es eigene Themen und Partnerkataloge in Zusammenarbeit mit externen Institutionen, beide sind angebotsorientiert für diverse Bildungsbedarfe der Fachseiten	eigener Trainingsanbieter intern sowie extern über Partner zu zahlreichen Themen Bildung	K1
E	150	402 – 418	beide Seiten sind relevant, entweder der Mensch hat den gewissen Anspruch selbst oder die nächsthöhere FK soll identifizieren was gebraucht wird, Talentmanagement ist nachfrageorientiert durch die Fachseiten	bezüglich eines Bildungsanspruchs kann dieser aus dem Menschen selbst, seiner FK als Sparringspartner oder nachfrageorientiert durch Fachbereiche entstehen (Talentmanagement)	K1
E	151	421 – 428	PE umfasst alle Maßnahmen, die einen MA auf einem bestimmten Bildungs-, Kenntnis-, Fähigkeitenstand fachlich, methodisch oder persönlich weiterentwickeln, individuell, gruppen- oder bereichsbezogen	PE betrifft die Weiterentwicklung von MA hinsichtlich fachlicher, methodischer oder persönlicher Kompetenzen	K1
E	152	432 – 439	gemäß dem altruistischen Gedanken haben Mitarbeiter selbst in gewissen Maßen eine Verantwortung, jeder MA sollte für ein UN arbeiten mit dem er einen bestimmten Identifikationsgrad hat sonst ist er kein glaubwürdiger Vertreter, er sollte die Strategie den Anspruch und seinen Beitrag kennen	altruistische Verantwortung wird von MA gefordert, sie sollten sich mit dem UN identifizieren und einen eigenen Beitrag leisten um glaubwürdige Vertreter zu sein	K2.1
E	153	440 – 456	unmittelbare Führungskräfte haben die Verantwortung, ggü. ihren MA im kontinuierlichen Veränderungsprozess transparent zu kommunizieren	FK haben eine Verantwortung ihre Mitarbeiter durch wiederholte Kommunikation zu informieren und so zu verantwortlichem Handeln zu bewegen	K2.1
E	154	464 – 484	Herausforderung ist die richtige Balance zu finden, zwischen methodischen, sozialen, fachlichen Kompetenzen, Führungsleitbildern und Strategieoffensiven, Nachhaltigkeit soll als Thema nicht inflationieren ein Sinnzusammenhang muss darstellbar sein wie Vision, Strategie, Marktzugang, Markenkern, Kultur zueinander finden	Nachhaltigkeit wird auf vielen Ebenen grundsätzlich und operativ betrachtet, bevor es in einer Strategieformulierung oder einem Führungsverständnis verankert würde muss eine strategische und eine Passungsdiskussion stattfinden	K3
E	155	467 – 470	ein CEO kann ein Thema neu besetzen und wichtige Dimensionen aufzeigen, die alle ihre Berechtigung haben	gerade auf Vorstandsebene müsste das Thema begründet getragen werden	K3
E	156	496 – 499	es muss immer einen Bezugspunkt geben, fachlich oder interessengeleitet, man kann das Thema Nachhaltigkeit nie "out of the blue" platzieren	um das Thema Nachhaltigkeit als FK bei MA zu platzieren, muss es immer einen Bezugspunkt geben	K1.1
E	157	504 – 512	der fachliche Bezug wäre der natürliche, es kann auch ein überfachlicher sein, wenn der Anspruch ethischer oder sozialer Art ist aber die Herleitung das Thema Nachhaltigkeit an MA zu bringen muss da sein, dies hängt aber von individuellem Führungsverständnis und Interesse ab	eine überfachliche Herleitung durch einen ethischen, sozialen Anspruch ist je nach individuellem Interesse der FK und dem Führungsverständnis ebenso möglich, Bezug muss gegeben sein	K1.1
E	158	514	fachliche Ergebnisse kann man sehen	fachliche Ergebnisse sind erkennbar	K4

E	159	517 – 522	nachhaltiges Management kann man durch die Mitarbeiterbefragung messen über die Fragen zum Führungsverhalten und Engagement, die Korrelation mit Gesundheit es gibt verbindliche Prozesse zur Analyse der Ergebnisse und bestimmte Schwellwerte	nachhaltiges Management wird durch die Mitarbeiterbefragung gemessen	K4	
E	160	526 – 529	ich finde spannend, herausfordernd dass mir Nachhaltigkeit mit den 3 Dimensionen hilft zu sagen das was ich tue wird kontinuierlich hinterfragt und weiter ausgerichtet zudem kann ein sinnvoller Beitrag geleistet werden	die Motivation für Nachhaltigkeit liegt im Hinterfragen des Tun und Handelns sowie kontinuierlicher Verbesserung und einem sinnvollen Beitrag bei guter Ausführung	K2	
E	161	532 – 533	Führungsverantwortung ist verantwortliches Handeln gegenüber Individuen, Unternehmen und auch der Gesellschaft	Führung ist verantwortliches Handeln gegenüber Individuen, Unternehmen, der Gesellschaft	K1	
F	162	11 – 16	PE bedeutet aus einer globalen, ganzheitlichen Sicht wir gestalten Prozesse, Instrumente, Maßnahmen und MA und FK zu befähigen, die jetzigen und zukünftigen Anforderungen an ihren Job erfüllen zu können, Auftraggeber ist die Unternehmensleitung bzw. Strategie	PE bedeutet globale, ganzheitliche Prozessdefinition inkl. Instrumente und Maßnahmen, sodass MA und FK befähigt werden jetzige und zukünftige Anforderungen zu erfüllen im Auftrag der Unternehmensstrategie bzw. der Unternehmensleitung	K1	K 1 Verständnis von Personalentwicklung · globale Prozessdefinition um Bedarfe zu erfüllen · Verfolgung strategischer Ziele · interne Trainings sind verhaltensbezogen · "training on the job" soll überwiegen · Methodenmix kennzeichnet Qualität der Trainings
F	163	20 – 26	es geht nicht um individuelle Betreuung sondern strategische Ziele ganzheitlich durch Weiterbildungsmaßnahmen vorzubereiten	PE ermöglicht durch Weiterbildungsmaßnahm en die Verfolgung strategischer organisatorischer Ziele, betrifft weniger individuelle Betreuung	K1	· FK muss MA befähigen, gewisses Verhalten zu zeigen · FK ist Vorbild · Unterstützung von PE bei Change · interner DL, Fachabteilungen geben Impuls für Kampagne
F	164	30 – 43	"Learning on the Job" wird stark fokussiert, nicht nur Training	"on the job" Lernen ist gewünscht und wird stark forciert	K1.1	
F	165	48 – 48	im Weiterbildungskatalog zielt eine Kompetenz auf Nachhaltigkeit ab	der Weiterbildungskatalog beinhaltet Nachhaltigkeit	K1.1	K 1.1 Spezifische Personalentwicklung · "on the job" Lernen forciert · Weiterbildungskatalog enthält Nachhaltigkeit · Zertifizierungen durch Branche vorgeschrieben · Online-Schulung zu Compliance · Umwelttrainings von Behörden · festgeschriebene Kompetenz "nachhaltige Lösungen vorantreiben" · Kompetenzmodell gibt gewünschtes Verhalten global vor · generische Beschreibungen der Kompetenz im Dialog präzisieren · konkretes Format nicht festlegbar · pro MA jährlich Ziele der Weiterentwicklung · Freiräume der Festlegung von Maßnahmen
F	166	52 – 58	bedingt durch die Branche ist der Erwerb staatlich, gesetzlich vorgegebene Trainingsmaßnahmen und Zertifizierungen Pflicht im Sinne der Nachhaltigkeit, dem Umweltschutz, die müssen nachgewiesen und alle paar Jahre erneuert werden	aufgrund der Branche sind Arbeitslizenzen und Zertifizierungen im Umweltbereich vorgeschrieben, also hat PE dort einen Bezug	K1.1	
F	167	64 – 75	auch ökonomische Nachhaltigkeit lässt sich durch klassische PE Themen abdecken, es gibt den Anspruch, dass jeder Mitarbeiter für seinen Bereich unternehmerisch verantwortlich handelt, kaufmännische Entscheidungen treffen	für jeden MA gilt der Anspruch in seinem Bereich unternehmerisch verantwortungsvoll zu handeln	K2.1	
F	168	75 – 89	soziale Nachhaltigkeit ist nicht in der PE sondern unter Kulturmanagement, Veranstaltungsmanagement, Sponsoring , das Unternehmen übernimmt an Standorten soziale Verantwortung und MA können sich ehrenamtlich engagieren, das UN spendet	soziale Verantwortung wird eher über das Format Sponsoring, Ehrenamt durch die Unternehmensleitung und MA unterstützt	K2.1	
F	169	94 – 98	als Schnittstelle wird das Thema Compliance angesehen, konformes Verhalten der MA bezüglich gewisser Richtlinien, als online-Training mit Quiz	zu Compliance gibt es ein online-Training mit Quiz	K1.1	

F					
F	170	98 – 99	in-house Trainings sind verhaltensbedingte Trainings	intern werden verhaltensbedingte Trainings organisiert	K1
F	171	100 – 101	Umwelttrainings werden von entsprechenden Behörden, Interessenverbänden angeboten	Umwelttrainings werden von Behörden, Interessenverbänden geleitet	K1.1
F	172	102 – 105	bei technischen Trainings sind Erfahrungen in Arbeitszeitstunden gefordert, ein Schein reicht nicht aus sondern Praxiserfahrung	technische Fertigkeiten bedürfen Praxiserfahrung in der Handhabung	
F	173	105 – 109	gewünscht ist ein Großteil "training on the job", dies wird durch teilweise durch Vorschriften eingeschränkt sodass das klassische Format bleibt	"training on the job" soll überwiegen, wird aber durch Vorschriften zum Teil eingeschränkt	K1
F	174	110 – 112	gute Trainings sind durch sehr gute Didakten, Praxisfälle, Diskussionsrunden gekennzeichnet	ein Methodenmix kennzeichnet gute Trainings	K1
F	175	121 – 125	eine der 8 Unternehmenskompetenzen heißt "Nachhaltige Lösungen vorantreiben", jeder MA entscheidet strategisch und handelt konsequent, um wirtschaftliche, ökologische und gesellschaftliche Vorteile langfristig zu erzielen	explizit festgeschriebene Kompetenz für den Handlungsraum eines MA "Nachhaltige Lösungen vorantreiben"	K1.1
F	176	125 – 127	eine Kompetenz ist ein Verhalten, sobald es ein festgeschriebenes Kompetenzmodell gibt, zeigt dies welches Verhalten gewünscht ist	ein Kompetenzmodell gibt vor, welches Verhalten gewünscht ist	K1.1
F	177	127 – 129	jede Kompetenz ist auf zwei Ebenen definiert, einmal "diese Kompetenz zeigen bedeutet" und "in dieser Kompetenz Führung zeigen bedeutet"	jede Kompetenz beschreibt das erwartete Verhalten von MA und FK einheitlich und global gültig	K1.1
F	178	129 – 131	als Führungskraft muss man einerseits Mitarbeiter befähigen, ein gewisses Verhalten zu zeigen und gleichzeitig mit seinem eigenen Verhalten Vorbild sein	eine FK muss MA befähigen, ein gewisses Verhalten zu zeigen und selbst Vorbild sein	K1.1
F	179	131 – 136	jede Kompetenz ist generisch beschrieben, wie Verständnis und Interesse für eine nachhaltige Zukunft sowie vorausschauendes Denken, Planen und Suchen nach dauerhaften Lösungen	generische Beschreibungen der Kompetenz: Verständnis für nachhaltige Zukunft, verantwortungsvolles Handeln	K1.1
F	180	136 – 142	Kompetenzen sind generisch und es liegt am Vorgesetzten und dem MA selbst diese für den entsprechenden Verantwortungsbereich zu füllen, im Dialog zwischen den beiden müssen die Beschreibungen von Nachhaltigkeit für den eigenen Arbeitsbereich präzisiert werden	generische Beschreibungen der Kompetenzen müssen im Dialog von FK und MA präzisiert werden und im Arbeitsbereich befüllt werden	K1.1
F	181	143 – 147	es ist daher kein spezifisches Format festlegbar, aber das PE-Instrument des Kompetenzrahmens hilft	ein konkretes Format ist nicht festlegbar aber als Instrument zur Ausrichtung dient das Kompetenzmodell	K1.1
F	182	151 – 160	für jeden Mitarbeiter werden aus den 8 Kompetenzen pro Jahr 2-3 ausgewählt in denen er sich entwickeln soll als "Wie-Faktor" neben der Leistungsmessung (Zahlen, Budget), keinen Einfluss hat ob die Kompetenz der Nachhaltigkeit ausgewählt wird (keine technische Verfolgung)	für jeden MA werden jährlich Kompetenzen zur Weiterentwicklung ausgewählt	K1.1
F	183	167 – 176	in der Mitarbeiterbefragung gibt es keine explizite Themenbatterie zu Nachhaltigkeit, viele Fragen zielen aber darauf ab, wie Arbeitssicherheit, Arbeitsbedingungen, Freiräume Entscheidungen zu treffen	in der Mitarbeiterbefragung indirekte Schnittstellen zum Thema Nachhaltigkeit	K2.2

K 2 Verständnis von Nachhaltigkeit
· Thema des Arbeitsalltags
· persönliche Einstellung und Verhalten
· aufgrund Industrie starker Schwerpunkt auf Außenwirkung

K 2.1 Verantwortung
· jeder MA soll verantwortungsvoll handeln
· soziale Verantwortung über Sponsoring, Ehrenamt
· jeder MA in seinem mikro-Wirkungskreis
· Menschen anhalten Verantwortung zu übernehmen

K 2.2 Messung
· in Mitarbeiterbefragung indirekt
· kein eigener Themenblock

K 2.3 Organisation
· durch Anbindung der Abteilung an UN-Leitung Wichtigkeit betont

K 3 Austausch Personalentwicklung und Nachhaltigkeit
· bisher kein Auftrag Training über Nachhaltigkeit zu konzipieren

K 4 Kampagne der PE zu Nachhaltigkeit
· PE kann keinen direkten Mehrwert liefern, Nachhaltigkeit ist verhaltensbezogen
· Format muss "Diskutieren, Informieren" sein
· nur im Gesamtkontext vermittelbar, argumentativ passender Deckmantel
· Thema wäre unpassend
· große Kampagne nicht unbedingt sinnvoll, notwendig
· PE soll Freiräume geben, Menschen befähigen sich Gedanken zu machen
· Aufklärung appellierender Art liegt eher bei Kommunikation
· PE ist kein bevorzugter Kanal

F	184	181 – 185	falscher Rückschluss wäre zu sagen, weil Nachhaltigkeit keinen eigenen Themenblock hat ist kein Platz dafür in der UN-Strategie, es ist ein hohes Thema aber die Mitarbeiterbefragung zielt auf Zufriedenheit ab, keine business Befragung	Mitarbeiterbefragung zielt primär auf Zufriedenheit ab, Nachhaltigkeit keine eigenen Fragen	K2.2
F	185	189 – 194	Nachhaltigkeit ist nicht im HR-Bereich angesiedelt sondern unter HSSSE (Health, Safety, Sustainability, Security, Environment) mit einer Referenting, AL ist direkter MA des Vorstandsvorsitzenden	durch die Anbindung der zuständigen Abteilung an die Unternehmensleitung wird Wichtigkeit betont	K2.3
F	186	197 – 198	es findet bei der Konzipierung von Trainings kein Austausch statt, in-house Aufträge für die PE beinhalten das Thema Nachhaltigkeit bisher nicht	bisher kein Auftrag ein Training zu konzipieren, dass Nachhaltigkeit befasst, kein Austausch	K3
F	187	218 – 220	das Thema Nachhaltigkeit ist ein sehr lebendiges aus dem aktiven Arbeitsalltag und hat viel mit einer persönlichen Einstellung und Verhaltensorientierung zu tun	Nachhaltigkeit ist ein aktives Thema aus dem Arbeitsalltag und hat viel mit persönlicher Einstellung und Verhalten zu tun	K2
F	188	220 – 222	PE stößt an seine Grenzen als Training einen direkten Mehrwert zu liefern, Nachhaltigkeit verhaltensbezogen ist, was eigentlich jeder für sich mitberücksichtigen sollte	PE als Training kann keinen direkten Mehrwert liefern, da Nachhaltigkeit verhaltensbezogen ist	K4
F	189	222 – 229	hypothetisch, zukünftig wäre allenfalls das Format "diskutieren, informieren" passen, nicht aber ein Schulungsformat	das Format zu Vermittlung von Nachhaltigkeit kann eher "Diskutieren, Informieren" sein, als "Schulen"	K4
F	190	239 – 255	Nachhaltigkeit in allen Facetten in alle Denkprozesse einzuschleusen kann nur im Gesamtkontext nicht aber als alleinstehende Maßnahme stehen, wenn es die ganze Organisation durchdringen soll, verpflichtend und breitflächig dann nur im Kontext damit die MA verstehen weshalb das Training notwendig ist, gerade Nachhaltigkeit ist zwar wichtig aber nicht greifbar, um ein Seminar oder E-Learning anzubieten muss ein Reiz oder Sinn damit verbunden sein, es muss über flankierende Maßnahmen begleitet werden, in eine Kampagne eingebunden	Nachhaltigkeit kann breitflächig nur im schlüssigen Gesamtkontext vermittelt werden, um Akzeptanz und Verständnis bei den MA zu gewinnen muss es mit einem Reiz oder Sinn verbunden sein	K4
F	191	262 – 264	Nachhaltigkeit als ganzheitliches Konzept durch eine Kampagne aufzusetzen dient der Wissensvermittlung sodass MA ihr Verhalten daran ausrichten können und zudem nochmal eine strategische Orientierung geben was der UN-Leitung wichtig ist	Kampagne zu Nachhaltigkeit dient der Wissensvermittlung mit anschließender Verhaltensänderung und gibt Orientierung über Ziele der UN-Leitung	K4
F	192	271 – 275	das UN ist vor dem Hintergrund der Chemie bezogen auf Nachhaltigkeit, Ökologie sehr umstritten daher macht die UN-Kommunikation viel Öffentlichkeitsarbeit, Kampagnen	aufgrund der Industrie starker Schwerpunkt auf Nachhaltigkeit in der Außenwirkung	K2
F	193	275 – 282	eine Kampagne "Wie kann jeder Einzelne durch sein Verhalten - nach dem Motto viele kleine Menschen, viele kleine Schritte etwas tun" ist ein neuartiges Aufhängen von Nachhaltigkeit, sehr ungewohnt	eine interne Nachhaltigkeitskampagne würde das Thema sehr ungewohnt, neu positionieren	K4

F	194	289 – 298	klarer Appell im Konzern zu bestehenden Themen wie Arbeitssicherheit, Gesundheit sind kleine Puzzelteile, die eine große Kampagne gibt es nicht, auch muss nicht alles was wichtig ist in eine Kampagne verpackt werden, das Thema ist zu divers	es gibt diverse nachhaltige Puzzelteile in bestehenden Themen, aber keine große Kampagne dies ist nicht immer notwendig und sinnvoll insbesondere für solch ein diverses Thema	K4
F	195	301 – 305	Nachhaltigkeit mit seinen 3 Säulen betrifft jeden MA in seinem eigenen Mikrokosmos, jeder kann für seinen Wirkungskreis Nachhaltigkeit bewirken	jeder MA egal welche Karrierestufe kann in seinem mikro-Wirkungskreis alle 3 Säulen der Nachhaltigkeit beachten	K2.1
F	196	305 – 307	ich finde es sehr wichtig, Menschen zu ihrer Verantwortung zu bringen, nachhaltige Lösungen zu entwickeln	Menschen müssen angehalten werden Verantwortung zu übernehmen	K2.1
F	197	307 – 312	es soll generisch definiert sein, damit es Freiräume gibt sodass jeder nachdenken kann, was es für ihn bedeutet, die Summe sind viele kleine Maßnahmen	generische Definitionen bieten Freiräume für eigene Interpretation und Festlegung von Maßnahmen	K1.1
F	198	313 – 321	man kann nichts vorgeben oder als PE-ler definieren, jeder MA muss Freiräume haben das Thema zu überdenken, klassische Trainingsformate sind unangebracht, weil dies bedeutet "andere erzählen wie etwas laufen oder nicht laufen kann", es muss aber darum gehen Menschen Freiräume zu geben sich Gedanken zu machen und Entscheidungen zu treffen	es ist eine unternehmenskulturelle Frage doch die Unterstützung von PE liegt primär darin Freiräume zu geben, Menschen zu befähigen sich selbst Gedanken zu machen	K4
F	199	331 – 333	eine vorgeschaltete initiative Aufklärung ist allerdings nicht Aufgabe der PE, informierendes, appellierendes liegt in der Hand der UN-Kommunikation bzw. HSSSE Abteilung	vorgeschaltete initiative Aufklärung ist informierender, appellierender Art und nicht Aufgabe der PE sondern der UN-Kommunikation oder Nachhaltigkeitsabteilung	K4
F	200	334 – 336	PE kann sich darüber Gedanken machen, wie ein Kulturwechsel bedingt werden kann und mit Formaten des Change Management, der Moderation unterstützen	PE kann als Handlanger mit Expertise zu Change Management, Moderation unterstützen	K1
F	201	337 – 341	wenn die PE einen Workshop zum Thema "FK befähigen, bei ihren MA mehr Verantwortlichkeit zum Thema herzustellen" moderiert ist das eine DL, die Fachabteilung gibt den Impuls	Fachabteilungen geben den Impuls für gewünschte Kampagnen, die PE ist interner DL	K1
F	202	350 – 354	man kann eine Verhaltensänderung durch PE-Instrumente Richtung Nachhaltigkeit nur erreichen in einem größeren Rahmen eingebettet, also Einzelmaßnahmen, ein Puzzelteil in einem großen Konzept, funktioniert nicht als Alleinstellungsgeschichte	Verhaltensänderung Richtung Nachhaltigkeit ist ein einzelnes Puzzelstück und gelingt nur eingebettet in einen größeren Rahmen	K4
F	203	357 – 368	PE ist kein bevorzugter Kanal für Nachhaltigkeit, es liegt mehr auf der Informationsebene, per Definition sind die Auftraggeber von PE die UN-Leitung, Vorstand, Strategie, solange kein konkreter Auftrag zu Nachhaltigkeit kommt sind es eher subtile Sachen, die das Thema vertreten, es sind viele kleine Rädchen die nicht explizit unter dem Stichwort Nachhaltigkeit laufen	PE ist kein bevorzugter Kanal für Nachhaltigkeit, das Thema liegt auf der Informationsebene, es gibt implizit viele subtile Traingsmaßnahmen die an das Thema angrenzen, aber keinen globalen top-down Auftrag für ein umgreifendes roll-out	K4
F	204	372 – 373	wenn das Thema bei PE verortet werden sollte, ist es Argumentationssache zu schauen unter welchem Deckmantel	eine Platzierung des Themas, Nachhaltigkeitstrainings bei PE bedarf eines argumentativ passenden Deckmantels	K4

G	Nr.	Zeilen	Text	Zusammenfassung	Code
G	205	2 – 8	bei einer Betrachtung von PE-Maßnahmen muss zwischen Beschäftigtengruppen differenziert werden, Büro- und Betriebsmenschen oder auch Teilzeitkräften die per se und auf Nachhaltigkeit bezogen unterschiedlich viel PE bekommen	unterschiedliche Beschäftigtengruppen erhalten unterschiedlich viele PE-Maßnahmen	K1
G	206	11 – 22	innerhalb der Konzerninitiativen werden E-Learning Module konzipiert wie zum Thema "Go Green" oder Compliance die in manchen aber nicht allen Einheiten Pflicht sind es gibt keine einheitliche Regelung	zu bestimmten Konzerninitiativen gibt es E-Learnings die nicht unbedingt verpflichtend sind	K1
G	207	25 – 34	großer Konzern in seinen Einheiten sehr zerfasert, viele Tochtergesellschaften, viele Ausgliederungen, nicht jede Einheit wird zentral von der PE verfolgt sondern hat ihre eigene PE mit eigenen Zielen, zentral angebotene Nachhaltigkeitstrainings müssen nicht angenommen werden, kein Zwang oder Kontrolle	großer Konzern mit stark zerfaserten Einheiten mit eigener PE, kein Kontrollierungszwang bei zentralen Angeboten	K1.1
G	208	39 – 74	das Organigramm des Bereichs Personal ist sehr kompliziert, unterteilt in Vorstandsbereiche, Zentralbereiche einzelner HR-Themen, einzelne Abteilungen die allesamt strategisch arbeiten, die Service-NL beinhaltet alle operativen Einheiten	Bereich Personal ist aufbauorganisatorisch in viele Einheiten zerteilt, die Zentralbereiche arbeiten strategisch, die Service-NL führt operativ aus	K1.1
G	209	69 – 74	die Service NL HRD unterstützt die Strategen durch operative Ausführung, Organisation von Schulungen, Trainer, Evaluation	Service NL macht die gesamte operative Arbeit	K1.1
G	210	117 – 118	Nachhaltigkeit ist als eigene Abteilung, ungefähr 10 Kollegen im Vorstandsvorsitzenden	Nachhaltigkeit im Vorstandsvorsitzenden Bereich verortet	K2.1
G	211	120 – 126	bekannt sind die eher zufällig, über den Einsatz als HR-Beobachter im AC, bei der Auswahl von Trainees	wenig konkret fachliche Interaktion zwischen HR und Nachhaltigkeit	K3
G	212	128 – 132	Nachhaltigkeitsstrategie hat drei Facetten, GO Green, GO Help und GO Teach, ökologisch da benzin- u. energieintensives UN	Nachhaltigkeit dreiteilig auf Umwelt, Soziales und Bildung bezogen	K2
G	213	132 – 138	Training entwickelt mit teils banalen Inhalten trotzdem musste Bewusstsein geschaffen werden, das Verhalten jedes einzelnen MA macht einen Unterschied	Trainings für ökologische Nachhaltigkeit beinhalten viele relativ kleine Sachen, das Verhalten jedes einzelnen MA macht einen Unterschied	K3
G	214	147 – 152	die SNLHRD und jeder Standort hat einen GO Green Beauftragten, im weitesten Sinne auch PE durch Tipps, E-Mails, Rundschreiben	in SNLHRD bundesweit Beauftragte für Umwelt verteilt, die im weitesten Sinne PE machen	K1.1
G	215	155 – 164	weite Auffassung von PE und Anhänger des 70-20 Zielmodells, 70% persönliche Entwicklung "on the job", 20% "near the job" und 10% nur PE durch Präsenzseminare oder Web	70-20 Zielmodell, 70% "on the job", 20% "near the job" und 10% nur PE durch Seminare	K1
G	216	169	berufliche Erstausbildung zählt nicht zu PE sondern wirklich unter Ausbildung	berufliche Erstausbildung zählt nicht zu PE	K1
G	217	171 – 173	die 10% Seminare sind zum Großteil Präsenz, technisch ist E-Learning nicht möglich, gerade im Betrieb	10% reine PE sind zum großen Teil Präsenztrainings	K1
G	218	176 – 183	im Talentprogramm für Beamte viele interne Trainer, Vorteil ist sie kennen die Praxis im Konzern, bei gewissen fachlichen Themen nur Externe einsetzbar die teilweise didaktisch schwach sind, Referenten im offenen Seminargeschäft 70% externe Trainer	nach Möglichkeit interne Trainer, im offenen Seminargeschäft überwiegen externe Trainer	K1.1

K 1 Verständnis von Personalentwicklung

- je nach Beschäftigtenart verschieden häufig Maßnahmen
- E-Learnings zu gewissen Konzerninitiativen nicht verpflichtend
- 70/20 Modell, 70% on the job, 20% near the job, 10% Seminare
- Ausbildung zählt nicht dazu
- 10% reine PE zum Großteil Präsenztrainings
- bei Fachthemen Frontalunterricht
- PE nicht verantwortlich für Nachhaltigkeitsumsetzung

K 1.1 Organisation

- großer Konzern, stark zerfaserte Einheiten mit eigener PE
- kein Kontrollierungszwang bei zentralen Angeboten
- Zentralbereiche strategisch, Service NL operative Ausführung
- in Service NL bundesweit Nachhaltigkeits-Beauftragte
- im offenen Seminargeschäft überwiegen externe Trainer

K 2 Verständnis von Nachhaltigkeit

- Nachhaltigkeit hat drei Facetten, Bildung, Soziales und Umwelt
- Thema Energiesparen ist tief verankert
- gesellschaftliches Engagement punktuell

K 2.1 Organisation

- Nachhaltigkeit im Vorstandsbereich

K 2.2 Bewusstsein und Gründe

- durch positive Markt- und Kundenreaktion
- ökonomische Gründe, nicht aus Überzeugung
- positive Außenwirkung, attraktives Arbeitgeberimage
- je weiter weg von Zentrale desto weniger Bewusstsein
- Nachhaltigkeit nur, wenn es messbaren Nutzen hat

G					K	
G	219	185 – 191	Einkaufsabteilung für Trainingsanbieter deutschlandweit, mit ungefähr 100 Rahmenverträge, Datenbank zum Abruf, aber bei langer Betriebspraxis arbeitet man immer mit den gleichen zusammen	Rahmenverträge mit Trainingsanbietern deutschlandweit, bei langer Zusammenarbeit gleiche Trainer		**2.3 Messung** · keine Messung in Mitarbeiterbefragung · Teilnehmerzahl zu globalem Freiwilligentag
G	220	196 – 204	bei Sachthemen Frontalunterricht, Selbstkompetenz-Themen erst ein Impuls dann Selbstarbeit wie bei Work-Life Balance, langsam darauf hin arbeiten was einem wichtig ist und wie man zukünftig mit WLB umgehen möchte, Führungsthemen viel Gruppenarbeit und kollegiale Beratung	wenn Fachthemen trainiert werden eher Frontalunterricht sonst viel Einzel- und Gruppenarbeit	K1	
G	221	214 – 221	Nachhaltigkeit wäre ein Misch-Thema zwischen Sach- und persönlicher Kompetenz, als Format passt Seminar mit viel Gruppenarbeit, selbst Verbesserungsmöglichkeiten erarbeiten	Nachhaltigkeit ist ein Misch-Thema zwischen Sach und Selbstkompetenz	K3	**K 3 Schnittstelle Personalentwicklung und Nachhaltigkeit** · wenig konkrete fachliche Interaktion · Trainings für ökologische Nachhaltigkeit · Misch-Thema zwischen Sach- und Selbstkompetenz · teilweise Engagement während der Arbeitszeit · Impuls, Infos für Engagement von Kommunikation · bei Energiekosten-Einsparungen nachhaltige PE · zentraler Sponsor nötig für konzernweite Durchsetzung · zu stark zerfasert für einheitliche Unternehmenskultur · Interesse von Personen entscheidet · Nachhaltigkeit wird als individuelles Thema gesehen
G	222	227 – 232	schwierig Verantwortung anzulernen, das Thema Nachhaltigkeit wurde anfangs belächelt, aber da die ökologischen Initiativen auf dem Markt gut ankommen, Geschäft gemacht wird geht es in die Köpfe der MA, wenn es für den Kunden wichtig ist wieso nicht auch für uns, Bewusstsein geschaffen	Bewusstsein für Nachhaltigkeit wird durch positive Markt- und Kundenreaktion in den Köpfen der MA verstärkt	K2.2	
G	223	239 – 243	Gründe sind Personalmarketing, als attraktiver nachhaltiger AG dazustehen, ökonomisches Thema des Geldsparens, wenn es in der Außenwirkung niemanden interessieren würde, ob das UN nachhaltig ist und kein Geld gespart würde, würde es nicht gemacht	Gründe für Nachhaltigkeit sind ökonomischer Art und positive Außenwirkung durch Image als attraktiver, nachhaltiger AG	K2.2	
G	224	247 – 248	Nachhaltigkeit wird nicht ausschließlich aus Überzeugung verfolgt, es ist ein Wirtschaftsunternehmen, das sich am Markt behaupten muss	Nachhaltigkeit nicht aus altruistisch, philanthropischer Sicht sondern als Wirtschaftsunternehmen das sich am Markt behaupten muss	K2.2	
G	225	257 – 266	im Rahmen von GO Teach Unterstützung von Schulen, hängt von persönlichem Engagement der MA ab, wird vom UN dahingehend gefördert dass es während der AZ geschehen darf, aber kein konzernweiter Aufruf zur Teilnahme sondern individuelle Initiative	Unterstützung des UN bei sozialen Aktivitäten durch Freistellung, aber Initiative hängt von persönlichem Engagement ab	K3	
G	226	271 – 273	Anstoß für ein gesellschaftliches Engagement kommt über interne Informationen oder persönliche Kontakte	Impuls für Engagement durch Unternehmenskommunikation, verfügbare Informationen	K3	
G	227	287 – 281	PE sieht sich weniger verantwortlich für Nachhaltigkeitspersonalentwicklung oder die Umsetzung der Strategie, dafür gibt es die Abteilung, obwohl die nicht auf die Einheiten durchgreifen kann	PE nicht verantwortlich für Nachhaltigkeitsumsetzung, die Abteilung kann aber nicht auf alle Einheiten durchgreifen	K1	
G	228	281 – 283	bei konkreten Angaben der Energiekosten-Einsparung ist die PE tatsächlich nachhaltig	in Bereichen mit konkreten Zielen wie Energiekosten-Einsparung spezifische PE	K3	
G	229	291 – 292	wenn es einen zentralen Sponsor gäbe, der sagt das müssen wir jetzt ausrollen in Gesamtdeutschland wäre es ein Thema	Nachhaltigkeit würde zum umfänglichen konzernweiten, bundesweiten Thema wenn es einen zentralen Sponsor gäbe	K3	

G	230	299 – 308	es gibt keinen globalen "mindset Gedanken" weil der Konzern zu zerfasert, zu groß ist mit völlig unterschiedlichen Kulturen, es gibt nicht eine UN-Kultur, Versuche eine einheitliche Kultur zu schaffen werden scheitern, viel durch Zukäufe gewachsen, die eigene Kultur mitbringen	für eine einheitliche UN-Kultur im Sinne eines "mindset" ist der Konzern zu zerfasert, völlig unterschiedliche Subkulturen	K3
G	231	318 – 321	was CO2 Minderung betrifft, Energie einsparen ist das mindset bis weit herunter verankert, die Initiativen GO Help und GO Teach eher punktuell, eher die Personen die direkt damit zu tun haben	das Thema Energiesparen ist tief verankert, gesellschaftliches Engagement punktuell durch direkt in Bezug stehende MA	K2
G	232	323 – 334	je näher in Kontakt, je näher an der Zentrale desto eher Unterstützung der Nachhaltigkeitsstrategie, Betriebsmitarbeiter haben keinen Bezug	je weiter weg von der Zentrale, angrenzenden Arbeitsbereichen desto mehr bröckelt Unterstützung von Nachhaltigkeit	K2.2
G	233	340 – 351	in der Mitarbeiterbefragung keine Frage zu Nachhaltigkeit, einzige Zahl die veröffentlicht wird ist zum "Global Volunteer Day", MA die außerhalb der AZ an sozialen Projekten teilnehmen, besondere Projekte werden kommuniziert, weltweite Teilnahme	keine Messung oder Befragung zu Nachhaltigkeit, Teilnehmerzahl des globalen Freiwilligentages wird kommuniziert	K2.3
G	234	364 – 367	bei dem wirtschaftlichen Druck unter dem wir stehen wird Nachhaltigkeit nur dann stärker forciert, wenn es messbar wirtschaftlich etwas bringt, die Aussage "je nachhaltiger wir sind, desto nachhaltiger werden wir in der Öffentlichkeit wahrgenommen, desto mehr Geschäft machen wir" genügt nicht	Nachhaltigkeit wird nur stärker forciert wenn es messbar wirtschaftlich etwas bringt aufgrund des wirtschaftlichen Drucks	K2.2
G	235	377– 380	ein Kollege hätte ein anderes Bild vermittelt, vermutlich hätte ein Nachhaltigkeitsbeauftragter gesagt es wird wahnsinnig viel gemacht von dem ich nichts weiß	Personen haben unterschiedlich viel Interesse an dem Thema und können es je nach Position vorantreiben	K3
G	236	382 – 386	bei der Durchsetzung von nachhaltiger Verantwortung bei MA geht es um die Frage der Wertigkeit, Nachhaltigkeit wird als persönliches Thema angesehen, jeder Einzelne muss sich damit beschäftigen, aber es wird nicht als Trainingsthema verstanden	die Einschätzung der Wertigkeit von Nachhaltigkeit ist bestimmend, es wird als individuelles Thema angesehen nicht als PE-Thema	K3
H	237	3 – 12	Nachhaltigkeit hat viel mit Umweltschutz zu tun, Gesundheit, Sicherheit, in Bezug auf PE bedeutet es effektiv, langjährig, voraus schauend, nachhaltig ist auch das Talent Development mit 80% interner Besetzung, viel "entry level hires" und nur 4% externe "experienced" Experten, also nachhaltige Nachfolgeplanung und Entwicklung	Nachhaltigkeit in engem Bezug zu Umweltschutz, Gesundheit, Sicherheit und im PE sowie Talent Development selbst durch nachhaltige Planung und Entwicklung verankert	K2
H	238	19 – 31	Gesundheit durch Ergonomie-Schulungen, Sicherheitsschulungen in den Werken vertreten, "standardized work" in der Automobilindustrie als optimaler Bewegungsablauf, Schulungen nicht formale "classroom trainings" sondern am Arbeitsplatz mit regelmäßige Rückkoppelung, kontinuierlicher Optimierungsprozess	Gesundheit durch Ergonomie und Sicherheitsschulungen in den Werken, "standardized work" und kontinuierliche Optimierung	K2
H	239	42 – 46	es gibt eine Standardschulung Spritzguss, die MA befähigt, Tanks zu entwickeln und produzieren die dazu führen dass die Umweltbelastung geringer ist	indirekt, durch eine lange Kette wird mit der Entwicklung nachhaltiger Produkte und Technologien auf Umweltschonung geachtet	K2

K 1 Verständnis von Personalentwicklung

- Vorgesetztenverantwortung
- Prozesse von PE definiert, gestellt
- die eigentlichen PE-ler sind die Führungskräfte
- Kernprozesse sind Zielvereinbarungen zur Weiterentwicklung
- parallel Talent Reviews
- PE ist Service Provider für MA und FK
- kommerzielle Seminaranbieter nicht angesehen
- "Training on the Job" forciert
- Ausbildung organisatorisch getrennt
- PE-ler sind Coach, Mentor auf keinen Fall Lehrer
- Wertekern der Maßnahmen sind Grundwerte der Menschheit

H				Umwelt bzw. Nachhaltigkeit und Personalbereich werden	
H	240	48 – 49	viel direkter ist schwierig, Umwelt und Personalabteilung das ist sehr weit weg	als weit entfernt wahrgenommen	K3
H	241	50 – 53	Nachhaltigkeit wird aus Fachbereich gesteuert, weil das die Experten sind	Nachhaltigkeit wird vom Fachbereich gesteuert	K2.1
H	242	53 – 65	mit onboarding, Trainingsplanung, Job Profiles werden Vorgesetzte unterstützt, diese müssen dann überprüfen ob etwas wirklich passiert das ist in der UN-Kultur der Anspruch an FK, die werden durch Kennzahlen daran gemessen, HR unterstützt mit Schulungen, der Planung aber die Verantwortung ("ownership") liegt beim Vorgesetzten	Vorgesetztenverantwortung wird betont, Prozesse werden von HR gestellt und nachgehalten	K1
H	243	69 – 75	jeder MA bekommt beim "Welcome Day" eine grundsätzliche Einführung zu EHS, Quality, Umwelt zudem werden onboarding-Pläne der Vorgesetzten getrackt um zu schauen ob alles Sinn macht, ebenso werden Job Profile von HR Business Partner und FK gemeinsam erarbeitet	es gibt eine grundsätzliche Einführung in an Nachhaltigkeit angrenzende Themen, Job Profile und onboarding-Pläne liegen in der Verantwortung der FK werden aber durch HR getrackt	K1.1
H	244	78 – 79	Pflicht-Schulung zu Sicherheit einmal jährlich, ebenso Vorgesetzten-Verantwortung aber Kontrolle durch HR	Sicherheitsschulung verpflichtend einmal jährlich	K1.1
H	245	82 – 87	bei Einstellung Fokus auf Absolventen, Frauen in technischen Berufen, Diversity, hat etwas mit Nutzen zu tun, insofern kein soziales Engagement	bei Neueinstellung Fokus auf Absolventen, Diversität, aufgrund des Nutzens	K1.1
H	246	88 – 94	soziales Engagement und Nachhaltigkeitsabteilung gibt es nicht direkt	keine eigene Nachhaltigkeitsabteilung und keine Initiativen für soziales Engagement	K2.1
H	247	98 – 110	Compliance Beauftragte und Compliance Training, keine Geschäftstätigkeit in korrupten Ländern, strenge Vorgaben bzgl. Geschäftsgebaren, Vertragsabschluss, Bestechung, ebenso Schulung zu Diversity, klare Botschaft dass Diskriminierung tabu ist, auch Beleidigungen, Schaffung einer Kultur der Wertschätzung, nicht direkt Nachhaltigkeit, gesteuert durch Führung, Kultur oder der rechtlichen Seite	Compliance und Diversity Trainings, klare Botschaften gegen Diskriminierung, Schaffung einer Kultur der Wertschätzung hat nicht direkt Bezug zu Nachhaltigkeit	K1.1
H	248	112 – 114	die Abteilung EHS hat einen globalen Lead, Gesundheit, Sicherheit und Umwelt	EHS als Abteilung mit Bezug zu Nachhaltigkeit mit globalem Lead	K2.1
H	249	117 – 121	körperliche Belastung ist in Werken höher aber auch für MA in der Verwaltung einmal jährlich Schulung Sicherheit, Gesundheit	Gesundheitskurse und Angebote für Werksmitarbeiter und Angestellte	K1.1
H	250	123 – 127	PE hat als ein strategisches Ziel das Talent Development, das ist Boni-relevant für das Senior Management, PE sind eher diejenigen die Prozesse definieren, FK beraten, Strategien entwickeln, als eigentliche PE-ler gelten die FK	PE definiert Prozesse und berät, entwickelt Strategien, die eigentlichen PE-ler sind die FK	K1
H	251	133 – 140	der PE-Cycle hat Kernprozesse, Jahresziele für MA-Entwicklung, Überprüfung Mitte des Jahres und Jahresgespräch am Ende, parallel dazu Talent Reviews um MA mit Potenzial zu entwickeln, aufgrund Leistungsgap oder Entwicklungswunsch	PE Kernprozesse sind Zielvereinbarungen zur Entwicklung und parallel Talent Reviews	K1

K 1.1 Spezifische Personalentwicklung

- grundsätzliche Einführung in nachhaltige Themen
- Job Profile, Onboarding Pläne werden geprüft
- einmal jährlich Sicherheitsschulung
- Compliance und Diversity Training
- klare Botschaften gegen Diskriminierung
- Gesundheitskurse
- interne Trainer für technische Schulungen, Train-the-Trainer Ausbildung
- externe Trainer für Führung, Soft Skills
- HR misst Wirksamkeit
- Classroom-Training häufig per Video
- großer E-Learning Pool
- "Learning on the Job" durch Career Conversation Training formalisiert

K 2 Verständnis von Nachhaltigkeit

- enger Bezug zu Umweltschutz, Gesundheit, Sicherheit
- nachhaltige Planung, Entwicklung im Talent Development
- indirekt durch Entwicklung nachhaltiger Produkte, Technologien
- wegen Effizienzdruck der Branche, Gesetzen, Kundenanforderungen
- nur Demografie, Fachkräftemangel betrifft PE

K 2.1 Organisation

- keine eigene Nachhaltigkeitsabteilung, sondern EHS
- keine Initiativen für soziales Engagement

K 2.2 Messung

- ökologische Nachhaltigkeit muss messbar sein, nahe am Wirkungsraum
- soziale Nachhaltigkeit über Employer Branding messen

H	252	141 – 143	PE liefert den Prozess, die Tools, Trainings, Coachings, 360° Feedback, online Assessments, interne Trainer für technische Schulungen, externe Trainer für Soft Skills und Führung	PE liefert den Prozess, generell interne Trainer für technische Schulung und externe Trainer für Soft Skills oder Führung	K1.1
H	253	143 – 147	PE ist Service Provider, um die FK und MA dabei zu unterstützen, dass Bedarfe des UN erfüllt werden, dass ein guter Job gemacht wird, Nachfolger bereit stehen, Prozesse wenn die Leistung nicht stimmt	PE ist Service Provider für die Führungskräfte und Mitarbeiter	K1
H	254	151 – 158	der Input kommt aus den Fachabteilungen, viel Dinge sind sehr technisch, interne Train-the-Trainer didaktische Ausbildung, Unterstützung wenn gefragt, Input kommt nur bei Social Skills und Führungsskills von der PE	technischer Input aus den Fachabteilungen, interne Train-the-Trainer Ausbildung, Input für Social und Führungsskills von der PE	K1.1
H	255	161 – 174	es ist Teil des Jobs technische Trainings zu geben, die Experten müssen selbst Bescheid wissen, nur wenn keine interne Expertise dann externe Trainer, HR misst die Wirksamkeit der Trainings ist aber weit weg	Trainer kommen aus den Fachbereichen außer es sind HR-spezifische Trainings, HR misst Wirksamkeit	K1.1
H	256	178 – 184	wir glauben an "on the job" Learning und geben für Soft Skills wie Präsentationstechnik und Rhetorik kein Geld aus, Trainingsinstitute nicht positiv gesehen	kommerzielle Seminaranbieter für Soft Skills nicht angesehen, "on the job" Learning wird hochgehalten	K1
H	257	188 – 193	an Formaten werden Classroom-Trainings häufig per Videokonferenz genutzt, da Experten auf der Welt verteilt, großes E-Learning Tool der Konzernmutter, On-the-Job Trainings sind das Wichtigste, im Werk und Angestelltenbereich	Classroom-Trainings häufig per Videokonferenz da Experten global verstreut, großer E-Learning Pool, On-the-Job Training wird als wichtigstes Format gesehen	K1.1
H	258	193 – 198	On-the-Job Training bedeutet ausprobieren, Feedback holen, Coaching erhalten, Selbstreflektion, Peer-Consulting, Mentoring, Transfer-Coaching, virtuelle kurz-Coachings so wenig wie möglich vortragsmäßig	On-the-Job Training bedeutet ausprobieren und selbst reflektieren, Feedback, Coaching, Mentoring erhalten	K1
H	259	203 – 228	On-the-Job Training ist für ein bestimmtes Problemlösungstool das sehr zentral ist formalisiert, andernfalls ist es durch das HRD Tool "Career Conversation Training" formalisiert, in dem FK lernen, Entwicklungspläne zu schreiben mit möglichst wenig Trainings, "Teaching" ist ein wichtiges Element, MA werden ins kalte Wasser geschmissen und sollen aus Fehlern lernen, aber FK, Peer oder Mentor sind nahe dran	Learning on-the-job ist durch "Career Conversation Training" formalisiert, in dem FK lernen Entwicklungspläne zu schreiben	K1.1
H	260	231 – 237	berufliche Erstausbildung hat eine eigene Abteilung, organisatorisch getrennt, Teil des operativen HR-Geschäfts aber nichts mit PE zu tun	Ausbildung ist organisatorisch von PE getrennt	K1
H	261	242 – 266	was hätte PE davon, das Thema Nachhaltigkeit bezogen auf Wirtschaftlichkeit, Umwelt, Soziales zu unterstützen, die Aufgabe von PE ist es UN-Probleme zu lösen, es muss einen klaren unternehmerischen Sinn und Zweck haben, wirtschaftlich gesehen wird viel getan um nachhaltig wettbewerbsfähig zu sein, dem Demografiedesaster und Fachkräftemangel zu begegnen	es ist nicht die Aufgabe von PE, Nachhaltigkeit zu fördern, sondern Unternehmensprobleme zu lösen	K3

K 3 Schnittstelle Personalentwicklung und Nachhaltigkeit

- werden als weit entfernt wahrgenommen
- nicht Aufgabe von PE
- fraglich wie entscheidend Grad der Nachhaltigkeit ist
- Mitarbeiterunterstützung eingeschränkt
- würde nicht zur Kultur passen, Irritationen auslösen
- wirtschaftlichem Nutzen betrifft Kern der PE, ungenutzte Potenziale umwandeln
- aus politischen Gründen Umsetzung begrenzt, keine Belehrung Erwachsener
- Bewusstsein schaffen möglich
- Erziehung nicht möglich, Verantwortung nur aus Überzeugung
- Kollektiv kann man nicht motivieren
- kein Engagement aus Zwang
- Dogmatismus vermeiden

K 4 Vorschlag einer Kampagne

- ein Workshop müsste aktiv gestaltet sein
- eventuell wird es zur Gewohnheit
- Flexibilität in der Ansprache
- individuelle Motivatoren beachten
- auf unmittelbares Arbeitsumfeld bezogen

H					
H	262	260 – 266	ist es denn ein Problem des UN nur so und so stark nachhaltig zu sein, es wird nicht von PE gesteuert weil es andere Experten besser können, es gibt Spezialisten für Umwelt	fraglich ob der Grad der Nachhaltigkeit kritisch ist, zudem wird das Thema von den spezialisierten Experten betreut	K3
H	263	269 – 274	ein konzernweites roll-out einer ganzheitlichen Nachhaltigkeitsstrategie wird nicht als Aufgabe der PE gesehen, ebenso kein Vorteil durch eine Steuerung von HR, die Experten und Ressourcen sind in einer anderen Abteilung	ganzheitliche Nachhaltigkeit wird nicht als Aufgabe von HR gesehen	K3
H	264	276 – 283	die Automobilindustrie fordert extreme Effizienz und jährliche Steigerung, auch durch Materialrecycling, MA hätten kein Verständnis für Nachhaltigkeitsstrategie und möchten Probleme schnell, unkompliziert gelöst haben	Automobilindustrie fordert hohe Kosten-Effizienz, für Nachhaltigkeitsstrategie gäbe es keine MA Unterstützung	K3
H	265	289 – 301	Nachhaltigkeit würde nie offiziell mit einer eigenen Abteilung bestehen, es gibt aber viele Vorschriften, die in die Richtung gehen, von den Kunden viel Druck effizient zu sein, das Thema begleitet ständig ist aber nicht zentral gesteuert sondern durch Gesetze und Kundenanforderungen, gerade in Werken durch Produktivität sehr präsent, außer bei Demografie, Fachkräftemangel kommt der Push nicht aus der PE sondern durch Experten aus unterschiedlichen Abteilungen	Nachhaltigkeit entsteht unter dem Effizienzdruck von Gesetzen, Vorschriften und Kunden nur bei Demografie, Fachkräftemangel liegt die Verantwortung bei PE	K2
H	266	295 – 296	es würde nicht zur Kultur passen einen Nachhaltigkeitsbeauftragten zu haben, das würde Irritationen auslösen	Nachhaltigkeitsbeauftragt er würde nicht zur Kultur passen und Irritationen bei den MA auslösen	K3
H	267	306 – 316	ein Thema das vorstellbar wäre ist aus sogenannten talentierten "Bildungsverlierern" erfolgreiche Auszubildende zu machen, sinnvoll aus der PE zu steuern, soziales Projekt und wirtschaftlicher Nutzen für das UN, es betrifft den Kernbereich der PE ungenutzte Potenziale von Menschen entdecken und in Verhalten, Kompetenzen umwandeln	ein vorstellbares sozial-wirtschaftliches Projekt mit konkretem Nutzen betrifft den Kern von PE, ungenutzte Potenziale entdecken und in Verhalten, Kompetenzen umwandeln	K3
H	268	316 – 320	auf Umwelt bezogen keine Aufgaben für PE, klingt alles stark nach Oberlehrerin, PE-ler sollen nicht belehrend sein sondern konsequent Coach und Consultant, auf keinen Fall Lehrerin	PE-ler sollen Coach, Consultant sein auf keinen Fall belehrend, daher Motivation für umweltbezogene Ziele nicht Aufgabe von PE	K1
H	269	325 – 328	nicht aus lerntheoretischen sondern politischen Gründen stößt eine komplette Durchsetzung von Nachhaltigkeitsstrategie an seine Grenzen, erwachsene Menschen lassen sich nicht gerne belehren, PE soll Lernprozesse fördern	nicht aus lerntheoretischen sondern politischen Gründen ist eine ganzheitliche Umsetzung von Nachhaltigkeit begrenzt, Erwachsene lassen sich nicht gerne belehren	K3
H	270	328 – 345	Nachhaltigkeit hat viel mit Moral, Verantwortung zu tun, das zu vermitteln mutet arrogant an, alle PE-Maßnahmen sollen einen ethischen Kern haben, gerade Führung ohne Wertschätzung ist nicht möglich, PE soll nicht die moralische, belehrende Rolle einnehmen, der Wertekern ist sehr wichtig muss aber aus Dingen bestehen, über die sich ein großer Teil der Menschheit einig ist, Grundwerte "was du nicht willst was man dir tut, füg auch keinem anderen zu", aber es soll kein Wertemodell aufgedrückt werden	PE-Maßnahmen sollen Lernprozesse fördern, haben alle einen ethischen Kern, der Wertekern besteht aus Grundwerten der Menschheit, soll nicht oktroyiert werden, PE soll nicht die moralische, belehrende Rolle einnehmen	K1

H	271	351 – 376	PE könnte eventuell "awareness" schaffen und falls MA motiviert sind auch eine Veränderung des Verhaltens, die zur Gewohnheit wird, kein Seminar, sondern "awareness" herstellen, dann in den Arbeitsmodus, Workshop in dem Leute alles selbst erarbeiten	was das Lernen betrifft könnte PE "awareness" schaffen und durch einen aktiven Workshop MA Verhalten ändern, eventuell wird es zur Gewohnheit	K4
H	272	374 – 375	man kann MA nicht behavioristisch erziehen, gerade bei so einem Thema, davon muss jemand überzeugt sein oder nicht	Erziehung ist nicht möglich, von Nachhaltigkeit und Verantwortung müssen MA selbst überzeugt sein	K3
H	273	380 – 382	Workshop muss freiwillig sein, sehr viel Spaß machen, lustig sein und als Erholung empfunden werden	Workshop über Nachhaltigkeit muss freiwillig sein, Spaß machen und als Erholung empfunden werden	K4
H	274	382 – 388	Flexibilität sodass man für jeden Einzelnen die Motivatoren anspricht, es muss eine "Grund-awareness" geschaffen werden und dann Menschen auf unterschiedliche Art neugierig machen, sodass jeder in seine Richtung lernt und in eine andere Richtung awareness bekommt	Flexibilität nach einer "Grund-awareness" müssen MA individuell neugierig gemacht werden und in unterschiedliche Richtungen lernen	K4
H	275	389 – 397	MA mit ähnlichen Motivatoren konkrete Sachen erarbeiten lassen, muss sehr konkret sein und einen wahrnehmbaren Nutzen entstehen durch geänderte Verhaltensweisen, bezogen auf das unmittelbare Umfeld nah an der Realität der MA	MA mit ähnlichen Motivatoren können konkrete Dinge erarbeiten, muss auf reales unmittelbares Arbeitsumfeld bezogen sein und einen wahrnehmbaren Nutzen haben	K4
H	276	399 – 409	es muss nah an der Realität des Menschen sein, man kann kein Kollektiv motivieren sein Verhalten zu ändern, die meisten Menschen lernen weil es weh tut oder nützlich ist, das heißt erfolgreich kann es nur sein, wenn man individuelle Motivatoren von Menschen anspricht	ein Kollektiv kann man nicht motivieren, immer individuelle Motivatoren der MA ansprechen	K3
H	277	422 – 425	wenn man eine Nachhaltigkeitsstrategie implementiert muss ein Quick-Win monetär ablesbar sein und die Messbarkeit darf nicht weit weg liegen sondern muss den eigenen Wirkungsraum betreffen	ökologische Nachhaltigkeit muss messbar sein am besten monetär und nahe im eigenen Wirkungsraum	K2.2
H	278	430	soziale Nachhaltigkeit lässt sich über Employer Branding, wie gut das UN dasteht, wie viele Bewerbungen es erhält messen	soziale Nachhaltigkeit über Employer Branding messen	K2.2
H	279	433 – 450	MA sollen Dinge nicht tun, weil sie es müssen, nur wenn es zur Corporate Identity gehört, man dadurch konkrete Kompetenzen entwickelt, Teil der Ausbildung soziales Engagement, dann Erwartungen in Ordnung, Teil der Unternehmenskultur verknüpft mit Kompetenzentwicklung und Mehrwert	kein soziales Engagement aus Zwang, nur wenn es zur Kultur gehört und man gleichzeitig Kompetenzentwicklung, Wirtschaftlichkeit fördert ist die Erwartung angebracht	K3
H	280	452 – 453	rein altruistische Haltung kann schnell in Dogmatismus überschlagen; soll vermieden werden	Dogmatismus soll vermieden werden	K3

C.4 Inductive Forming of Categories Step 2

Schritt 2: Reduktion

Case	Category	Translation and Generalization	Reduction
A	**K 1 Verständnis von Personalentwicklung** · Kompetenzcenter · Führungskräfte zur Mitarbeiterentwicklung befähigen · berufliche Erstausbildung · technische Weiterbildung durch interne Mitarbeiter · Führungskräfte sollen sich im Job entwickeln · Aufstieg von Mitarbeitern als Erfolgsmessung der Entwicklungsmaßnahme · Maßnahmen aufgrund des Marktdrucks zurückfahren	Comprehension of HRD · Competence Center · Qualify managers for development of employees · Vocational training included · On-the-job training of executives · Career advancement as success indicator of personnel development · Technical education in-house · Investments subject to cost-saving measures	**C' 1 Comprehension of HRD** · Qualify managers for development of employees · Broad conception that requires actual and future perspective · Organizational development and development of competencies into a certain direction · Recruiting and Onboarding · Requirement planning: Development strategy to attract and retain talents · Help employees to progress in career · Global process definition and provision · Talent reviews in parallel to target agreements · HRD professionals as coach, consultant or mentor not teacher · Job profiles, onboarding plans are checked
A	**K 2 Verständnis von Nachhaltigkeit** · Potenzialeinschätzung und Führungskräfteentwicklung · eine Balance finden · nicht aus der ethischen Orientierung der Nachhaltigkeit selbst getrieben K 2.1 Soziale Nachhaltigkeit · soziale Projekte als Zeichen der gesellschaftlichen Verantwortung K 2.2 Organisation · spezifische Abteilung für alle Themen zuständig · keine Überprüfung, ob Nachhaltigkeitsbericht gelesen wird, Feedback ist erwünscht · Nachhaltigkeit im Stab organisiert	Comprehension of sustainability · Finding a balance · Projects show social responsibility · Own staff department · Readers of report not tracked but feedback encouraged	*C 1.1 Learning and Training Formats* · Executives shall be developed on the job · Technical education by internal staff · Learning through continuous repetition, excitement, appropriate format · Programs according to target group · Training offer does not mean training attendance · Online and offline training · Development ambition of person himself, of his supervisor or because of departmental needs · Development of functional, methodological, personal skills, leadership competencies · "Change" preferentially by external trainers · Mixed methods indicate high quality training · (Amount of) measures depend on type of employment · 70/20 model: 70% on the job, 20% near the job, 10% trainings · Specialized functional trainings as classroom teaching (via video if experts globally dispersed) · Learning on the job formalized through career conversation training
A	**K 3 Schnittstelle Personalentwicklung und Nachhaltigkeit** K 3.1 Nutzenaspekte · ein Mehrwert ist verbesserte Arbeitsqualität · Wirkung im Zeitversatz von 1-2 Jahren erkennbar K 3.2 Veranstaltungen · Infoveranstaltung für Trainees beinhaltet Nachhaltigkeitsthemen · nachhaltige Themen bei Trainings nur mit konkretem Bezug · umfassende Lehr- und Lernmaßnahmen nur wenn ein Vorstand erkennt, dass es im Sinne der Außen- und Innenwirkung wichtig ist	Interface of HRD and sustainability · Info events include topic for general awareness · Otherwise sustainability as topic only if specific relationship given · Time lag of effects on organization	*C 1.2 Organization of HRD* · Competence Center · Vocational training included rather seldom · Investments in HR-measures are subject to market pressure · More HR-departments in large companies · HR is support function · Differentiation between strategic and
B	**K 1 Verständnis von Personalentwicklung** · PE weitgreifend verstanden · bedarf eines Ist- und Zukunftblicks	Comprehension of HRD · Broad conception that requires an actual and future look · Development of competencies and	

- Kompetenzaufbau bei Mitarbeitern
- Organisationsentwicklung in eine bestimmte Richtung
- Recruiting zählt dazu
- Onboarding und Ausbildung sind Teil der PE
- Trainings werden durch interne Kollegen gegeben
- Standardpräsentationen kommen aus der Zentrale
- Führungskräfte vermitteln selbst gewisse Themenkomplexe
- nur in Ausnahmefällen externe Trainer

K 1.1 Organisation

- je größer die Firma, desto mehr Bereiche im Personal

K 1.3 Nachhaltigkeit durch Personalentwicklung

- Nachhaltigkeit für jeden Mitarbeiter strukturell verankert durch Jahreszielplanung, Bonusvereinbarungen
- Nachhaltigkeit integriert in Führungskräfteentwicklung und Ausbildung
- Nachhaltigkeit in Firmenwerten enthalten und daher "Muss"-Schulungsthema
- für Mitarbeiter, die einzelne Nachhaltigkeitsthemen betreuen spezielle Schulungen
- Teilnahme an Schulungen in Abhängigkeit von der Position, höhere Frequenz bei FK
- auf niedrigen Hierarchieebenen kommen nur Richtlinien an
- keine Nachhaltigkeitsschulung für alle Mitarbeiter außer Compliance
- hinter der Umsetzung von Nachhaltigkeit steckt persönliches Interesse der Führungskräfte
- Auszubildende werden für soziales Engagement von der Arbeit freigestellt
- Lernen durch häufige Wiederholungen des Themas
- Jahresziele für jeden Mitarbeiter und Commitment aus dem Vorstand erhöhen den Erfolg
- Nachhaltigkeit integrativ, nicht als Randthema behandeln

| B | K 2 Verständnis von Nachhaltigkeit |

- ganzheitlicher, langfristiger schonender Umgang mit allen Ressourcen, auch dem Mensch
- Ebene 1: Nachhaltigkeit als Inhalt in Fachthemen
- Ebene 2: strukturelle Nachhaltigkeit der Trainings
- Ebene 3: methodische Nachhaltigkeit in der Durchführung
- wird stärker kommen aufgrund von Regulierungen, erhöhter Notwendigkeit, Werteveränderung bei Mitarbeitern
- der demografische Wandel zwingt zum Umdenken

---

of organization
- Recruiting, ~~Apprenticeship~~ and Onboarding
- ~~Managers should educate their employees~~
- Lecture on sustainability topics given by colleagues
- Executives train certain topics themselves
- More HR-departments in large companies
- Target planning and bonus agreements
- Sustainability topics in executive and vocational training
- Sustainability included in company values
- Training for specific subjects
- Participation depends on job position
- In lower hierarchy levels guidelines only
- No holistic sustainability training except about compliance rules
- Personal interest of executive promotes sustainability
- Social engagement during working time
- Learning occurs through continuous repetition
- ~~Goals enhance success~~
- Treat subject in integrative manner

Comprehension of sustainability

- Long-term, cautious use of all resources, including the human being
- Level 1: Sustainability as content
- Level 2: Sustainability of trainings
- Level 3: Sustainability of methods
- Sustainability issues will occur increasingly due to regulations, necessity and value changes
- Demographic change forces a rethinking

---

operational talent management
- Complex architecture of HR
- Considerable need for coordination
- Cooperation with external training institutions
- Discrepancy between global guidelines and needs of national companies or subsidiaries
- Internal service provider

C 1.3 Measuring Success of HRD-Interventions
- Career advancement as success indicator
- Target planning and bonus agreements
- Employee survey to control success
- HR measures effectiveness of development plans implemented by executives

C' 2 Comprehension of Sustainability

Overall
- Finding a balance
- Long-term, cautious use of all resources, including the human being
- Closely related to environmental protection, health, safety
- Indirectly through products, technology
- Three facets: education, society, environment
- Saving of energy is strongly anchored
- Social engagement only selectively
- Topic of everyday work

Responsibility
- CR is economic, ecological, social responsibility
- Questioning of actions, continuous improvement, meaningful contribution

with Respect to HRD
- Level 1: Sustainability as content
- Level 2: Sustainability of trainings
- Level 3: Sustainability of methods
- Sustainability of HRD instruments
- Support of HRD in sustainability endeavors
- CR closely related to transformation, change
- Only demographic change, skills shortage affect HRD directly
- Talent management includes sustainability regarding personal development and work situation

C 2.1 Reasons for Sustainability
- Philanthropic and economic side
- Sustainability issues will occur increasingly due to regulations, necessity and value changes
- Demographic change forces a rethinking
- Personal interest as driver
- Utilitarian, economic reasons not goodwill
- Reasons and benefits involve all three

K 2.1 Nachhaltigkeit des Menschen

- Nachhaltigkeit betrifft auch die Person
- der Mitarbeiter stellt eine Säule dar
- persönliches Engagement und Interesse als Treiber

~~Sustainability concerns individuals as well~~
- Personal interest as driver

K 2.2 Kosten-Nutzen Abwägungen

- größter Hebel in Bezug auf Gesundheit der Mitarbeiter und Umwelt
- rein utilitaristische, wirtschaftliche Gründe kein Gutmenschentum
- Kontinuität in der Investition notwendig
- alle vier Säulen gleichstark fördern, im Verhältnis sind PE-Maßnahmen günstig

- Health and environment effects are greatest levers
- Utilitarian, economic reasons not goodwill
- Continuity in expenditures necessary
- Support four pillars equally

C | K 1 Verständnis von Personalentwicklung

- Talentmanagement beinhaltet Nachhaltigkeit bezüglich der persönlichen Entwicklung und der Arbeitssituation
- Entwicklungsprogramme angepasst an Zielgruppe (Karrierestufe), Eintrittsvoraussetzungen und Fokus
- kein ganzheitliches Training zu Nachhaltigkeit
- Anlaufstellen für diverse angrenzende Themen
- deutliches Werteverständnis, das gelebt wird
- Lernen von Themen hängt von Format der Vermittlung und Spannungsfaktor und Häufigkeit der Wiederholungen ab
- Mitarbeiterbefragung als Kontrolle des Erfolgs von Initiativen
- Trainings-Angebot ist nicht gleich Nutzung, Eigenleistung der Mitarbeiter ist gefordert
- Kompetenzen in Fach und Führung unterteilt
- Formate sind online und offline
- HR als unterstützender Unternehmensbereich

Comprehension of HRD
- Talent management includes sustainability regarding personal development and work situation
- Development programs according to target group
- ~~No holistic sustainability training~~
- Counseling for related topics
- Learning depends on format, ex~~citement, repetition~~
- Employee survey to control success
- Training offer is not equal to attendance
- Separation of functional and leadership competencies
- Online and offline training
- HR is support function

C | K 2 Verständnis von Nachhaltigkeit

- durch häufige interne Kommunikation werden Themen und soziales Engagement transportiert
- Gründe für Nachhaltigkeit kann man nicht trennen
- Nachhaltigkeit aufgrund des Wettbewerbsdrucks
- ständiger Kontakt zur Arbeitswelt (24/7 Erreichbarkeit) ist Gesundheitsrisiko

Comprehension of sustainability
- Frequent communication about social engagement
- Reasons and benefits involve all three pillars simultaneously
- Sustainability due to stress of competition

C | K 3 Aspekte der Mitarbeiter

- berufliche Vorerfahrungen prägen
- Themen sind bekannt, selbstverständlich oder neuartig

Aspects of employees
- Working experience determines if subject is known, unknown

C | K 4 Aspekte des Unternehmens

- Unternehmensgröße ermöglicht intensive Beschäftigung mit Themen
- Unternehmen erfolgreich, wenn es Mitarbeitern wohlergeht

Aspects of companies
- ~~Large size makes pursuit of sustainability issues possible~~
- Successful if employees are doing well

pillars simultaneously
- Sustainability due to stress of competition
- Situation calls for savings which are top priority
- Intrinsic motivation not sufficient for sustainable management
- Awareness, persecution due to positive customer response

C 2.2 Organization of Sustainability
- Frequently staff department directly linked to Executive Board
- CR not necessarily close to HR, localization of department is diverse
- Department for environment, health, safety
- Importance highlighted by direct link of department to executive board
- Continuity in expenditures necessary and equal support of all pillars
- German standards cannot apply in foreign subsidiaries

C 2.3 Measuring Success of Sustainability
- Realization of endeavors or initiatives often difficult
- Endeavor can only be fulfilled iteratively in long-term
- Readers of report not tracked but feedback encouraged
- Health and environment effects are greatest levers
- Indirectly measured in employee survey
- Ecological sustainability must be measurable monetarily
- Sustainability must not reduce economic success
- What is assessed has a lot of engagement is a question of perspective
- Definition of KPIs reflects seriousness

C' 3 Dissociation of HRD and Sustainability

- Perceived to be disconnected
- So far no assignment to conceptualize training on sustainability
- HRD not responsible for sustainability implementation
- HRD not filtered by "how sustainable"
- Little concrete professional interaction
- Not a task of HRD to promote sustainability
- Direct and indirect bridges
- In some cases initially random interaction has grown
- Content not mediated systematically, holistically
- Functional demands and guiding principles are decisive

D	K 1 Verständnis von Personalentwicklung	Comprehension of HRD	C' 4 Existing HRD Approaches for Sustainability
	· Entwicklungsstrategie, um Talente zu gewinnen und halten · Bedarfsplanung · Unterscheidung Talent/Managemententwicklung und Personalentwicklung · Management und Talent Development sind strategisch · Personalentwickler arbeiten aktiv, geben Trainings · Veränderungsprozesse, Change Management besser durch externe Trainer · MA fördern, um höhere Positionen zu erreichen · Personalstrategie bedeutet Talentpool für zukünftige Bedarfe haben K 1.1 Nachhaltigkeit durch Personalentwicklung · jeder Mitarbeiter muss zu angrenzenden Themen online Schulungen absolvieren · verantwortungsvolle Führung, Vorleben und Kommunikation von Nachhaltigkeit · soziales Engagement fester Bestandteil des Trainee Programms · Motivation durch den Vorgesetzten wirkt positiv · soziales Engagement ist gute Tat für die Gesellschaft und ein Lernfeld, Chance zur Teamentwicklung · Führungskräfte für Verantwortung sensibilisieren · bei Neueinstellung Passung zur Kultur, Werten · Führungskräfte vermitteln eher nachhaltige Alltagsthemen · Ergebnisse von Nachhaltigkeit-Schulungen nicht kontrolliert · Trainings selbst können durch "follow-up", Feedback nachhaltig sein K 1.2 Organisation und Austausch · Vernetzung mit Kollegen die demografischen Wandel thematisieren · individuelle Wichtigkeit für Vorstand entscheidet über Verfolgung von Themen, Durchsetzung einer Kultur	· Development strategy to attract and retain talents · Requirement planning · Differentiation between strategic and operational talent management · Change conducted preferentially by external trainers · Help employees to progress in career · ~~Talent pool for future needs~~ · Online trainings about related topics · Responsible management, leading by example · Social engagement part of trainee program · Social engagement twofold useful, for society and team · Sensitize executives for responsibility · Mind person-organizational values and culture fit in recruiting · Executives rather convey everyday sustainability issues · Results of sustainability trainings not controlled · Follow-up make trainings sustainable · ~~Exchange with colleague responsible for demographic change~~ · Explicit significance for executive board steers pursuit and pervasion of subject	· No holistic sustainability training except about compliance rules · Info events include topic for general awareness · Sustainability topics in executive and vocational training · Online trainings about related topics · Certifications required by industry · Environmental training by authorities · Trainings and clear rules on environmental sustainability, protection · Annual safety training, diversity training, anti – discrimination directive, health courses · In lower hierarchy levels guidelines only · Projects and sponsorship show social responsibility · Social engagement allowed during working time · Social engagement part of trainee program · Corporate volunteering as professional framework · Counseling available for related topics · Mind person-organizational values and culture fit in recruiting · Executives rather convey everyday sustainability issues · Top-down and bottom-up mechanisms to promote engagement C 4.1 *Character of Topic and Formats used* · Mixed theme between self-competence and professional skills · Sustainability as topic in depth only if specific relationship given · Treat subject in integrative manner not peripheral · Reference point must always be given for employee involvement · Sustainability included in company values · Lecture on sustainability topics given by internal colleagues · Managers train certain topics themselves · Training for specific subjects as counselor · Participation and touch points depend on job position · Competency model including "promoting sustainable solutions" · Generic descriptions to be specified in dialogue · Format not to be set unitarily · Freedom of establishing measures C 4.2 *Control and Transparency of Interventions* · Results of sustainability trainings not controlled · Follow-up make trainings sustainable · No compulsive control concerning participation in central (online) training offers · Frequent communication about social engagement · Number of participants on global volunteer day announced
D	K 2 Verständnis von Nachhaltigkeit	Comprehension of sustainability	
	· drei Säulen, dritter Aspekt in soziale Säule und interne Seite der Mitarbeiter geteilt · demografischer Wandel bedingt nachhaltige Personalentscheidungen · Menschliche Säule bezogen auf Engagement in- und außerhalb der Branche · soziales Engagement für alle Mitarbeiter angeboten, gefördert · Neuigkeiten über soziales Engagement, Zukunftsthemen häufig kommuniziert · Umweltschonung deutliche Regeln, durch Kosten bestimmt · Nachhaltigkeit kann auf PE-	· ~~Three pillars, division of third one into society and employee~~ · ~~Demographic change induces sustainable HRM~~ · ~~News on social engagement spread frequently~~ · Clear rules on environmental protection · ~~Sustainability of HRD instruments~~ · Support of HRD in sustainability endeavors	

	Instrumente oder die Unterstützung durch PE bezogen sein		**C' 5 Benefits of HRD Support for Sustainability**
			C 5.1 Internal Success
	2.1 Nutzen • fördert attraktives Arbeitgeberimage, dient aber auch Nachhaltigkeit selbst • Nachhaltigkeitsthemen gehen mit Mitarbeiterbindung einher	• Employer image upgraded • Employee loyalty, retention	• Companies prosper if employees are doing well • Employee loyalty and retention • Functional results are visible • Social engagement twofold useful, for society and team • Time lag of effects on organization
	2.2 Wirtschaftlichkeit • aufgrund des Wettbewerbs Druck in der Branche • Situation fordert Einsparungen, hat höchste Priorität • Nachhaltigkeit darf nicht wirtschaftlichen Erfolg mindern • für nachhaltiges Wirtschaften reicht intrinsische Motivation nicht	• ~~Result of competitive pressure in industry~~ • Situation calls for savings which are top priority • Sustainability must not reduce economic success • Intrinsic motivation not sufficient for sustainable management	*C 5.2 External Success* • Employer image upgraded • Measure social sustainability through employer branding • Due to industry strong focus on external visibility
E	**K 1 Verständnis von Personalentwicklung** • HR-Bereiche in Konzernen unübersichtlich, Architektur vielschichtig, erheblicher Abstimmungsbedarf • Diskrepanz zwischen globalen Vorgaben für HRD und Bedürfnissen der Ländergesellschaft • eigener Trainingsanbieter intern • externe Kooperation mit Trainingsinstitutionen • Bildungsanspruch aus Person selbst, seiner FK oder Bedarf von Fachbereichen • Weiterentwicklung fachlicher, methodischer, persönlicher Kompetenzen • Führung ist verantwortliches Handeln K 1.1 Nachhaltigkeit durch Personalentwicklung • ehrenamtliches Engagement einsehbar • Angebote/Gesuche und Erfahrungsberichte zu sozialen Projekten • abhängig von Interesse der Führungskräfte • FK implizit angehalten, Verantwortung zu leben • um Thema bei MA zu platzieren, muss es immer Bezugpunkt geben • überfachliche Herleitung durch ethischen Anspruch nur wenn Bezug gegeben K 1.2 Organisation und Austausch • "Corporate Volunteering" professionell durch CR Abteilung überwacht, beraten • CR Abteilung als Scharnier • Top-Down und Bottom-Up Mechanismen, um Engagement zu fördern	Comprehension of HRD • Complex architecture of HR • Considerable need for coordination • Discrepancy between global guidelines and needs of national companies • ~~Internal training provider~~ • Cooperation with external training institutions • Development aspiration of person himself, of his supervisor or because of departmental needs • Development of functional, methodological, personal skills • ~~Leadership is acting responsibly~~ • ~~Social engagement is visible~~ • ~~Offers, requests for social projects~~ • ~~Depends on interest of executives~~ • ~~Executives are implicitly encouraged to take responsibility~~ • Reference point must always be given for employee involvement • Corporate volunteering as professional framework • Top-down and bottom-up mechanisms to promote engagement	**C' 6 Individual Employees and Sustainability** • Working experience determines if sustainability or related subjects are known or unknown • Sustainability seen as individual topic • Call for altruistic responsibility of employees • Personal interest and commitment of executive promotes sustainability • Responsible management, leading by example • Explicit significance for executive board steers pursuit and pervasion of subject • The further away from headquarters the less awareness **C' 7 Planning an HRD Campaign for Sustainability** • Topic would be unusual • Major campaign might not be sensible and not necessary • HRD is not a preferred channel • HRD cannot provide direct added value • Raising awareness is possible • Format must be "discuss and inform" • But appealing enlightenment is task of corporate communication • Discussion of fit before determination in strategy • Must be conveyed in overall context • Indoctrination of adults not appropriate, avoid dogmatism • Active participation • Direct link to work environment • Corporate responsibility only by conviction • No engagement under duress • Mind individual motivators • Values of measures are fundamental values of humanity • Only social projects to disclose unused potentials relate to the core of HRD • HRD should provide freedom, empower people to think
E	**K 2 Verständnis von Nachhaltigkeit** • CR ist wirtschaftliche, unternehmerische, gesellschaftliche Verantwortung • Impuls CR zu besetzen aus Verant-	Comprehension of sustainability • CR is economic, ecological, social responsibility • ~~Impetus came from procurement, energy, society~~	

wortlichkeiten im Einkauf, Energie, Gesellschaft · Dreiklang von Kosten, Umwelt, Gesellschaft · zunächst hohe Investitionen · Bestrebungen nur längerfristig, iterativ · Umsetzung häufig schwierig · Hinterfragen des Tuns, kontinuierliche Verbesserung und sinnvoller Beitrag	· Endeavor can only be fulfilled iteratively in long-term · Realization often difficult · Questioning of actions, continuous improvement, meaningful contribution	· Large corporations too frayed for uniform corporate culture · Consider limited staff support, possible irritation · Regard fit with company culture

K 2.1 Verantwortung

· philanthropische und wirtschaftliche Seite · altruistische Verantwortung von MA gefordert · Führungskräfte haben Verantwortung	· Philanthropic and economic side · Call for altruistic responsibility of employees · ~~Executives have responsibility~~

K 2.2 Organisation

· CR im Personalbereich, "Responsibility, Transformation, neue Lernformen" · CR eng verknüpft mit Transformation, Change · deutsche Standards können nicht in Ländergesellschaften gelten · Verortung von CR ist divers, nicht unbedingt nahe an HR/HRD	· CR closely related to transformation, change · German standards cannot apply in foreign subsidiaries · CR not necessarily close to HR, localization is diverse

E	**K 3 Schnittstelle Personalentwicklung und Nachhaltigkeit** · mittelbare und unmittelbare Brücken · "Corporate Volunteering" gibt der Verbindung einen professionellen Rahmen · anfänglich zufällige Interaktion ist gewachsen · PE wird nicht über "wie nachhaltig" gefiltert, fachliche Bedarfe und Konzernleitbild bestimmen · Inhalte über Nachhaltigkeit nicht vollständig, systematisch vermittelt · viele Einzelinitiativen · keine Besetzung des Themas, strategisch-konzeptionelle Betreuung · für Verankerung in Strategie Passungsdisskussion voranstellen · Vorstandsebene muss Thema tragen	Interface of HRD and sustainability · Direct and indirect bridges · ~~Corporate volunteering as professional setting~~ · Initially random interaction has grown · HRD not filtered by "how sustainable" · ~~Functional demands~~ and guiding principles are decisive · Content not mediated systematically, holistically · Discussion of fit before determination in strategy · ~~Executive board support~~
E	**K 4 Bewertung des Erfolgs** · Frage der Perspektive, was ist viel · Entwicklung von KPIs zeigt Ernsthaftigkeit · Mitarbeiterbefragung liefert Indizien · fachliche Ergebnisse erkennbar	Evaluation of success · Question of perspective · Definition of KPIs reflects seriousness · ~~Employee survey provides evidence~~ · Functional results are visible
F	**K 1 Verständnis von Personalentwicklung** · globale Prozessdefinition um Bedarfe zu erfüllen · Verfolgung strategischer Ziele · interne Trainings sind verhaltensbezogen · "training on the job" soll überwiegen · Methodenmix kennzeichnet Qualität der Trainings · FK muss MA befähigen, gewisses	Comprehension of HRD · Global process definition ~~to meet requirements~~ · ~~Pursuit of strategic objectives~~ · ~~Internal trainings have behavioral focus~~ · ~~Training on the job should outweigh~~ · ~~Executives enable employees to show certain behavior~~ · ~~Executives are role models~~

	Verhalten zu zeigen · FK ist Vorbild · Unterstützung von PE bei Change · interner DL, Fachabteilungen geben Impuls für Kampagnen K 1.1 Spezifische Personalentwicklung · "on the job" Lernen forciert · Weiterbildungskatalog enthält Nachhaltigkeit · Zertifizierungen durch Branche vorgeschrieben · Online-Schulung zu Compliance · Umwelttrainings von Behörden · festgeschriebene Kompetenz "nachhaltige Lösungen vorantreiben" · Kompetenzmodell gibt gewünschtes Verhalten global vor · generische Beschreibungen der Kompetenz im Dialog präzisieren · konkretes Format nicht festlegbar · pro MA jährlich Ziele der Weiterentwicklung · Freiräume der Festlegung von Maßnahmen	~~Support of HRD during organizational change~~ · Mixed methods indicate high quality training ~~Internal service provider, departments give impetus to campaigns~~ ~~Training catalogue includes sustainability~~ · Certifications required by industry ~~Online compliance training~~ · Environmental training by authorities · Competency model including "promoting sustainable solutions" · Generic descriptions to be specified in dialogue · Format not to be set unitarily ~~Annual development objectives per employee~~ · Freedom of establishing measures		
F	**K 2 Verständnis von Nachhaltigkeit** · Thema des Arbeitsalltags · persönliche Einstellung und Verhalten · aufgrund Industrie starker Schwerpunkt auf Außenwirkung K 2.1 Verantwortung · jeder MA soll verantwortungsvoll handeln · soziale Verantwortung über Sponsoring, Ehrenamt · jeder MA in seinem mikro-Wirkungskreis · Menschen anhalten Verantwortung zu übernehmen K 2.2 Messung · in Mitarbeiterbefragung indirekt · kein eigener Themenblock K 2.3 Organisation · durch Anbindung der Abteilung an UN-Leitung Wichtigkeit betont	Comprehension of sustainability · Topic of everyday work ~~Personal attitude and behavior~~ · Due to industry strong focus on external visibility ~~Every employee should act responsibly~~ · Social responsibility through sponsorship, volunteering ~~Encouraging to take responsibility~~ · Indirectly measured in employee survey ~~No separate thematic block~~ · Importance highlighted by direct link of department to executive board		
F	**K 3 Austausch Personalentwicklung und Nachhaltigkeit** · bisher kein Auftrag Training über Nachhaltigkeit zu konzipieren	Interface of HRD and sustainability · So far no assignment to conceptualize training on sustainability		
F	**K 4 Kampagne der PE zu Nachhaltigkeit** · PE kann keinen direkten Mehrwert liefern, Nachhaltigkeit ist verhaltensbezogen · Format muss "Diskutieren, Informieren" sein · nur im Gesamtkontext vermittelbar, argumentativ passender Deckmantel · Thema wäre ungewohnt · große Kampagne nicht unbedingt	HRD campaign for sustainability · HRD cannot provide direct added value · Format must be "discuss, inform" · Must be conveyed in overall context · Topic would be unusual · Major campaign might not be sensible, necessary · HRD should provide freedom, empower people to think		

	sinnvoll, notwendig • PE soll Freiräume geben, Menschen befähigen sich Gedanken zu machen • Aufklärung appellierender Art liegt eher bei Kommunikation • PE ist kein bevorzugter Kanal	• Appealing enlightenment is task of corporate communication • HRD is not a preferred channel
G	**K 1 Verständnis von Personalentwicklung** • je nach Beschäftigtenart verschieden häufig Maßnahmen • E-Learnings zu gewissen Konzerninitiativen nicht verpflichtend • 70/20 Modell, 70% on the job, 20% near the job, 10% Seminare • Ausbildung zählt nicht dazu • 10% reine PE zum Großteil Präsenztrainings • bei Fachthemen Frontalunterricht • PE nicht verantwortlich für Nachhaltigkeitsumsetzung	Comprehension of HRD • Different measures depending on type of employment • ~~E-Learning for certain company initiatives not mandatory~~ • 70/20 model: 70% on the job, 20% near the job, 10% trainings • ~~Vocational training not included~~ • Specialized functional trainings classroom teaching • HRD not responsible for sustainability implementation
	K 1.1 Organisation • großer Konzern, stark zerfaserte Einheiten mit eigener PE • kein Kontrollierungszwang bei zentralen Angeboten • Zentralbereiche strategisch, Service NL operative Ausführung • in Service NL bundesweit Nachhaltigkeits-Beauftragte • im offenen Seminargeschäft überwiegen externe Trainer	• ~~Large corporation, frayed units with own HRD~~ • No compulsive control concerning central training offers • ~~Central functions work strategically~~ • ~~Affiliated service departments execute operationally~~ • ~~Concerning open seminars external trainers outweigh~~
G	**K 2 Verständnis von Nachhaltigkeit** • Nachhaltigkeit hat drei Facetten, Bildung, Soziales und Umwelt • Thema Energiesparen ist tief verankert • gesellschaftliches Engagement punktuell	Comprehension of sustainability • Three facets: education, society, environment • Saving of energy is strongly anchored • Social engagement only selectively
	K 2.1 Organisation • Nachhaltigkeit im Vorstandsbereich	• ~~Sustainability connected to executive board~~
	K 2.2 Bewusstsein und Gründe • durch positive Markt- und Kundenreaktion • ökonomische Gründe, nicht aus Überzeugung • positive Außenwirkung, attraktives Arbeitgeberimage • je weiter weg von Zentrale desto weniger Bewusstsein • Nachhaltigkeit nur, wenn es messbaren Nutzen hat	• Awareness, persecution due to positive customer response • ~~Economic reasons, not conviction~~ • ~~Positive external effects on employer image~~ • The further away from headquarters the less awareness • ~~Sustainability only if benefits measurable~~
	2.3 Messung • keine Messung in Mitarbeiterbefragung • Teilnehmerzahl zu globalem Freiwilligentag	• ~~No measurement in survey~~ • Number of participants on global volunteer day announced
G	**K 3 Schnittstelle Personalentwicklung und Nachhaltigkeit** • wenig konkrete fachliche Interaktion • Trainings für ökologische Nachhal-	Interface of HRD and sustainability • Little concrete professional interaction • Trainings on environmental

	tigkeit · Misch-Thema zwischen Sach- und Selbstkompetenz · teilweise Engagement während der Arbeitszeit · Impuls, Infos für Engagement von Kommunikation · bei Energiekosten-Einsparungen nachhaltige PE · zentraler Sponsor nötig für konzernweite Durchsetzung · zu stark zerfasert für einheitliche Unternehmenskultur · Interesse von Personen entscheidet · Nachhaltigkeit wird als individuelles Thema gesehen	sustainability · Mixed theme between self-competence and professional skills · ~~Engagement allowed during working time~~ · ~~Impetus comes from corporate communications~~ · ~~Sustainable HRD regarding energy efficiency~~ · Too frayed for uniform corporate culture · Sustainability seen as individual topic
H	**K 1 Verständnis von Personalentwicklung** · Vorgesetztenverantwortung · Prozesse von PE definiert, gestellt · die eigentlichen PE-ler sind die Führungskräfte · Kernprozesse sind Zielvereinbarungen zur Weiterentwicklung · parallel Talent Reviews · PE ist Service Provider für MA und FK · kommerzielle Seminaranbieter nicht angesehen · "Training on the Job" forciert · Ausbildung organisatorisch getrennt · PE-ler sind Coach, Mentor auf keinen Fall Lehrer · Wertekern der Maßnahmen sind Grundwerte der Menschheit K 1.1 Spezifische Personalentwicklung · grundsätzliche Einführung in nachhaltige Themen · Job Profile, Onboarding Pläne werden geprüft · einmal jährlich Sicherheitsschulung · Compliance und Diversity Training · klare Botschaften gegen Diskriminierung · Gesundheitskurse · interne Trainer für technische Schulungen, Train-the-Trainer Ausbildung · externe Trainer für Führung, Soft Skills · HR misst Wirksamkeit · Classroom-Training häufig per Video · großer E-Learning Pool · "Learning on the Job" durch Career Conversation Training formalisiert	Comprehension of HRD · ~~Development is responsibility of executives~~ · ~~Processes defined and provided~~ · Target agreements as core process for development · Talent reviews held in parallel · ~~HRD as service provider for employees and managers~~ · ~~Commercial training providers not considered reputable~~ · ~~On-the-Job Training reinforced~~ · ~~Vocational training organized separately~~ · HRD professionals as coach, consultant, mentor not teacher · Values of measures are fundamental values of humanity · ~~Basic introduction to sustainability issue~~ · Job profiles, onboarding plans are checked · Annual safety training, ~~compliance~~ and diversity training, anti-discrimination directive, health courses · ~~Internal technical education~~ · HR measures effectiveness · Classroom training often via video · ~~Large E-Learning pool~~ · Learning on the job formalized through career conversation training
H	**K 2 Verständnis von Nachhaltigkeit** · enger Bezug zu Umweltschutz, Gesundheit, Sicherheit · nachhaltige Planung, Entwicklung im Talent Development · indirekt durch Entwicklung nachhaltiger Produkte, Technologien · wegen Effizienzdruck der Branche, Gesetzen, Kundenanforderungen · nur Demografie, Fachkräftemangel betrifft PE	Comprehension of sustainability · Closely related to environmental protection, health, safety · ~~Sustainable talent management~~ · Indirectly through products, technology · ~~Efficiency pressures in industry, regulations, laws, customer requirements~~ · Only demographic change, skills shortage affect HRD directly

	K 2.1 Organisation · keine eigene Nachhaltigkeitsabteilung, sondern EHS · keine Initiativen für soziales Engagement	· Department for environment, health, safety
	K 2.2 Messung · ökologische Nachhaltigkeit muss messbar sein, nahe am Wirkungsraum · soziale Nachhaltigkeit über Employer Branding messen	· Ecological sustainability must be measurable · Measure social sustainability through employer branding
H	**K 3 Schnittstelle Personalentwicklung und Nachhaltigkeit** · werden als weit entfernt wahrgenommen · nicht Aufgabe von PE Nachhaltigkeit zu fördern · fraglich wie entscheidend Grad der Nachhaltigkeit ist · Mitarbeiterunterstützung eingeschränkt · würde nicht zur Kultur passen, Irritationen auslösen · nur soziales Projekt mit wirtschaftlichem Nutzen betrifft Kern der PE, ungenutzte Potenziale umwandeln · aus politischen Gründen Umsetzung begrenzt, keine Belehrung Erwachsener · Bewusstsein schaffen möglich · Erziehung nicht möglich, Verantwortung nur aus Überzeugung · Kollektiv kann man nicht motivieren · kein Engagement aus Zwang · Dogmatismus vermeiden	Interface of HRD and sustainability · Perceived to be disconnected · Not a task of HRD to promote sustainability · Limited staff support, would provoke irritation · No fit with culture · Only social projects to disclose unused potentials relate to the core of HRD · Indoctrination of adults not appropriate, avoid dogmatism · Raising awareness is possible · Corporate responsibility only by conviction · No engagement under duress
H	**K 4 Vorschlag einer Kampagne** · ein Workshop müsste aktiv gestaltet sein · eventuell wird es zur Gewohnheit · Flexibilität in der Ansprache · individuelle Motivatoren beachten · auf unmittelbares Arbeitsumfeld bezogen	HRD campaign for sustainability · Active participation · Direct link to work environment · Mind individual motivators

References

Aguinis, H. (2011). Organizational responsibility: Doing good and doing well. In S. Zedeck (Ed.), *APA handbook of industrial and organizational psychology*, Vol. 3 (pp. 855-897). Washington, DC: American Psychological Association.

Andre, J. M. (2013). Plan do stabilise repeat: How to lead change successfully. *Management Services, 57*(1), 42-47.

Ardichvili, A. (2013). The role of HRD in CSR, sustainability, and ethics: A relational model. *Human Resource Development Review, 12*(4), 456-473.

Ardichvili, A., & Jondle, D. (2009). Ethical business cultures: A literature review and implications for HRD. *Human Resource Development Review, 8*(2), 223-244.

Argyris, C. (1977). Double-loop learning in organizations. *Harvard Business Review, 55*(5), 115-125.

A.T. Kearney (2015). *Mehr Mut zu entschlossener Umsetzung und Führung: Nachhaltigkeit in Unternehmen in Deutschland* [Online]. Available at: http://www.atkearney.de/documents/856314/5548246/BIP+Nachhaltigkeit+in+Unternehmen+in+Deutschland.pdf/4138ed54-11a3-4d3f-b69a-205d9e85c755 (Accessed: 18 September 2015).

Banerjee, S. B. (2011). Embedding sustainability across the organization: A critical perspective. *Academy of Management Learning & Education, 10*(4), 719-731.

Bansal, P. (2005). Evolving sustainably: Longitudinal study of corporate sustainable development. *Strategic Management Journal, 26*(3), 197-218.

Barney, J. B. (2002). *Gaining and sustaining competitive advantage* (2nd ed.). Upper Saddle River, NJ: Pearson Prentice Hall.

Baron, R. M., & Kenny, D. A. (1986). The moderator–mediator variable distinction in social psychological research: Conceptual, strategic, and statistical considerations. *Journal of Personality and Social Psychology, 51*(6), 1173-1182.

Baumgartner, R. J., & Ebner, D. (2010). Corporate sustainability strategies: Sustainability profiles and maturity levels. *Sustainable Development, 18*(2), 76-89.

Bierema, L., & Callahan, J. L. (2014). Transforming HRD: A framework for critical HRD practice. *Advances in Developing Human Resources, 16*(4), 1-16.

Bisnode Deutschland GmbH (2015). *Hoppenstedt Firmendatenbank Suchstrategie Firmen* [Online]. Available at: http://www.hoppenstedt-firmendatenbank.de/suche/firmen.html (Accessed: 16 April 2015).

Bluestone, A. S. (2011). Process of Change: What it really takes. *Journal of Financial Planning*, p. 21.

Bogner, A., & Menz, W. (2009). The theory-generating expert interview. In A. Bogner, B. Littig, & W. Menz (Eds.), *Interviewing experts* (pp. 43-80). New York i.a.: Palgrave Macmillan.

Bogner, A., Littig, B., & Menz, W. (2014). *Interviews mit Experten: Eine praxisorientierte Einführung*. Reihe Qualitative Sozialforschung, R. Bohnsack, U. Flick, C. Lüders, & J. Reichertz (Hrsg.). Wiesbaden: Springer.

Bortz, J., & Döring, N. (2006). *Forschungsmethoden und Evaluation für Human- und Sozialwissenschaftler* (4. Aufl.). Heidelberg: Springer.

Boud, D., Cressey, P., & Docherty, P. (Eds.). (2006). *Productive Reflection at Work: Learning for Changing Organizations*. London: Routledge.

Boudreau, J.W., & Ramstad, P.M. (2005). Talentship, talent segmentation, and sustainability: A new HR decision science paradigm for a new strategy definition. *Human Resource Management, 44*(2), 129-36.

Bowen, H. R. (1953). *Social responsibilities of the businessman*. New York: Harper & Row.

Brewster, C., & Larsen, H. H. (Eds.). (2000). *Human resource management in Northern Europe: Trends, dilemmas and strategy*. Oxford: Blackwell.

Caligiuri, P., Mencin A., & Jiang, K. (2013). Win–win–win: The influence of company sponsored volunteerism programs on employees, NGOs, and business units. *Personnel Psychology, 66*(4), 825-860.

Carlowitz, H. C. (1713). *Sylvicultura oeconomica oder hauswirthliche Nachricht und Naturgemäße Anweisung zur wilden Baumzucht*. Leipzig.

Carrol, A. B. (1991). The pyramid of corporate social responsibility: Toward the moral management of organizational stakeholders. *Business Horizons, 34*(4), 39-48.

Carrol, A. B. (1999). Corporate social responsibility: Evolution of a definitional construct. *Business & Society, 38*(3), 268-295.

Cho, J. Y., & Lee, E. (2014). Reducing confusion about grounded theory and qualitative content analysis: Similarities and differences. *The Qualitative Report, 19*(32), 1-20.

Cooper, H. (1998). *Synthesizing research: A guide for literature reviews* (3rd ed.). Thousand Oaks, CA: Sage.

Corporate Leadership Council (2004). *Employee Engagement Survey: Executive Summary* [Online]. Available at: http://www.stcloudstate.edu/humanresources/_files/documents/supv-brown-bag/employee-engagement.pdf (Accessed: 07 September 2015).

Cummings, T. G., & Worley, C. G. (2001). *Organization Development and Change* (7th ed.). Cincinnati, OH: Southwestern College Publishing.

Daily, B.F., & Huang, S. (2001). Achieving sustainability through attention to human resource factors in environmental management. *International Journal of Operations and Production Management, 21*(12), 1539-1552.

Denyer, D., & Tranfield, D. (2009). Producing a systematic review. In D. A. Buchanan, & A. Bryman (Eds.), *The Sage handbook of organizational research methods* (pp. 671-689). Thousand Oaks, CA: Sage.

Diesendorf, M (2000). Sustainability and sustainable development. In D. Dunphy, J. Benveniste, A. Griffiths, & P. Sutton (Eds.), *Sustainability: The corporate challenge of the 21st century* (pp. 19-37). Sydney: Allen & Unwin.

Dyllick, T., & Hockerts, K. (2002). Beyond the business case for corporate sustainability. *Business Strategy and the Environment, 11*(2), 130-141.

Ebner, D., & Baumgartner, R. J. (2006). *The relationship between sustainable development and corporate social responsibility*. Corporate Responsibility Research Conference, Dublin.

econsense - Forum Sustainable Development of German Business e. V. (2015). *Econsense currently has 32 members from various industries* [Online]. Available at: http://www.econsense.de/en/members/ (Accessed: 16 April 2015).

Elkington, J. (1997). *Cannibals with forks: The triple bottom line of 21st century business.* Oxford: Capstone.

Epstein, M. J., & Yuthas, K. (2014). *Measuring and improving social impacts: A guide for nonprofits, companies, and impact investors.* San Francisco: Berrett-Koehler.

Ernst & Young (2012). *Six growing trends in corporate sustainability* [Online]. Available at: http://www.ddline.fr/wp-content/uploads/2012/11/SixTrends-RSE.pdf (Accessed: 06 September 2015).

Ernst & Young (2014). *Pflicht oder Kür? Nachhaltigkeitsberichterstattung in Deutschland: Standortbestimmung* [Online]. Available at: http://www.ey.com/Publication/vwLUAssets/EY_Studie_-_Pflicht_oder_Kuer/$FILE/EY-Studie-PflichtoderKuer-2014.pdf (Accessed: 18 September 2015).

EU Commission (2011). *Communication from the commission of the European Parliament, the Council, the European Economic and Social Committee of the Regions: A renewed EU strategy, 2011-14 for Corporate Social Responsibility.* Brussels, Belgium.

EU Commission (2014). *Directive 2014/95/EU of the European Parliament and of the Council of 22 October 2014 amending Directive 2013/34/EU as regards disclosure of non-financial and diversity information by certain large undertakings and groups.* OJ L 330, 1-9.

Fenwick, T. (2005). Conceptions of critical HRD: Dilemmas for theory and practice. *Human Resource Development International, 8*(2), 225-238.

Fenwick, T., & Bierema, L. (2008). Corporate social responsibility: Issues for human resource development professionals. *International Journal of Training and Development, 12*(1), 24-35.

Fernández, E., Junquera, B., & Ordiz, M. (2003). Organizational culture and human resources in the environmental issue: A review of the literature. *International Journal of Resource Management, 14*(4), 634-656.

Fink, A. (2005). Conducting research literature reviews: From the internet to paper (2nd ed.). Thousand Oaks, CA: Sage.

Flick, U. (2015). *Introducing research methodology: A beginner's guide to doing a research project* (2nd ed.). Thousand Oaks, CA i.a.: Sage.

Fowler, S. J.; & Hope, C. (2007). Incorporating sustainable business practices into company strategy. *Business Strategy and the Environment, 16*(1), 26-38.

French,W. L., Bell, C., & Zawacki, R. A. (Eds.). (1999). *Organization development and transformation: Managing effective change* (5th ed.). New York: McGraw-Hill.

Frey, B. S., & Jegen, R. (2001). Motivation crowding theory. *Journal of Economic Surveys, 15*(5), 589-611.

Gallup (2015). *Only 15% of employees in Germany are engaged* [Online] Available at: http://www.gallup.com/businessjournal/183851/employees-germany-engaged.aspx (Accessed: 18 September 2015).

Garavan, T. N. (1995). Stakeholders and strategic human resource development. *Journal of European Industrial Training, 19*(10), 11-16.

Garavan, T. N., & McGuire, D. (2010). Human resource development and society: Human resource development's role in embedding corporate social responsibility, sustainability, and ethics in organizations. *Advances in Developing Human Resources, 12*(5), 487-507.

Garavan, T. N., Heraty, N., Rock, A., & Dalton, E. (2010). Conceptualizing the behavioral barriers to CSR and CS in organizations: A typology of HRD interventions. *Advances in Developing Human Resources, 12*(5), 587-613.

GEPA mbH - The Fair Trade Company (2015). *Mission: GEPA-Kriterien* [Online]. Available at: http://www.gepa.de/gepa/mission/gepa-kriterien.html (Accessed: 18 September 2015).

German Academic Association for Business Research (2015). *VHB jourqual journal rating* [Online]. Available at: http://vhbonline.org/en/service/jourqual/ (Accessed: 16 April 2015).

German Council for Sustainable Development (2015). *The Sustainability Code – Benchmarking sustainable economy* [Online]. Available at: http://www.nachhaltigkeitsrat.de/uploads/media/RNE_The_Sustainability_Code_Tex t_no_47_January_2015.pdf (Accessed: 02 September 2015).

Ghosh, B. N., & Chopra, P. K. (2003). *A dictionary of research methods.* Leeds i.a.: Wisdom House.

Glaser, B. G., & Strauss, A. L. (1967). *The discovery of grounded theory: Strategies for qualitative research.* Chicago: Aldine.

Gläser, J., & Laudel, G. (2010). *Experteninterviews und qualitative Inhalsanalyse* (4. Aufl.). Wiesbaden: VS Verlag.

Global Reporting Initiative (2015). *Sustainability Disclosure Database* [Online]. Available at: http://database.globalreporting.org (Accessed: 02 September 2015).

Gminder, C.U., Bieker, T., Dyllick, T., & Hockerts, K. (2002). Nachhaltigkeitsstrategien umsetzen mit einer sustainability balanced scorecard. In S. Schaltegger, & T. Dyllick (Hrsg.), *Nachhaltig managen mit der Balanced Scorecard: Konzept und Fallstudien* (S. 95-147). Wiesbaden: Gabler.

Gollan, P. J. (2006). High involvement management and human resource line sustainability. *Handbook of Business Strategy, 7*(1), 279-286.

Goodpaster, K. E. (2007). *Conscience and corporate culture.* Malden, MA: Blackwell.

Griffiths, A., Dunphy, D., & Benn, S. (2005). Corporate sustainability: Integrating human and ecological sustainability approaches. In M. Starik, S. Sharma, C. Egri, & R. Bunch (Eds.), *New horizons in research on sustainable organisations: Emerging ideas, approaches and tools for practitioners and researchers* (pp. 166-186). Suffolk: Greenleaf.

Guerci, M., Radaelli, G., Siletti, E., Cirella, S., & Shani, A. B. R. (2015). The impact of human resource management practices and corporate sustainability on organizational ethical climates: An employee perspective. *Journal of Business Ethics, 126*(2), 325-342.

Harmon, J., Fairfield, K. D., & Wirtenberg, J. (2010). Missing an opportunity: HR leadership and sustainability. *People & Strategy, 33*(1), 16-21.

Hatcher, T., & Aragon, S. R. (2000a). Rationale for and development of a standard on ethics and integrity for international HRD research and practice. *Human Resource Development International, 3*(2), 207-219.

Hatcher, T., & Aragon, S. R. (2000b). A code of ethics and integrity for HRD research and practice. *Human Resource Development International, 11*(2), 179-185.

Haugh, H. M., & Talwar, A. (2010). How do corporations embed sustainability across the organization? *Academy of Management Learning & Education, 9*(3), 384-96.

Helfat, C. E., Finkelstein, S., Mitchell, W., Peteraf, M. A., Singh, H., Teece, D. J., & Winter, S. G. (Eds.). (2007). *Dynamic capabilities: Understanding strategic change in organizations.* Oxford: Blackwell.

Helfferich, C. (2011). *Die Qualität qualitative Daten: Manual für die Durchführung qualitativer Interviews* (4. Aufl.). Wiesbaden: VS Verlag.

Hermanns, H. (1995). Narrative Interviews. In U. Flick, E. v. Kardorff, H. Keupp, L. v. Rosenstiel, & S. Wolff (Hrsg.), *Handbuch Qualitative Sozialforschung,* 2. Aufl. (S. 182-185). München: Psychologie Verlags Union.

Hitchcock, D., & Willard, M. (2009). *The business guide to sustainability: Practical strategies and tools for organizations* (2nd ed.). London: Earthscan.

Hitzler, R. (1994). Wissen und Wesen des Experten: Ein Annäherungsversuch – zur Einleitung. In R. Hitzler, A. Honer, & C. Maeder (Hrsg.), *Expertenwissen: Die institutionalisierte Kompetenz zur Konstruktion von Wirklichkeit* (S. 13-30). Opladen: Westdeutscher Verlag.

Hopkins, M. (2003). *The planetary bargain: Corporate social responsibility matters.* Sterling, VA: Earthscan.

Horwitz, F. M. (1999). The emergence of strategic training and development: The current state of play. *Journal of European Industrial Training, 23*(4/5), 180-190.

Jabbour, C. J. C., & Santos, F. C. A. (2008). The central role of human resource management in the search for sustainable organizations. *The International Journal of Human Resource Management, 19*(12), 2133-2154.

Jaffee, D. (2001). *Organization theory: Tension and change.* Singapore: McGraw-Hill.

Jensen, P. E. (2005). A contextual theory of learning and the learning organization. *Knowledge and Process Management, 12*(1), 53-64.

Ji, L., Huang, J., Liu, Z., Zhu, H., & Cai, Z. (2012). The effects of employee training on the relationship between environmental attitude and firms' performance in sustainable development. *The International Journal of Human Resource Management, 23*(14), 2995-3008.

Johnson, G., Whittington, R., & Scholes, K. (2010). *Exploring strategy* (9th ed.). Harlow i.a: Prentice Hall.

Jones-Christensen, L., Peirce, E., Hartman, L. P., Hoffman, W. M., & Carrier, J. (2007). Ethics, CSR, and sustainability education in the Financial Times top 50 global business schools: Baseline data and future research directions. *Journal of Business Ethics, 73*(4), 347-368.

Kant, I. (1788). Kritik der praktischen Vernunft. In W. Weischede (Hrsg.) *Werksausgabe Bd. VII.,* 4. Aufl., 1978 (S. 103-302). Frankfurt/Main: Suhrkamp.

Kauffeld, S., Lorenzo, G., & Weisweiler, S. (2012). Wann wird Weiterbildung nachhaltig? – Erfolg und Erfolgfaktoren beim Lerntransfer. *PERSONALquaterly, (64)*2, 10-15.

Kira, M., van Eijnatten, F. M., & Balkin, D. B. (2010). Crafting sustainable work: Development of personal resources. *Journal of Organizational Change Management, 23*(5), 616-632.

Kochan, T. A. (2008). Social legitimacy of the HRM profession: A US perspective. In P. Boxall, J. Purcell, & P. Wright (Eds.), *The Oxford Handbook of Human Resource Management* (pp. 599-619). Oxford: Oxford University Press.

Kotter, J. P. (2007). Leading change: Why transformation efforts fail. *Harvard Business Review, 85*(1), 96-103.

Krippendorff, K. (1980). *Content analysis: An introduction to its methodology.* Beverly Hills: Sage.

Kuchinke, K. P. (2001). Why HRD is not an academic discipline. *Human Resource Development International, 4*(3), 291-294.

Kuchinke, K. P. (2010). Human development as a central goal for human resource development. *Human Resource Development International, 13*(5), 575-585.

Lamnek, S. (2010). *Qualitative Sozialforschung* (5. Aufl.). Weinheim, Basel: Beltz.

Langer, A. (2010). Transkribieren – Grundlagen und Regeln. In B. Friebertshäuser, A. Langer, & A. Prengel (Hrsg.). *Handbuch Qualitative Forschungsmethoden in der Erziehungswissenschaft,* 3. Aufl. (S. 515-525). Weinheim, München: Beltz.

Lee, K.-H., & Ball, R. (2003). Achieving sustainable corporate competitiveness: Strategic link between top management's (green) commitment and corporate environmental strategy. *Greener Management International, 44,* 89-104.

Lee, M. (2001). A refusal to define HRD. *Human Resource Development International, 4*(3), 327-341.

Lee, M. (2007). Human resource development from a holistic perspective. *Advances in Developing Human Resources, 9*(1), 97-110.

Lee, M. (2010). Shifting boundaries: The role of HRD in a changing world. *Advances in Developing Human Resources, 12*(5), 508-23.

Lewin, K. (1951). *Field theory in social science: Selected theoretical papers.* New York: Harper.

Liebowitz, J. (2010). The role of HR in achieving a sustainability culture. *Journal of Sustainable Development, 3*(4), 50-57.

Luhmann, N. (1984). *Soziale Systeme: Grundriß einer allgemeinen Theorie.* Frankfurt/Main: Suhrkamp.

Lünendonk GmbH & Orizon GmbH (2013). *Arbeitsmarkt 2013 – Perspektive der Arbeitnehmer* [Online]. Available at: https://www.orizon.de/fileadmin/user_upload/Presselounge_Texte_PDF/2013-11-14_Attraktiver_Arbeitgeber_Zeitarbeit.pdf (Accessed: 18 September 2015).

MacKenzie, C., Garavan, T., & Carbery, R. (2011). *Corporate social responsibility: HRD as a mediator of organizational ethical behavior.* Paper presented at the 12th International HRD Conference, University of Gloucestershire, Cheltenham, UK.

MacKinnon, D. P., Coxe, S., & Baraldi, A. N. (2012). Guidelines for the investigation of mediating variables in business research. *Journal of Business and Psychology, 27*(1), 1-14.

Mayer, H. O. (2004). *Interview und schriftliche Befragung: Entwicklung, Durchführung und Auswertung* (2.Aufl.). München: Oldenbourg.

Mayring, P. (2002). *Einführung in die Qualitative Sozialforschung: Eine Anleitung zum qualitativen Denken* (5. Aufl.). Weinheim, Basel: Beltz.

Mayring, P. (2010). *Qualitative Inhaltsanalyse: Grundlagen und Techniken* (11. Aufl.). Weinheim, Basel: Beltz.

Mayring, P. (2014). *Qualtitative content analysis: Theoretical foundation, basic procedures and software solution.* Klagenfurt: Social Science Open Access Repository.

McGuire, D., & Cseh, M. (2006). The development of the field of HRD: A Delphi study. *Journal of European Industrial Training, 30*(8), 653-667.

McLean, G. N., & McLean, L. (2001). If we can't define HRD in one country, how can we define it in an international context? *Human Resource Development International, 4*(3), 313-326.

Meister, J. C., & Willyerd, K. (2010). Mentoring mill: Delivering the feedback gen Y craves is easier than you think. *Harvard Business Review, 88*(5), 68-72.

Merriman, K. K., & Sen, S. (2012). Incenting managers toward the Triple Bottom Line: An agency and social norm perspective. *Human Resource Management, 51*(6), 851-872.

Meuser, M., & Nagel, U. (2009). Das Experteninterview – konzeptionelle Grundlagen und methodische Anlage. In S. Pickel, G. Pickel, H.-J. Lauth, & D. Jahn (Hrsg.), *Methoden der vergleichenden Politik- und Sozialwissenschaft* (S. 465-479). Wiesbaden: VS Verlag.

Morgeson, F. P., Aguinis, H., Waldman, D. A., & Siegel, D. S. (2013). Extending corporate social responsibility research to the human resource management and organizational behavior domains: A look to the future. *Personnel Psychology, 66*(4), 805–824.

Mueller, K., Hattrup, K., Spiess, S.-O., & Lin-Hi, N. (2012). The effects of corporate social responsibility on employees' affective commitment: A cross-cultural investigation. *The Journal of applied psychology, 97*(6), 1186–1200.

Nielsen (2014). *Doing well by doing good* [Online]. Available at: http://www.nielsen.com/content/dam/nielsenglobal/apac/docs/reports/2014/Nielsen-Global-Corporate-Social-Responsibility-Report-June-2014.pdf (Accessed: 18 September 2015).

Oerter, R. & Montada, L (Hrsg.). (2008). *Entwicklungspsychologie* (6. Aufl.). Weinheim: Beltz.

Pfeffer, J. (2010). Building sustainable organizations: The human factor. *Academy of Management Perspectives, 24*(1), 34-45.

Pistrang, N., & Barker, C. (2012). Varieties of qualitative research: A pragmatic approach to selecting methods. In H. Cooper (Ed.), *APA Handbook of Research Methods in Psychology,* Vol. 2. Research Designs (pp. 5-18).Washington, DC: American Psychological Association.

Pless, N. M., & Maak, T. (2011). Developing responsible global leaders through international service-learning programs: The Ulysses experience. *Academy of Management Learning & Education, 10*(2), 237-260.

Porras, J. I., & Silvers, R. C. (1991). Organization development and transformation. *Annual Review of Psychology, 42*, 51-78.

Porter, M. E. (1987). From competitive advantage to corporate strategy. *Harvard Business Review, 65*(3), 43-59.

Porter, M. E., & Kramer, M. R. (2011). Creating shared value: How to reinvent capitalism – and unleash a wave of innovation and growth. *Harvard Business Review, 89*(1/2), 62-77.

Pundt, A., Martins, E., Horsmann, C. S., & Nerdinger, F.W. (2007). Gesellschaftliche Verantwortung als Unternehmenswert: Qualitative und Quantitative Untersuchungen der Sicht von Führungskräften, Betriebsräten und Vertretern des HR-Managements. *Wirtschaftspsychologie, 9*(1), 31-39.

Ramus, C. A., & Killmer, A. B. C. (2007). Corporate greening through prosocial extrarole behaviors: A conceptual framework for employee motivation. *Business Strategy and the Environment, 16*(8), 554-570.

Rimanoczy, I., & Pearson, T. (2010). Role of HR in the new world of sustainability. *Industrial and Commercial Training, 42*(1), 11-17.

Rupp, D. E., Ganapathi, J., Aguilera, R. V., & Williams, C. A. (2006). Employee reactions to corporate social responsibility: An organizational justice framework. *Journal of Organizational Behavior, 27*(4), 537-543.

Salzmann, O., Ionescu-Somers, A., & Steger, U. (2005). The business case for corporate sustainability: Literature review and research options. *European Management Journal, 23*(1), 27-36.

Schaltegger, S., Windolph, S. E., & Harms, D. (2010). *Corporate Sustainability Barometer: Wie nachhaltig agieren Unternehmen in Deutschland?* Lüneburg, Frankfurt/Main: Centre for Sustainability Management der Leuphana Universität Lüneburg, PriceWaterhouseCoopers.

Schein, E.H. (1990). Organizational culture. *American Psychologist, 45*(2), 109-119.

Scholz. C., & Müller, S.(2014). The HR-department as driver for sustainability. In C. Scholz, & J. Zentes (Eds.), *Beyond Sustainability* (pp. 52-68). Baden-Baden: Nomos.

Scully-Russ, E. (2012). Human resource development and sustainability: Beyond sustainable organizations. *Human Resource Development International, 15*(4), 399-415.

Sheehan, M., Garavan, T. N., & Carbery, R. (2014). Sustainability, corporate social responsibility and HRD. *European Journal of Training and Development, 38*(5), 370-386.

Society of Human Resource Management (2011). *Advancing sustainability: HR's role* [Online]. Available at: https://www.shrm.org/Research/SurveyFindings/Articles/Documents/11-0066_AdvSustainHR_FNL_FULL.pdf (Accessed: 18 September 2015).

Society of Human Resource Management (2015). *Employee job satisfaction and engagement 2014: Optimizing organizational culture for success* [Online]. Available at: http://www.shrm.org/Research/SurveyFindings/Documents/2015-Job-Satisfaction-and-Engagement-Report.pdf (Accessed: 18 September 2015).

Spranger, E. (1928). *Types of men: The psychology and ethics of personality* (P. J. W. Pigors, Trans.). Halle: Max Niemeyer.

Sroufe, R., Liebowitz, J., & Sivasubramaniam, N. (2010). Are you a leader or a laggard? HR's role in creating a sustainability culture. *People & Strategy, 33*(1), 34-42.

Steurer, R., Langer, M. E., Konrad, A., & Martinuzzi, A. (2005). Corporations, stakeholders and sustainable development I: A theoretical exploration of business-society relations. *Journal of Business Ethics, 61*(3), 263-281.

Sukserm, T., & Takahashi, Y. (2012). Self-efficacy as a mediator of the relationships between learning and ethical behavior from human resource development in corporate social responsibility activity. *Asia-Pacific Journal of Business Administration, 4*(1), 8-22.

Swanson, R. A. (2001). Human resource development and its underlying theory. *Human Resource Development International, 4*(3), 299-312.

Swanson, R. A., & Holton, E. F. III (2001). *Foundations of human resource development.* San Francisco: Berrett-Koehler.

Tomé, E. (2011). Human resource development in the knowledge based and services driven economy. *Journal of European Industrial Training, 35*(6), 524-539.

Ulrich Walter GmbH/ Lebensbaum (2015). *Über unser Unternehmen* [Online]. Available at: http://www.lebensbaum.com/de/ueber-uns/unser-unternehmen (Accessed: 18 September 2015).

United Nations (1992). *Framework convention on climate change.* United Nations, New York.

United Nations (1997). *Kyoto protocol to the United Nations Framework Convention on Climate Change, conference of the parties on its third session,* FCCC/CP/1997/L.7/Add.1, 10 December.

United Nations Conference on Environment and Development (1992). *Agenda 21* [Online]. Available at: http://www.un.org/Depts/german/conf/agenda21/agenda_21.pdf (Accessed: 23 April 2015).

Valentin, C. (2006). Researching human resource development: Emergence of a critical approach to HRD enquiry. *International Journal of Training and Development, 10*(1), 17-29.

Van Marrewijk, M. (2003). Concepts and definitions of CSR and corporate sustainability: Between agency and communion. *Journal of Business Ethics, 44*(2), 95-105.

Vithessonthi, C. (2009). Corporate ecological sustainability strategy decisions: The role of attitude towards sustainable development. *Journal of Organisational Transformation and Social Change, 6*(1), 49-64.

Von Kettler, B. (2010). (R)evolution der Arbeit: Warum Work-Life Balance zum Megathema wird und sich trotzdem verändert. Wie konkrete Handlungsempfehlungen und gezielte Projekte aussehen, In S. Kaiser, & M. J. Ringlstetter (Hrsg.), *Work-Life Balance, Erfolgsversprechende Konzepte und Instrumente für Extremjobber* (S. 139-153). Berlin, Heidelberg: Springer.

Waite, A. M. (2013). Leadership's influence on innovation and sustainability. *European Journal of Training and Development, 38*(1/2), 15-39.

Walker, P. (2007). Supporting the change agents. *Greener Management International, 54,* 9-22.

Wall, F., & Leitner, S. (2012). Die Relevanz der Nachhaltigkeit für unternehmerische Entscheidungen. *Controlling, 24*(4/5), 255-260.

Weston, J. F., Mitchell, M., & Mulherin, J. H. (2004). *Takeovers, restructuring, and corporate governance* (4. Aufl.). Upper Saddle River, NJ: Pearson Prentice Hall.

Wilcox, T. (2006). Human resource development as an element of corporate social responsibility. *Asia Pacific Journal of Human Resources, 44*(2), 184-196.

Wirtenberg, J., Harmon, K. D., Russell, W. G., & Fairfield, K. D. (2007). HR's role in building a sustainable enterprise. *Human Resource Planning, 30*(1), 10-20.

Witzel, A. (1982). *Verfahren der qualitativen Sozialforschung: Überblick und Alternativen.* Frankfurt/Main u.a.: Campus-Verlag.

Woodward, N. H. (2008). New breed of Human Resource leader. *HR Magazine, 53*(6), 52-56.

World Commission on Environment and Development (1987). *Our common future* [Online]. Available at: http://www.un-documents.net/our-common-future.pdf (Accessed: 23 April 2015).

World Health Organization (1986). *The Ottawa charter for health promotion* [Online]. Available   at: http://www.who.int/healthpromotion/conferences/previous/ottawa/en/index.html (Accessed: 07 September 2015).

XING AG (2015). *XING is the social network for business professionals* [Online]. Available at: https://corporate.xing.com/index.php?id=138&tx_ttnews[tt_news]=0&tx_ttnews [pointer]=0&tx_ttnews[backPid]=0&cHash=0&cat=0&L=1 (Accessed: 16 April 2015).

Young, W., Davis, M., McNeill, I. M., Malhotra, B., Russell, S., Unsworth, K., & Clegg, C. W. (2013). Changing behaviour: Successful environmental programmes in the workplace. *Business Strategy and the Environment,* doi: 10.1002/bse.1836.

Zadek, S. (2001). *The civil corporation: The new economy of corporate citizenship.* London: Earthscan.

Zidan, S. S. (2001). The Role of HRD in economic development. *Human Resource Development Quarterly, 12*(4), 437-443.